THE BABYSITTER

THE BABYSITTER

MY SUMMERS WITH A SERIAL KILLER

Liza Rodman

and

Jennifer Jordan

ATRIA BOOKS

New York   London   Toronto   Sydney   New Delhi

An Imprint of Simon & Schuster, Inc.
1230 Avenue of the Americas
New York, NY 10020

First Atria Books hardcover edition March 2021

ATRIA BOOKS and colophon are trademarks of Simon & Schuster, Inc.

For information about special discounts for bulk purchases,
please contact Simon & Schuster Special Sales at
1-866-506-1949 or business@simonandschuster.com.

The Simon & Schuster Speakers Bureau can bring authors to your live event. For
more information or to book an event, contact the Simon & Schuster Speakers
Bureau at 1-866-248-3049 or visit our website at www.simonspeakers.com.

Interior design by A. Kathryn Barrett

Manufactured in the United States of America

1   3   5   7   9   10   8   6   4   2

Library of Congress Cataloging-in-Publication Data

Names: Rodman, Liza, author. | Jordan, Jennifer, author.
Title: The babysitter : my summers with a serial killer /
Liza Rodman and Jennifer Jordan.
Description: New York, NY : Atria Books, [2021] | Includes
bibliographical references and index.
Identifiers: LCCN 2020033280 (print) | LCCN 2020033281 (ebook) |
ISBN 9781982129477 (hardcover) | ISBN 9781982129491 (ebook)
Subjects: LCSH: Costa, Antone Charles, –1974. | Rodman, Liza. | Serial
Murderers—Massachusetts—Provincetown—Biography. |
Serial Murders—Massachusetts—Provincetown.
Classification: LCC HV6248.C669 R63 2021 (print) | LCC HV6248.C669
(ebook) | DDC 364.152/32092 [B]—dc23
LC record available at https://lccn.loc.gov/2020033280
LC ebook record available at https://lccn.loc.gov/2020033281

ISBN 978-1-9821-2947-7
ISBN 978-1-9821-2949-1 (ebook)

To the women

One need not be a Chamber—to be Haunted—
—Emily Dickinson

A NOTE ON OUR PROCESS

This is a hybrid work of memoir and narrative nonfiction. Liza's story is subject to the limitations of her memories from childhood. We understand that others who were there will have differing recollections. However, those events involving Tony Costa and his crimes are taken directly from the original records and source documents—police reports and detectives' notes, prosecution and defense interviews, the trial transcript, Tony's exhaustive medical and psychological testing, including his nine polygraphs, his prison diary as well as what he called his "factual novel" of his life and crimes, and clippings from the extensive media coverage. We were also fortunate to have more than fifty hours of digitally preserved tape recordings of interviews conducted with Tony Costa during his fifteen months in the Barnstable County Jail. Finally, we tracked down and spoke with dozens of people who knew Tony as well as those who were there and witness to the time, place, and events herein.

While quotes are taken directly from interviews, articles, letters, transcripts, and documents, we have made minor grammatical changes for the sake of clarity and readability. And lastly, some of the names and identifying details have been changed.

Prologue

LIZA'S NIGHTMARE

2005

"Close your eyes and count to four," he whispered. I felt his breath on my cheek. The barrel of the gun was hard and cold against my forehead.

I counted, and when I opened my eyes, he was gone.

I sat up quickly in bed, gasping, my body soaked with sweat.

What the hell was that?

It was pitch-dark in the room—not even a sliver of the moon to offer some light.

Damn. Another nightmare.

I'd been having them for almost two years, during which they had become more and more violent and vivid, and in each I was hunted by an anonymous man with a knife or a gun. I would struggle to recognize him, but he kept his face turned away from me. Then, just as he'd find my hiding place, I'd wake with my heart pounding and adrenaline coursing through my legs until they ached.

But this nightmare was different. In this dream, I was a young girl again, probably about nine or ten and in my summer pajamas walking down a long hotel hallway. Suddenly the elusive man blocked my path, backed me up against the wall, and pointed a gun at my head. I looked up at him and I finally saw his face. It was a man I hadn't seen since I was a child in Provincetown, Massachusetts.

Tony Costa.

Tony had been hired as a handyman to fix torn screens and leaky faucets in the seaside motel where my mother worked summers as a housekeeper. Everybody thought Tony was great, especially me. He was part of the revolving door of so-called babysitters my mother corralled to look after me and my younger sister, Louisa. Mom was notorious for being able to find a babysitter faster than she could say the word. She'd stop people in the supermarket or the post office or at the gas pump and ask, "Do you babysit?" Mostly the person would just stare at her, wondering why a mother would hire a random stranger to look after her children with less care than she would a plumber or a car mechanic. But sometimes they said sure. Tony was one of those, and he turned out to be one of the good ones. In fact, he was one of the few kind and gentle adults in my life during those turbulent years. But then in 1969, when I was ten years old, Tony disappeared. I didn't know why; I just knew he was gone.

So why was Tony Costa now in my dreams, holding a gun to my head and smiling with teeth better suited to a wolf? What I remembered about him was all good; in fact, Tony was a nice guy who never yelled, never hit, never made me feel small and ugly and unwanted. I had been afraid of my mother but never of Tony. So when he suddenly appeared, threatening and frightening in the dream, it confounded me.

With nowhere else to turn, I did something I learned long ago not to—I asked Mom for help. I invited her to dinner, and when she arrived at Tim's and my house, she was already teetering as she climbed the front porch. She was seventy by then, and everywhere she went, she carried a plastic sixteen-ounce water bottle of gin in her purse.

"Those were some wild days," she said, seated at my counter and swirling the ice around in her snifter. She was clearly enjoying the memory of those summers on Cape Cod when she was a pretty divorcée, barely thirty years old, spending most of her free time closing down the various bars and dance clubs with her own revolving door of suitors. She took a long pull on her gin and settled back into her chair while I put the last of the seasoning in the soup simmering on the stove.

"Did something happen to me back then that you're not telling me?" I said, suddenly wondering if it had.

"What do you mean, *happen to you*?"

"With Tony Costa."

"Tony Costa? Why are you still thinking about him?"

"I wasn't until I had a nightmare about him."

"Oh, Christ, you and your dreams," she said, snort-laughing as she took a sip of her drink.

"Well, this one was pretty horrible. But I don't get it. He was always so nice to me," I said. "What do you remember about him?"

She was quiet for a moment too long, and I stopped stirring and waited. She was just staring into the bottom of her glass. Mom rarely paused to contemplate her words, so I watched, curious as to what was going to come out of her mouth.

"Well," she said, watching the gin swirl around the glass. "I remember he turned out to be a serial killer." She said it calmly, as if she were reading the weather report.

I felt sick. I had always had several disjointed memories about murders that occurred in Provincetown during the years we lived there, but no one ever told me who had committed them. The bits and pieces I remembered involved hideous crimes—shallow graves and hearts being carved out of bodies and teeth marks on corpses.

I suddenly had an image, as clear as the pot of soup on the stove in front of me, of my two little tan feet up on the dashboard of the Royal Coachman Motel's utility truck. Sand was stuck between my toes, and there were flecks of old red polish on my big toenails. I loved how tan my feet would get during the long, shoeless summer, and with them poised on the dash in front of me, I would turn them this way and that, admiring their smooth brown skin. I was never pretty like my mother, but, I thought, at least I had her pretty feet. Driving the motel's truck, always, was Tony Costa.

I shook my head to clear the image and turned back to Mom.

"A serial killer? Tony, the babysitter?"

"Oh, for Christ's sake," she said, "don't be so dramatic. He wasn't your *babysitter.*" Her eyes narrowed in emphasis. "He was the *handyman.*"

I felt as if someone had sucker punched me in the gut.

"Handyman at the motel . . . ," I said, my words trailing off as I envisioned its long hallway and recognized it from the nightmare.

"But Louisa and I went all over the Cape with him," I sputtered. "He took us on his errands and out to the dump and out to the Truro woods. Tony was the *Cape Cod Vampire*? Our Tony? A *serial killer*?" My words were tumbling out of me.

"Yeah, so what?" she said, again reaching for her gin. "He didn't kill *you*, did he?"

1

TONY

Antone Charles "Tony" Costa was born just after midnight on August 2, 1944, in Cambridge, Massachusetts. His mother, Cecelia, had married his father, Antone Fonseca Costa, in 1928, and they spent the next fifteen years trying to conceive. She finally got pregnant, and Antone—a US Navy Reserve carpenter's mate—returned to the Pacific to fight the war. She would never see him again, and he would never meet his namesake. On April 21, 1945, Antone F. drowned in New Guinea while trying to rescue a fellow seaman during the final days of World War II. Tony was eight months old.

Only five months after Antone's death, a very much unmarried Cecelia got pregnant by a man who was fourteen years her junior. Joseph Bonaviri was the owner of a small masonry business in Somerville, a working-class neighborhood north of Boston. After all the problems she had getting pregnant with Antone, her relationship with the young mason proved immediately fruitful, if not a tad unseemly in her Catholic and largely immigrant neighborhood. They married in May 1946, and six weeks later they welcomed a son, Vincent "Vinnie" Bonaviri, born almost two years after his half brother, Tony.

Tony grew into a bright-eyed, good-looking boy. But as he matured, he became fascinated, even obsessed, with his deceased father and begged Cecelia to tell him about brave Antone, the war hero, over and over, like a favorite bedtime story. He later said he remembered tiny details of his father's funeral, even though he'd been only four years old when the burial was finally held. He sat for hours poring through the trunk of his father's possessions the navy had sent home from the Pacific. Tony's favorite items were his father's dress uniform; his posthumous commendation for bravery, which Tony proudly took to school and showed his classmates; and a knife big enough to be called a dagger[1] kept in a handmade leather sheath. Cecelia answered as many of Tony's questions about his father as she could, but the boy's curiosity about who the missing father was, what he was like, and most of all, how he died, seemed to haunt him.

When he was seven, Tony told his mother "a man" was visiting him in his bedroom at night and talking to him. Cecelia showed him a picture of his father and Tony said, "That's him." Tony never revealed whether those visits of "a man" were pure fantasy, the obsessions of a son haunted by his absent father, a young child's nightmares, or if Tony was in fact being "visited" by a male intruder.

Every summer, Cecelia took Tony and Vinnie down to her sister's house in Provincetown, where she worked cleaning motel rooms while the boys had the run of the town. Even though Cecelia was born in Provincetown, Tony and Vinnie were seen as outsiders, "wash-ashores," and often made to feel somehow different by the local kids. The brothers were so inseparable they became known as Tonyandvinnie, Vinnieandtony,[2] but Tony resented having his younger brother tag along and mocked him at every turn, chanting, "Vinnie, the skinny little ginnie [*sic*] with the ravioli eyes, put him in the oven and make french fries."[3]

One of the boys with whom Tony and Vinnie played those summers was Frank Gaspar, who lived in Provincetown year-round and was part of the close-knit Portuguese community where fathers worked processing fish in the Atlantic Coast Fisheries plant and mothers cooked sea clams with linguica or mackerel *vinha d'alhos* for Sunday dinner and yelled to each other over the back fences, sometimes in a polyglot of languages. Frank and his family lived for the summertime, when there was regular money coming in, and they dreaded the misery of the cold months, when heat and hot water were luxuries they rarely could afford.

From the beginning, Tony was different from the other kids—somehow cooler, smarter, and more "inside himself" than anyone else. Frank Gaspar felt as if Tony were "not there, even though he was."[4]

One day, a gaggle of boys was headed to the beach, and Frank told Tony to hold up while he got something out of his yard.

"Time and tide wait for no one," Tony announced. First pointing to himself and then to Vinnie, he said, "I'm time and he's tide."

Frank thought that was just about the smartest thing he'd ever heard.

In those days, boys collected coupons from the back of comic books and used them to order magic kits, slingshots, X-ray glasses, kryptonite rocks, and toy soldiers. But rather than cheap comic book toys, Tony ordered a taxidermy kit from the Sears catalog. Vinnie later said Tony's taxidermy craft was "a lot of baloney; he couldn't stuff a sausage."[5] Nevertheless, Frank observed that Tony kept on killing and disemboweling small animals, even though he never finished a trophy that anyone saw.

During the winter months back in Somerville, Tony kept his taxidermy kit in the basement of their triple-decker on Hudson Street in the Winter Hill neighborhood, home to infamous mobster Whitey Bulger's eponymous gang. Tony spent untold hours experimenting with chemicals and fiddling with the instruments. Later, neighbors would claim a number of their small pets, cats in particular, went missing during those years, but no one at the time associated those mysterious disappearances with anything but bad luck, certainly not with young Tony Costa.

Whether or not Tony spent too much time with dead animals and his taxidermy kit, he did spend enough time on his studies to become a gifted and popular student. When Tony was eleven, Joseph Bonaviri put him to work at his masonry company. Tony was able to figure in decimals in his head, balancing columns of cash income, outlay, unemployment insurance, Social Security deductions, and tax entries, all of which were accurate enough to survive an auditor's inspection. Bonaviri nicknamed his stepson the Whiz Kid, and in school he earned commendations for "splendid cooperation and honesty." His English teacher said he was a gentle young man and that there was something lovable about him.

Before Tony turned twelve, when he was in Provincetown for the summer, a local teenager lured him into his basement, tied him up, and raped him.[6] As with most sexual assaults of children, then and now, the attack was never reported to police, and Tony never revealed publicly who had raped him or if it happened more than once. Tony would only say it was an "older kid." And more than fifty years later, in 2009, Tony's ex-wife still refused to identify the attacker, saying only that the man was still alive and still living in Provincetown. However, she did disclose "it was just one of the experiences that nestled in [Tony's] psyche."[7]

Tragically, it might not have been the only sexual assault Tony suffered during his summers in Provincetown. Cory Devereaux, a local boy who would become one of Tony's young followers, said he and several other boys were sexually molested "every fucking Sunday"[9] by Father Leo Duarte*, the parish priest at St. Peter the Apostle Catholic Church in Provincetown. When Devereaux was seven years old, he said the priest drugged him and the other altar boys with a shot glass of spiked wine, telling them it was "the blood of Christ." Then, one by one, Duarte took the boys "in the back" of the church. Unlike Tony's attack by the "older kid," Devereaux's alleged attack *did* get reported after he was found unconscious on the street and taken to the police. Then, in front of his mother; the town doctor, Dr. Daniel Hiebert; and the chief of police, Francis Marshall, the story came tumbling out.

"They tried to pin it on my stepfather, but it was Duarte. That much I know. But the fuckers did nothing," Cory said, his anger and hatred of the Catholic Church and the powers that protected its pedophile priests still palpable sixty years later.

Regardless of whom Tony's attacker was or how Tony felt about the rape, he said that it was then that he began to lose his faith in God. While

---

* While the spelling of the priest's name is recorded in various places as both Duarte and Duart, the most common spelling is Duarte.

Tony would marry and christen his children in the Church, he wouldn't attend regular services until he was in prison serving time for first-degree murder. Then he went nearly every day.

On August 2, 1960, Tony turned sixteen, and with some of the money from his father's death benefits, Cecelia bought him his first car, a second-hand jalopy. He adored the car and rented space in a neighbor's garage in Somerville so he wouldn't have to leave it on the street at night. But with the garage came the neighbor's daughter, Donna, who, according to Tony, was "an annoying skinny little pest,"[9] a teenybopper with a crush on him.

One could hardly blame the girl for thinking that Tony liked her. The year before, when Donna was thirteen, Tony began taking her down into his basement, where he bound her hands, laid her on a pool table, and pulled down her underpants. Tony claimed that he just "looked at her." Then, in November 1961, according to Tony, Donna gave him a key to her house so he could come upstairs when her parents were asleep. He did, but as he stood over her bed, she screamed, and he ran out of the house. Several days later, Tony tried to drag her into his basement. She screamed again, and he slapped her hard across the face. She ran home, and when she was questioned about the bruise, she told her mother Tony "wouldn't let me go."[10] She went on to tell her parents about how several nights before she had awoken to find him standing over her bed, fondling her through her nightgown. Despite their differing accounts, Tony was arrested and charged with assault and battery and breaking and entering with intent to commit a felony (rape). He told the court he was just trying to find out why she "hated my guts." The judge didn't buy it. Although there was no evidence that Tony had broken into the apartment, he nonetheless was convicted of both charges and given a one-year suspended sentence, three-year probation, and ordered to get out of Somerville for good.

Cecelia did as the court demanded and sent him to Provincetown to live with her sister until things cooled down with the authorities. But things didn't cool down, and several months later, Cecelia and Vinnie packed their bags and joined Tony in Provincetown. Along with Somerville, Cecelia left Joseph Bonaviri behind for good. While Bonaviri paid $50 a week for Vinnie's child support, he never again had anything to do with the Whiz Kid.

2

LIZA

My mother married my father so they could finally have sex. She got a kick out of saying it. Truth was, she adored Dad when they were both sixteen and she first saw him at a party in Bridgewater at his family's funeral home, of all places. He was playing a piano which stood in the corner near an empty casket stand, and he was belting out "Pennies from Heaven." She was hooked, but she was dead serious about only getting married so she could have sex. Good Catholic girls, among which she considered herself, didn't have sex before marriage. Not in 1958 anyway. Years later, when I asked about their wedding night, she laughed, remembering my father jumping around their hotel room "holding on to his thing, poor bastard," as they tried to avoid pregnancy with Catholic birth control: withdrawal. It didn't work. I was born exactly nine months after that night, and my sister, Louisa, twenty-two months after that.

Their marriage had begun well enough, but by the time I was four, the soft murmurs from behind their closed bedroom door had been replaced by fighting so loud and ferocious it sent me and Louisa to the cubbyhole crawl space in our bedroom to hide, covering our ears and crouching amid the dusty suitcases stored there. But hiding didn't work. Our house was tiny, and their screaming pounded through the thin walls.

As best we could make out from all the yelling, she was *sick to damn death* of our father, and she wished he'd *do us all a favor and jump off the damn Sagamore Bridge*, and she was just about ready to pack up his bags and throw him out on his *damn ass* and be done with his *damn shit once and for all*! He could tell his *damn lies* to someone else. She was *through*.

And then one night, she really was.

When Dad came home that night, he tried to explain himself but Mom would hear none of it. Their fighting once again sent me and Louisa to the crawl space, where we fell asleep. Mom finally found us, dragged us out, and put us to bed. In the morning, two of the dusty suitcases were packed and sitting in the hall. Before we knew what hit us, Dad was gone.

He didn't say goodbye.

After she threw him out, Mom was desperate to finally be free of Dad. But everybody knew Catholics didn't divorce. *Ever.* She had tried her whole life to be a front-row kind of Catholic, so she hoped she was in pretty good standing for getting some special favors from Father Francis Shea, the same priest who had married her and Dad four years before. But, turned out she was wrong.

"You can't get a divorce. It's simply not done," Father Shea said, and sat back in his chair, scowling.

"What about an annulment?" she asked.

"It's too late for that," Father Shea said. "Listen, if you won't think about yourself, Betty, think about the girls. If you are determined to get a divorce, they'll be damned in the eyes of the Holy Father," he said, and crossed himself. "The only eyes that matter."

"I am *very* determined to get a divorce." She was surprised that the words came out cold rather than compliant.

Father Shea rose from his chair and smoothed the front of his cassock. "Then I think it's time for you to leave my office," he said, motioning toward the door. "I can't help you."

She left and slammed the door—hard enough, she hoped, to dislodge the crucifix hanging over the threshold. She was glad she made it to the car before her tears started.

Mom told the story a lot. It was another of her favorites and one of many I heard while eavesdropping on her phone calls to Joan, Mom's best friend since college. We called her Auntie because she and Mom were as close as sisters. Mom would sit on the floor under the phone that hung on the kitchen wall—her legs outstretched with a tall glass of rum and Coke balanced between her thighs—put her plaid beanbag ashtray next to her, light a little cigar or one of her Virginia Slims cigarettes, and vent her fury. Her mother, my nana Noonan, told me that's what girlfriends did: they talked to each other until they were all talked out and calm. I wondered why it never worked with Mom.

"The Catholic Church is a *cult*, and that Father Shea is a *weasel*," Mom told Auntie, blowing a gust of cigarette smoke above her head. "He owed me that annulment. He *owed* me."

I never knew what that meant, but I could see how sad and angry his denunciation made her. For one thing, she started to swear, a lot. She had always said *damn* and *shit* and *bastard* and *bitch*, but now she was pissed, *fucking pissed*, at having spent so much of her young life on her knees genuflecting to the *fucking cult*. While the swearing was real, I also think she loved to shock Auntie, who "wouldn't have said *shit* if she had a mouthful of it," according to Mom. So Mom said it for her, and then some. She told Auntie she was done, *fucking done* with all the *goddamn Catholic bullshit*. And she was. While she still forced Louisa and me to go every Sunday until our confirmations, *she* was through.

So Mom went to court and got herself a regular *fucking* divorce.

After Dad left, I kind of hoped that Mom's anger would leave too. But instead it only got worse, and with Dad not there to absorb some of her rage, she came after me with both barrels. When they were in high school together, she had played on the basketball team, and because she gritted her teeth when she dribbled the ball from one end of the court to the other, Dad had nicknamed her "the Fang." Now, she gritted those teeth at me as she backhanded my face, over and over. I learned not to cry, not to protest, not to fight back, because the few times I had, she'd really railed on me. Challenging her only fueled her rage. So I would stand there and stare her down as the welt grew on my cheek.

"Mummy hates you," Louisa said once after I had gotten smacked for bumping into the kitchen table and spilling her rum and Coke.

I slapped Louisa when she'd said it. She was right, but I didn't want her to know it, never mind speak it out loud.

So I became very good at finding places to hide from my mother. I spent hours, sometimes entire days alone reading Nancy Drew mysteries or playing house with my dolls; at least in those make-believe houses I could create a normal family in a world of love, comfort, and, most of all, safety.

Meanwhile, I waited for Dad to come back and save me, to take me with him wherever he had gone.

3

TONY

By December 1961, when Tony enrolled in Provincetown High School to finish his senior year, he had grown into a handsome young man. He was tall, slender, and powerfully built, with a cleft chin, strong jawline, smooth olive complexion, and a head of thick dark hair. Upon Tony's admission to PHS, the principal, presumably unaware that the young man was on probation for assault and battery, breaking and entering, *and* attempted rape, noted in his file that he "seems to be a gentleman."[1] He was kind and polite, particularly with adults, always using *sir* and *ma'am*. He also gave off an air of sensuality like a fragrance and if he flashed his wide grin, he could turn a junkyard dog into a squirming puppy.

When Tony traveled the halls of PHS, he wouldn't just walk—he'd strut, thinking himself an utterly "cool cat," in the parlance of the 1960s. As one witness would later describe him: "He was cool because he had reserve. He was cool because he had poise. He was cool because he had for authority a quiet scorn. . . . He was cool because he did his thing regardless of what people thought. He was cool because he went after anything he wanted with breathtaking directness."[2]

Even though Tony's family members were working-class Portuguese immigrants and his mother a chambermaid who survived during the winter months on welfare and Vinnie's child support, he thought of himself as a city kid, somehow better and smarter than his Provincetown classmates. He complained that the other kids in his class were "boobs" who threw spitballs and snapped paper clips at each other with rubber bands all day.

Instead of his classmates, he preferred hanging out with young teenagers who looked up to him like some sort of an older, hip hero, a role Tony was all too happy to cultivate.

One day in the spring of 1962, just weeks before his graduation, he approached a group of eighth-grade girls gathered on the sidewalk in front of the Lobster Pot on Commercial Street. He wore polished black shoes with pointed toes, black chinos, and a sport jacket, and the girls watched the high school senior approach with something like wonder. He was moving toward *them*.

One of the girls, Judy, said, "That's my cousin," as Tony approached.

When she introduced him to the other girls, he held out a pack of Juicy Fruit gum, assuring them there was "plenty more where this came from." Judy noticed a ring on his pinkie finger and complimented it.

"I'm hoping to find a chain and just the right neck to adorn. Any ideas?" he said, giving the girls his best smile. "Well, I am off to the library so I shall bid all of you lovely ladies adieu."[3]

And just like that, thirteen-year-old Avis Lou Johnson fell in love; for the first time in her young life, her future looked bright. Her mother had raised her with an iron fist after her father had disappeared from their life when Avis was just four years old. The abandonment broke Avis's young heart. When she saw Tony stride up to her and her friends, she felt as if a missing piece in her life had miraculously reappeared. She had written long passages in her diary about the day when she would meet a rich man who'd give her the love she craved and buy her everything she wanted. Instead, she met Tony Costa.

Within days of their meeting on the street, Avis and Tony were "an item," but when her mother got wind of it, she tried to shut down the young love. Marian Johnson thought—as did many Provincetown mothers and fathers—that there was something terribly wrong with the seventeen-year-old Tony Costa sniffing around Avis and her friends, handing out sticks of gum and flirting with them about who would wear his ring around their neck.

Avis, however, was undeterred. She had known Tony most of her life as a summer kid, but when she saw him sauntering toward her and her girlfriends that April morning in 1962, she felt as if she were looking at her future, a future she imagined away from her mother's stifling control and away from having to care for her sister, Carol, who had contracted lupus, a burden that fell heavily on Avis's shoulders. When she complained about having to do Carol's chores, like taking out the garbage or walking the dog, her mother would snap, "You should be grateful you can walk." As Carol's condition worsened, chronic pain caused the young girl to become something of a recluse, and Avis would regale her with stories of school, biking all over Provincetown, digging for clams in the bay, and, most of all, boys. After Avis and Tony began dating, Carol lived vicariously through Avis's hushed confessions of heavy petting and, eventually, of their sex.

In her older, wiser boyfriend, Avis saw someone who would give her the grown-up life she wanted, and she dreamed of marrying him, playing the name "Mrs. Avis Costa" through her head over and over like a tape. After her confirmation at St. Peter's, she walked out of the church and saw Tony waiting at the bottom of the stairs, looking like Elvis Presley in his usual outfit of a blazer, pressed chinos, and black shoes, his hair slicked back with Vaseline and a sly smile on his face. As she walked down the steps toward him, she felt like she had gotten married, instead of confirmed.[4]

Marian's fears about Tony only worsened after she learned that he was on probation for an attempted rape back in Somerville only a year before. But it was too late.

"He wanted me then; we wanted each other,"[5] Avis said.

Because she was only thirteen, they needed her mother's approval to get married, but Marian refused to grant it. They decided to force her hand by intentionally getting pregnant. He would pick her up at school and they would drive out to the Provincetown dump or Pilgrim Springs to have sex, both places close enough for her to get back to school before her next class. When time wasn't an issue, they drove out to Truro's infamous lovers' lane— a clearing in the dense woods behind the Pine Grove Cemetery—where they would spot the signs of litter left behind by others who'd been there before them with a similar purpose but decidedly different aim: used condoms. It took them six months, but Avis finally conceived, as well she might since they had sex nearly every day, sometimes both morning and night.[6]

With the deed done, Marian Johnson put her signature to the marriage license, but she was far from happy about it.

"You deliberately seduced her," she told Tony. "You don't have a conscience or a decent instinct. . . . You know it, your relatives know it . . . you are marrying her just to save yourself from jail."[7]

On April 20, 1963, one day shy of the eighteenth anniversary of his father's death, Tony and Avis married at St. Peter's with Father Duarte presiding. Already four months pregnant, Avis fainted at the altar, and Tony had to hold her up through the long mass. Later, at the reception in her grandmother's living room, she vomited up her breakfast. Avis was fourteen years old.

Kids grew up fast in Provincetown. Between the free-wheeling artists, the freedom-seeking homosexuals, the free-love hippies, and the unending supply of drugs and alcohol that flowed through the town like hot lava, young children turned into savvy and often troubled teenagers overnight. It didn't help that the locals who stayed on past Labor Day and lived in the shuttered, desolate town fought poverty, depression, addiction, and domestic violence through a long, gray winter that stank of rotting fish.

Avis Johnson Costa was no exception. By the fall of 1963, she had met the man of her dreams, gotten pregnant, then married, and had her first child, Peter—all before she turned fifteen. But, while the lovestruck teenage girl envisioned a life of security, romance, and, best of all, freedom with her charming older husband, Tony quickly crumbled under the weight and responsibility of being a husband and father. He'd often leave their cramped apartment after an argument and walk the beaches and dunes, sometimes all night. A few months into their marriage, Tony got drunk and sat on the couch crying.

"My feet are staring at me! Go get me a towel to cover them!"

Avis did, but it was all she could do not to roll her eyes at his histrionics.

Another time, Tony collapsed in her arms, sobbing, "I can't do this. I have to get away from here."[8]

"Fine," she said, rapidly wearying of her fragile husband. "Go. I have the best part of you—Peter."

Tony stayed; even though his life felt suffocating, Avis was his anchor, and without her he feared he'd drift away with the next high tide. And although he belittled her, reminding her of her lack of a high school education and mocking her crooked teeth and plain looks, he needed her and she knew it. For all of his failures as a father and husband, Tony loved Avis and baby Peter, perhaps as much as he was capable, but he was unable to give them what he himself most craved: a solid family life, safety, and an end to the increasingly dark and disturbing thoughts roiling through his head.

The first year of their marriage, they lived in a first-floor apartment on Hughes Road in Truro that Avis felt was haunted. Night after night she'd wake to an ominous visage standing at the end of their bed. She'd rouse Tony, crying, "Do you see it? Right there?" He never did, but her belief that something was there was so strong, he once grabbed a rifle he kept next to the bed, aimed it where she pointed, and shot a hole through the wall right above Peter's crib, who by this point was wailing. While Tony wondered if the possible ghost was a poltergeist of his dead father, Avis began to believe it was the grim reaper and that his portent of death was always lurking, ready to reach out and take someone she needed, or worse, someone she loved.

Through it all, they fought. Money was always tight even though Cecelia had given them $2,450 ($20,250 in today's dollars) for a wedding present—$450 in savings bonds and $2,000 she had saved of his father's $10,000 naval insurance policy. But, by early 1964, less than a year after their marriage, Tony had burned through all of it (which is perhaps not surprising given that he "thanked" his mother for the gift by telling her,

"The money means nothing to me. I'd rather have my father," as if she had had any control over Antone's fate).

Their arguments only got worse when Tony's inability to secure regular work forced them to borrow money from people all over town. Feeling indebted particularly rankled Tony.

"We owe them nothing," he told Avis.

Calling those who had loaned them money "ignorant jerks," he insisted, "They ought to pay me just for speaking to them."[9]

4

LIZA

Mom loved being behind the wheel; it didn't seem like she cared where we were going, so long as it was somewhere else. And with Dad out of the picture, Louisa and I spent a lot of time in the back seat of her Chevy Malibu. On the longer drives, Louisa mostly slept, especially at night, propped up against her door behind the passenger seat, but I sat wide awake right behind Mom, counting the oncoming headlights on the other side of the road. As she drove, I asked her questions about where we were going, how long until we'd get there, what we would do when we arrived, until she said, "Do you ever shut up? Go to sleep," and I went back to counting headlights and twirling my already curly hair around my index fingers—a nervous habit I'd picked up from watching my dad, who also twirled his. But as soon as I started, she'd bark, "Stop that twirling, you look like Denny Dimwit." I didn't know who that was, but I didn't like the sound of it, so I'd tuck my fingers under my thighs to keep them out of my hair.

Sometimes when we were driving home late from Auntie and Uncle Hank's house, after a long night of them drinking at the kitchen counter, she'd drive with her head almost all the way out the window to keep herself awake. One of those nights, the blue lights of a police cruiser pulled us over.

"Shit!" Mom said, pulling to the side of the road, the tires biting through gravel.

I heard her rummage through her purse and then put two or three pieces of gum into her mouth, muttering "shitshitshit" as she watched the cop in the rearview mirror walk up to our car. The car filled with the smell of cinnamon gum as the flickering beam of the cop's flashlight approached. Usually she was able to smile and laugh and pat the officer's arm through the open window and just get a warning to "take it easy, young lady. Wouldn't want anything to happen to you and those pretty girls of yours." *Pretty girls.* I loved that. She would laugh and thank him, and then we'd be back on the road, driving so slow it seemed like we could walk home faster. But after she had finally been stopped by a cop she couldn't sweet-talk, and she lost her license for ninety days; it didn't keep her from driving, but it sure slowed her down for a while.

On the longer drives, she'd forget we were in the back seat and would sing along with the radio, partly to keep herself awake, partly because she loved the sound of her own voice. I sang along too, but not out loud; that would have just made her mad. I learned to memorize the lyrics just like I memorized her stories. One she loved to tell was about the night I was born. It always began with Mom shivering on her gurney as the nurse wheeled her into the hallway of the obstetrics ward at Brockton Hospital, patted her shoulder and then disappeared. Mom lay there, cold, miserable, and alone, wanting a cigarette in the worst way. The hallway was empty except for other women in labor, screaming and moaning on their gurneys.

Why in hell am I waiting out here in the damn hallway? she wondered.

As one of her contractions ebbed, Mom leaned over the edge of the gurney and vomited her dinner onto the gray linoleum floor. Her head spun, and her eyes wouldn't quite focus.

Where the hell is everybody?

The next thing she remembered I was born.

She called it "the worst night of her life."

I never knew why she loved to tell that story so much.

My mother named me after herself, Elizabeth, but everybody—Mom, Dad, my sister, grandparents, aunties, uncles, cousins—called me Liza. I asked her why she named me Elizabeth but never called me Elizabeth and she shooed me away, saying, "I don't know. I don't remember." But come to think of it, she was never called Elizabeth either. Everybody always called her Betty.

I think she assumed she was going to love me when I was born, but by the time she realized she didn't, it was too late to take her name back. *Not everybody automatically loves their babies, you know*, I once heard her say to a friend. The words scared me; *doesn't everybody love their babies?* She didn't hate me, but I don't think she liked me very much. And she certainly didn't show me any affection—hugs, caresses, a kiss on my cheek? Never. I didn't know why, but it felt as if Mom had it in for me right from the start. She loved to tell people that when I was born, I looked just like Bob Hope—Bob Hope with a bad case of eczema. She always laughed and laughed telling that story.

As I grew older and taller, she said I looked like Bambi because my legs were too long and skinny for my body.

"You're too tall for a girl," she'd say, as if I could do anything about it. Or, "Can't you do something about that hair? It looks like a mess of steel wool." She also said my ears stuck out "like your father's . . . But don't worry, Elizabeth Taylor had hers pinned back, and we can pin your hound-dog ears back too if we have to." I didn't much like the sound of that. But I knew her real problem with me wasn't my Dumbo ears or my tall, skinny Bambi legs, or that I had been an ugly baby with a bad skin rash; it was that every day I became a little bit more like my father. I was even beginning to laugh like him.

5

TONY

Tony Costa assumed all women, including one as young as Avis, ironed their sons' and husbands' clothes, right down to their boxer shorts, and kept an immaculate house, where pets were only allowed in the basement—like his mother did. But unlike Cecelia, Avis hated housework. Nonetheless, early in their marriage she reluctantly bowed to his demand that there never be so much as a dirty dish in the sink; otherwise, he often threatened, she could always return to her mother's house. "Dirty dishes make him mad," she later confided.[1] Cecelia was no help; rather than offer a hand to her overwhelmed daughter-in-law, she criticized everything about Avis—her appearance, her housekeeping, her mothering, and mostly her care of "my Tony," as Cecelia always called him. When Avis and a girl-friend would see her walking across Conant Street, they'd groan, "Oh no, here she comes."

Avis learned to cook and sew and wash the laundry on a scrub board in the bathroom tub, but as hard as she tried to keep a clean and tidy house, Tony was never satisfied. He found fault with just about every aspect of her, berating her privately and in front of their friends and family, calling her a simpleminded ding-a-ling, a neglectful mother, and an abysmal wife. Their bickering soon devolved into violence; Avis reported to a family doctor that Tony had hit her and the baby more than once. Within a year of their wedding, they consulted a lawyer about a divorce but were told they couldn't just say they didn't love each other anymore and end their marriage. It didn't work that way, particularly with a young child already in the picture. Not only had they both grown up Catholic, but the no-fault divorce was yet to come; in the 1960s, a couple had to have cause *and* proof that the marriage was over.

So they soldiered on in their sad and volatile dysfunction, but Tony was determined to bring some excitement back into their sex life. It had been a long time since their dangerous and delicious lovemaking in the back seat of his car out in the Truro woods.

He had heard about a "wild" book, full of pictures and instructions on different sexual positions. It was called the Kama Sutra. He found a copy in Molly Malone Cook's East End Bookshop on Commercial Street and quickly tucked it into his jacket, lest the salesgirl know he was into "some kinky shit." After looking through the pictures, he screwed a thick metal hook "not meant for hanging plants"[2] into his and Avis's kitchen ceiling. He told her that hanging by her feet would get her high from the rush of blood to her head and heighten her sexual pleasure. Panting with the effort, he fastened her into the rig, but it only made her dizzy to the point of passing out, and he let her down. Then with considerable effort, he pulled himself up, secured the rope, and masturbated as he swung at the end of it. Avis watched as Tony hung on the hook. She felt "ready to puke, for something I had loved was there, dead, hanging like a gutted deer, turning slowly in the lamplight. After that I had only pity for Tony, and that is the worst thing that can happen between two married people—pity. I found that out."[3]

He put her on the hook two or three more times before that "thrill" paled, and then he tied her to their bed and burned her with a cigarette.[4] Thankfully, that "game" was also short-lived.

Next, he told Avis that he had gone to parties in Somerville where the boys would put pillows over the girls' faces until they passed out so that they could "then do whatever we wanted to them." He insisted that he and Avis do the same thing and put a plastic bag over her face until she lost consciousness.[5] At least once, he demanded that she beat him with a belt while he masturbated. He also inserted a wooden phallus into her vagina, insisting she was "too tight." Avis found that "just plain silly" because

Tony's penis was smaller than the phallus. Still other times he had her "finish him off" after he'd masturbated almost to the point of orgasm, or he'd kneel on the floor by the bed and rub her naked body while he masturbated. All of this she did with a growing weariness.

Tony was probably engaging in hypererotic sex because he was becoming numb to stimuli and had to have ever more dangerous and volatile sex in order to be at all aroused, let alone reach orgasm. As odd and unsettling as it was, fifteen-year-old Avis had no idea this wasn't what every married couple did, particularly with Tony insisting it was.

"I learned everything I knew about sex from Tony, including birth control, which is how I got pregnant," Avis said.[6]

One friend later said, "She was just fourteen or fifteen—a baby having babies. What did she know?" But without achieving any sexual satisfaction herself and missing what had been their more normal lovemaking during their dating days, Avis soon became depressed over the pressure and guilt Tony applied to get her to take part in his increasingly perverse sex acts.

Night after night she lay awake, sleepless with anxiety. While their sex (most of which was his masturbation) left him momentarily satisfied, it left her drained and disillusioned. She realized Tony seemed to be able to perform sexually only if she was unconscious or doped to the point of near catatonia from chloral hydrate, a powerful sedative now known more commonly as a mickey, or the date rape drug, which Tony kept in his taxidermy kit.[7] Avis asked him why he wanted to have sex with her only when she was unconscious, "like I'm dead, Tony." While she wished there was an adult she could talk to who'd "listen and understand," at the same time she also didn't want people to know there might be something wrong with Tony.[8] She was left alone with her burgeoning fear and anxiety.

After her last time hanging on the hook and desperate for sleep, Avis opened Tony's taxidermy kit and took out his bottle of chloral hydrate. She sat on the edge of their bed where Tony lay sleeping, unscrewed the cap, and swallowed the entire vial. She passed out, pitching headfirst onto the floor with a loud thud, waking Tony. Unable to rouse her, he wrapped the baby in a blanket and Avis in her robe, and drove them to their family physician, Dr. Daniel Hiebert, frantically ringing the nighttime emergency bell until the doctor came to the door. For the next several hours, the men pumped Avis's stomach, forced coffee down her throat, and walked her back and forth through the office until the drug had cleared her system.[9]

While the police ruled the overdose a suicide attempt, they told Tony if she had died he would have been charged with manslaughter. Afterward, she refused to engage in his increasingly bizarre sex acts, and as a result they all but stopped having sex. But there was at least one exception to the abstinence, and in the spring of 1965, their second child, Michael, was born. Tony was not yet twenty-one, and Avis only sixteen.

6

LIZA

My mother had big dreams and fancy tastes; she wanted to travel, spend her summers on the beach, and, mostly, find a handsome man who would put a huge diamond on her finger. But her regular job as a home ec teacher at Stoughton High School didn't provide the money or the lifestyle for any of those things. So in the spring of 1966, when Auntie called to say there was a summer job at a motel that Auntie's husband, Uncle Hank, co-owned and had just finished building on the Cape, Mom was thrilled. It was a first step toward all of her dreams, especially meeting a rich man, even though her father, Grampa Georgie, said only whores and circus freaks lived in Provincetown. Or maybe he said Hyannis. Didn't matter which. Mom ignored him and got us ready to leave.

I found her in her bedroom packing.

"How long will it take us to get to Provincetown?" I asked as I plopped down on the bed to watch her pack.

"Get off-a there," she said, pushing me off the bed. "I just folded that."

Her push was hard, so I had to take a few steps to catch myself from falling. I stood in the door a safe distance away from her hands and feet, watching her resmooth the blouse I had sat on. Without knowing I was doing it, I started scratching at the angry red welts in the crooks of my arms and behind my knees. Mom told me the eczema I'd been born with only got worse after Dad left, spreading to my belly and the insides of my fingers and wrists. Some days it was worse than others, and my scratching left streaks of blood on my arms, legs, and clothes. Sometimes Grampa Georgie would run a bath with Epsom salts—he had a cure for everything, and for eczema it was a warm bath. For a while it helped the itching but not the rash; still, the baths always made me feel better.

"Stop that scratching!" Mom said, looking up from her packing. "You're only making it worse."

I forced my hands to my sides, even though the rash was bad that day with tiny bubbles of oozing pus on my arms and hands.

"So how long do you think it will take us to get there, Ma?" I tried again, fiddling against the itching burn on my arms.

Her hands slowed as she the folded the sleeves of the blouse, and I instinctively took another step back. She turned to me, her lips pressed together and her eyes narrowed to slits.

"How many times have I told you to call me *Mummy*?" she said through clenched teeth. "*Ma* sounds like something some half-breed dim-wit would say."

Half-breed. It would be years before I understood that if *I* sounded ig-norant then *she* too sounded ignorant, or worse, low-class. To her *Mummy* sounded highbrow, like something the Kennedys would say.

"How long will it take to get there, *Mummy*? Will we be there by dinner?"

"For Christ's sake, how should I know?" she said, putting the perfectly folded blouse into the suitcase on the bed and reaching for another to fold. "What do I look like? A road map? Go ask Grampa."

Nana and Grampa Georgie lived next door to us in West Bridgewater. He had built a little two-bedroom house on his land for Mom and Dad when they got married, and we'd lived in it ever since. I found Grampa Georgie where I usually did—in his basement, where along with a set of encyclopedias he had a shelf of little nip bottles of booze with white screw caps. I often wondered if Grampa Georgie didn't like his nips too much. Sometimes he tripped when he was only walking across the room, and other times he'd get mad at a tool and throw it across the barn yelling *God*damn *it!* Sometimes he'd yell at the car in front of him on the road:

LEARN HOW TO DRIVE, YA CHOWDAHHEAD! And his breath usually didn't smell very good, kind of sour and a little like vomit.

Everybody knew not to make Grampa Georgie mad on account of something called his Irish temper. I didn't know what that was and I didn't want to find out. But Mom knew. When she was about thirteen, she had sassed her mother, my nana, and before Mom knew it, Grampa had her over his knee, pulled her pants down, and spanked her like a toddler. She said that Grampa Georgie pulling her pants down and spanking her bare bottom at thirteen years old was just about the worst thing that ever happened to her. Unfortunately, Mom's shame at being spanked by her father didn't stop her from doing the same to me when it was her turn as a parent. I guess that's why Grampa Georgie and Nana never stopped her when she backhanded me. They'd taught her everything she knew about being a mom.

I came down the cellar stairs and saw Grampa Georgie leaning back in his chair with his big work boots propped on his metal desk. He had never gotten around to finishing his basement "office," so instead of walls there were just studs, and I loved to play between them. When he heard me on the stairs, he quickly took a last swallow of his nip and threw the empty bottle toward the trash can in the corner. It hit the metal can with a *clank* but bounced off the side and skittered across the floor.

"Hey there, Tootsie, whacha up to?" he said, smiling and wiping his mouth with the back of his hand.

I asked him how long it would take us to drive to Provincetown.

"Place is full of goddamn chowdahheads!" he muttered as he got up out of his chair. "I don't know why your mother is dragging you girls to the ends of the goddamn earth for the entire summer!" He went over to a rusty filing cabinet, pulled a map out of a drawer, and brought it back to the desk.

"Come over here, and I'll show ya," he said, switching on the light and clearing a space on the desk to smooth out the map.

"There, right there," he said, putting his finger on the map, "is P'town. And here"—he moved his finger slowly across the map—"right next to the Hockomock Swamp is West Bridgewater, where we live."

I looked at the route from West Bridgewater down to and over the Sagamore Bridge and then all the way out to the very end of Route 6 on Cape Cod—Provincetown. I thought of all the headlights I'd count along the way.

"Looks like a long way. How long will it take to drive there?" I said.

He thought about it as he studied the map. "I dunno. 'Bout a hundred miles. Shouldn't take ya mother longer than two, two and a half hours, depending on traffic. Especially the way she drives," he added with a chuckle. "She learned that from me." *Betty drives like a bat outta hell, just like me*, he loved to say.

He was right. We were there in a little over two hours. After we'd crossed over the Sagamore Bridge, I don't think she hit the brakes once.

We arrived a couple of days before the start of the Memorial Day weekend, the official kickoff to the summer season on Cape Cod. Mom's new job was head of housekeeping, which I knew was a fancy title for someone who changed beds and cleaned toilets. Still, she was thrilled to be working at the Royal Coachman Motel on Route 6A, just north of the Truro town line. It was so new it sparkled.

It was a motel unlike any other on the Outer Cape, where most motels were a handful of one-room, weather-beaten clapboard cottages along the two-lane highway. But the RC, as we called it, had 168 rooms on three floors, indoor and outdoor Olympic-size swimming pools, tennis courts, and a restaurant and cocktail lounge. The glossy brochures stacked on the front desk boasted, "None larger, newer or finer. Dancing and entertainment nightly."

It also promised a summer of fun for me and Louisa playing with Auntie and Uncle Hank's two kids, four-year-old Gail and six-year-old Geoff. Our mothers were the kind of best friends who were practically inseparable, so we four had grown up together, and Gail and Geoff were more like our cousins or even our siblings. We spent so much time together that

Louisa even started to think that Uncle Hank was our father. I stopped telling her she was wrong because it seemed to make her feel better to believe that he was.

Mom and Auntie's first order of business was hiring a small army of maids to clean all those rooms. One was a short, plump woman with rounded shoulders and sad, deep-set eyes who spoke with a slight accent, Portuguese or Italian, I didn't know which. Her name was Cecelia, and she was only fifty-six but she was already bent by years of scrubbing toilets and floors in other people's houses and motels. Along with her pale yellow sweater, every day she wore her white imitation-leather shoes, half loafer half sneaker, laced so tight her ankles swelled over the tops.

I loved Cecelia right away. She was soft and patient and gave the best hugs I'd ever had. And even if her breath sometimes smelled sour, like Grampa Georgie's, I didn't mind because in the solid warmth of her arms, I knew that I was loved. Unlike my mother, Cecelia's eyes would light up when she saw me, and she made me feel that I belonged somewhere. When I was with her, talking for hours in the hotel's laundry room while she folded sheets and towels warm from the dryer, listening to her hum her church songs, I felt something I rarely did anywhere else. Safe.

7

TONY

Tony always seemed to be looking for work, and when he found it, he did a solid job—electrical, plumbing, carpentry, stonework, painting—he could do just about anything related to constructing or maintaining a building. Even when there wasn't a major construction job on the Outer Cape, he usually could find an odd job here or there because he was unlicensed and nonunion, and therefore cheaper labor for those hiring. The guys on his work sites said he did a "great job" *when* he worked, but he was unreliable and prone to impulsive and erratic outbursts that left him withdrawn and sullen if he didn't get his way. As his friends, including lifelong Province-town resident Bob Anthony, noted, "Tony always had to be right. About everything."[1] Avis agreed, saying that Tony "considered himself the sole judge on everything"[2] and "if he thought he was right and someone disagreed, he would flip."[3] That didn't go over well with his bosses and foremen, and it often isolated him from his peers, who merely laughed at his childish tantrums.

He had never been one to set goals for himself, and often he could barely muster the energy to get out of bed and read the daily want ads in the *Provincetown Advocate*. So work remained sporadic. With no regular job to go to, Tony did a lot of walking, usually the dunes where he could be alone, as well as up and down Commercial Street, running into friends and his young hangers-on. A favorite stop along his treks was the counter at Adams Pharmacy, where he would order a cup of tea and a small packet of Lorna Doones, and he would nurse the two while he listened to the older waitresses gossip. One dreary November morning, Tony sat at the counter with a friend who told him about a doctor in Wellfleet he was seeing for his alcoholism. Tony asked if the doc might be able to help him with his crumbling marriage and whatever it was that was gnawing at his stomach. Wellfleet was just far enough from Provincetown that nobody would have to know Tony's business. A week later, Tony hitchhiked the fifteen miles to Dr. Sidney Callis's office on Route 6 and walked into the gray clapboard building for the first time.

Dr. Sidney Callis had graduated from Kansas City College of Osteopathy and Surgery, which bestowed a DO (doctor of osteopathic medicine) but not an MD. Then, because of an interest in psychosomatic medicine dealing with emotional illness, Callis did part of his residency at Bridgewater State Hospital, an asylum for the criminally insane, south of Boston. In 1967, Bridgewater would be the subject of a damning documentary, *Titicut Follies* by Frederick Wiseman, which exposed brutal and often inhumane treatment of its inmates. After only a few months at Bridgewater, Callis considered himself qualified to act as a marriage counselor. By the time Tony walked into his office, Callis had been practicing medicine and doing counseling in Wellfleet for fifteen years.

Callis asked Tony a few preliminary questions and made note of the young man's hand-wringing and scratching of his ear, observing that his fingernails were bitten to the quick. Callis told Tony he suffered from a nervous condition, and rather than marriage counseling, he recommended an antianxiety medication. Callis gave him an envelope full of Solacen, each capsule containing 350 milligrams of tybamate, an otherwise safe tranquilizer when used as prescribed but potentially dangerous if abused, particularly when mixed with other drugs.

That evening, Tony took his first pill fifteen minutes before eating, as directed. But by the time Avis put his chocolate pudding dessert in front of him, he told her he couldn't pick up the spoon.

"Why not?" she said.

"Because it feels like it weighs twenty pounds," Tony said, and with that he promptly fell asleep, his head falling forward onto the table.

Avis was stunned and shook him awake.

"Jesus, Tony. Look at you," she said. "What did that quack give you?"

Years later Tony would describe his first experience with Solacen, saying it was like an "unholy orgasm" and that he "hadn't felt that good in a long time."[4]

Eventually, it would be revealed that Callis was being paid by the drug's maker, Wallace Pharmaceuticals, to write a study[5] on Solacen and its effects on patients, a practice that today could cost a doctor his or her license. Tony was not told he was part of a paid study, but he probably wouldn't have cared. In addition to writing Tony prescriptions, Callis gave him envelopes of free samples from a closet full of pharmaceuticals in his office.

On two occasions, and at Tony's urging, Avis went with him to see Dr. Callis for *her* "nervous condition." But the second and last visit didn't go well after Callis ridiculed her for not stepping up to her duties as a wife and mother. She tried to talk to him about her night terrors of the visiting visage, but Callis mocked her with a dismissive "Oh, come on!" He wrote her a prescription she didn't want for yet another Wallace Pharmaceuticals sedative, meprobamate, and quickly ended the visit. Avis refused to go back.

But Tony did go back, a total of nearly thirty visits over the next two and a half years, during which Callis prescribed more than twelve hundred pills.

One day in late 1965, Tony came home to find the apartment a mess and the two babies lying naked on the floor. By his own admission, Tony "went berserk." He dragged Avis into the bathroom screaming at her: "You're a slob, a born slob! A grubby little girl!" When he saw that she had put soiled diapers and dirty laundry into the bathtub, his anger turned to fury. He told Avis he was going to give her "a scrubbing you'll never forget; you first, and then those dirty diapers."[6] He threw her in the shower, turned the hot water on high, doused her with shampoo, and scrubbed her nearly raw with the back brush. It was an indignity that remained with Avis a long, long time.

His marriage in shambles, his work schedule sporadic at best, and now taking Solacen by the handful, Tony spent less and less time at home and more and more time walking the streets and sand dunes of Provincetown. What he really wanted was to get the hell out of Provincetown, and in late May 1966, he found the perfect excuse.

8

LIZA

When I was six, a couple of years after my parents had divorced, Dad—the *stinking liar*—showed up for the first time since he'd left. His car rolled into the driveway, and I ran to the front door. When he saw me standing there, he gave me a big, wide smile. I couldn't believe that he had finally come to rescue me from Mom.

Before I could open the door, she pushed past me out of the house and rushed across the lawn to where Dad's Pontiac sat idling.

She seemed to know he was coming, because she was already pissed as hell.

I cringed as I watched her approach the car. *Please don't make Dad disappear again.*

"Where's my money, Roddy?" she hissed at him, inches from his face. I heard from Grampa Georgie that my dad was lousy with money, and it must have been true; Mom always wanted it, and Dad never had it to give. He forever seemed to owe somebody something with nothing left over to give her, or us.

"I'll get you the money, Betty," he said, giving me a wink and a nod of his head toward the passenger seat. I ran down the steps and hopped in the car.

"Yeah, I've heard that before." She stood with her arms tightly crossed in front of her. "Make sure to have her back by six," she hollered as Dad backed the car onto Crescent Street. "In case you've forgotten, it's a school night. Don't be late."

So he's not rescuing me forever, I realized, *just for the day. Well, I'll take what I can get.*

At first, I was glad Louisa didn't come, but I wished she had when I saw that my date with Dad wasn't going to be spent on amusement park rides or eating cotton candy at the fair. Instead, he pulled into the driveway of his father's funeral home in Bridgewater, the same place Mom had fallen in love with Dad when she saw him play "Pennies from Heaven" on the piano.

"Let's go in and say hello to your grandmother."

"Gramma Dozie." It was short for "bulldozer," and she had earned the name. She was cross and crabby and always said what was on her mind, little of it nice. She was too tall and too skinny, with deep-set eyes that were always ringed with black circles, like she'd been punched. Dad insisted Dozie was a snappy dresser, but the few times I saw her, she was always in a housecoat, a cigarette in one hand, the other hand on her hip. I was terrified of her, and she wasn't crazy about me either. She was mad that Mom had divorced Dad and once told my aunt Judy, "I want nothing to do with Betty or those kids," and she meant it.

Dad looked over at me.

"Come on," he said. "Let's go."

I felt both of my index fingers go for my head, and I began twirling my hair. Sometimes it was the only thing that helped settle my nerves, and few things made me as nervous as Gramma Dozie (except, of course, Mom).

"Stop that twirling," Dad said. "Nothing's going to hurt you in there."

I wasn't so sure. Dozie and Grampa Chapmann lived in the funeral home, in the same house where dead people were stored in the morgue next door until their funerals. Then when it was time, the caskets were wheeled through the kitchen, sometimes during our Sunday breakfast, to the living room for viewing the next day. So I wasn't at all sure there wasn't something that could hurt me in there. Besides, even without the dead people being wheeled through, there was Gramma Dozie, standing on the porch with a cigarette and looking at Dad through the smoke. But when she saw me get out of the car, she threw the cigarette into the azalea bushes, turned, and disappeared into the house. The screen door slammed behind her.

I followed Dad past the big water fountain on the lawn and up the walkway, dragging my flip-flops along the uneven bricks. Grampa Chapmann met us on the porch, wiping his hands on an apron. He reached out and shook Dad's hand and then gave my head a pat-pat. I shrunk a little and couldn't help but wonder where that hand had been that it needed wiping.

Dad and Grampa talked as they walked into the front room. The curtains were closed, and a couple of dim lamps were lit in the corners. I stopped in the doorway and then took a step back.

At the far side of the room stood a casket, and it was open. I could just see the tip of a large white nose.

"Who do you have today?" Dad asked, walking over to the casket and looking in.

"Joe Rose," Grampa said. "Remember him? He ran the deli on Main Street."

"Sure," Dad said, leaning in to get a better look. "You did a good job, Dad. Good color. Not too much filler in the cheeks. But"—he plucked something from Joe's lip—"you left some suture on the poor guy."

Grampa chuckled. "Comes with the territory, I'm afraid," he said, taking the little piece of string from Dad and tucking it into his apron pocket.

Yuck.

"Come on, Liza. Don't be scared," Dad said, and walked back to where I stood. He put his hand on my shoulder and pushed me forward. "Come *closer.*"

I was quite sure I was close enough. It was hard to take a deep breath because the air stunk from all the flowers draped over the casket and in huge vases on the side tables and floor. I was beginning to get queasy, and for a terrible moment I thought I might throw up on the fancy carpet. I wanted nothing more than to run out of that room, out the front door, and down the street as fast as my legs would carry me. Instead, Dad took my hand and pulled me over to the casket.

"That's better," he said.

I peered over the edge of the casket at Joe Rose. He lay there, white and waxy, one hand resting on the other on his suit coat, his mouth set in a grim line. I swore I saw his chest move. And even though Grampa said he was dead, and I knew that he'd never talk or breathe or smile again, I was suddenly filled with terror that he would, that Joe Rose would rise up and look right at me and bare his yellow crooked teeth.

"Go ahead, touch him," Dad said.

Touch him? I thought. *Really?*

"Touch him," Dad said again, pushing at my elbow. "I don't want you afraid of a cadaver. It's the family business."

I squeezed my eyes shut, reached out, and with the tip of my finger gave Joe Rose a quick poke in his hard chest. It felt like poking a bag of flour. Then, before Dad could grab a hold of me, I turned and ran out of the room, through the front door, and out to the fountain. Leaning over the edge, I dunked my face into the cold water, hoping the shock of it would erase the image of poor, dead Joe Rose's face.

Later that night, I heard Mom downstairs on the phone with Auntie.

"That lying sonofa*bitch*! Roddy doesn't pay a dime of child support, and after two years he has the *nerve* to just show up, looking to take his precious little girl out for the afternoon? I only let her go because I wanted my money. But he didn't give me so much as one damn dollar. He's such a god*damn bastard*!"

She just yelled and yelled into the phone about how she was going to have him arrested. I hoped she wasn't serious, but she sure talked an awful *goddamn* lot about how "just plain *wrong*" it was that he didn't support his children.

But Dad got one thing right: Joe Rose would be the first and only corpse that scared me in the years to come. After that, a dead body was just another "customer" in the family funeral home.

9

TONY

Toward the end of May 1966, Tony finally found his excuse to leave town—leave Avis and the kids, leave their miserable apartment, and leave all his other problems behind. He met two girls, Bonnie Williams and Diane Federoff, who wanted a ride out to California, and he offered to take them, as if it were down to Hyannis rather than thirty-two hundred miles across the country.

They got as far as eastern Arizona before his beat-up 1959 Bonneville overheated. He'd driven more than twenty-six hundred miles since leaving Provincetown, and he'd done it with only a few quick stops, fueled by handfuls of various amphetamines he kept stashed in a coffee can under the front seat. After months of swallowing Solacen like aspirin, he'd started taking amphetamines to help bring him back "up." He'd finally stopped to rest when he was punch-drunk with exhaustion and feared running off the road. He pulled up at the Bonanza Motel outside Amarillo for a couple hours of sleep and a shower. If it hadn't been for the girls, he was sure he'd have already made it to San Francisco.

But the two of them were always demanding he pull over—to eat, to pee, or to stretch their legs. It was always something. Bonnie was worse than Diane; maybe she irked him more because she was plump, and for Tony it was just one more personal weakness. He had always kept himself trim, within five pounds of his ideal weight for his six feet—175 pounds. But more than Bonnie's weight, what most likely chafed him was that she was a true redhead—forthright, even fearless, in ways he knew he would never be; she demanded they stop even though he didn't want to and complained loudly at his car's lack of air-conditioning. "She had a real mouth on her," her sister later said.[1] Diane was the quieter of the two. She was also frail, almost fragile, and stunningly pretty with bright blue eyes, porcelain skin, and long blond hair. She was at once vulnerable and untouchable. Even though she was only sixteen, she reminded Tony of Peggy Lipton, a beautiful actress he'd seen on television. But still, both girls were annoying as hell, and he wished again, as he had a hundred times since leaving Cape Cod, that he'd never offered to give them a ride. But with the two babies and a very unhappy wife back in Provincetown, anything seemed better than listening to the incessant noise in his and Avis's claustrophobic apartment. So there he was—stranded on a remote section of highway with a dead car and two bothersome teenagers.

He'd met the girls at the Fo'csle tavern in Provincetown the week before. Shortened from "forecastle," the place on a ship where sailors sleep and spend their off-duty hours, the Fo'csle was dark and dank, with fish netting, lobster traps, and faded buoys hanging from the ceiling and half a dory sticking out of the far wall. The place reeked of stale cigarettes and urine, and its floor was warped by years of spilled beer and worse. But unlike the bars for tourists and summer people, with overpriced crab cakes and shrimp cocktails and a view of the ocean from their decks, the Fo'csle was a dive where short beers were fifteen cents and "schooners" were twenty-five. And it was one of the few places open year-round. Summer people wouldn't be caught dead in its dingy recesses. One observer at the time described its patrons as "an unapologetically wild bunch, a veritable Manson family minus the homicides. Swimming on acid and pumped up on speed, [they] shoplifted and stole bicycles. Some fucked everyone in town, sold drugs, failed invariably at menial jobs, and skipped out on the rent."[2] The description could have been written with Tony Costa in mind.

When Tony met the girls at the bar, they were broke, hungry, and badly needed a place to crash and a hot bath. They had run away from their homes in Florida and had been on the road for weeks, following the rides where they took them, ending up in Provincetown in late May. Tony later said they were groupies of various cover bands and found themselves at the Fo'csle after following one of the musicians to Cape Cod. Because Tony fancied himself a friend to the downtrodden, he suggested they could sleep on his couch until they figured out what they were going to do next. They jumped at the offer. When he appeared at home with his two grungy houseguests, Avis welcomed them, but after a week of the girls eating "everything but the mouse seed," Avis demanded Tony get "rid of them." The girls had been helpful enough looking after the babies, but she and Tony could barely afford to feed themselves and the boys, let alone the two strays from God only knew where.

Tony was already thinking of heading out to San Francisco, where he'd heard that in a neighborhood called Haight-Ashbury drugs were as cheap and plentiful as dime-store candy. He offered to take the girls along because they said one of their band members had a big house there and lots of money and drugs. Tony liked the sound of that.

On their way out the door, Bonnie and Diane stole Avis's only pair of good shoes. Unaware, Avis exchanged addresses with the girls so that they could write, and then stood on the porch holding one-year-old Michael on her hip and watched as the car pulled out of the driveway. When the car turned toward Route 6A, she saw Diane's thin, pale arm waving from the window. She never saw either girl again.

When Tony had offered the ride, he'd imagined a wild road trip; he had plenty of drugs, and the girls seemed amenable to just about anything he had in mind. But after a few hundred miles, the girls had become tiresome, singing loudly and off-key to the Mamas and the Papas hit single "Monday, Monday" whenever it came on the radio, or, even worse, "California, Here I Come!" Diane had a high, reedy voice, and when she sang, she squeaked the lyrics. It felt like his head was in a vise whenever they opened their mouths, and he yelled at them to "shut the hell up" until he was hoarse. And now his damned car was overheating in the middle of the godforsaken desert; the last town they went through had been at least an hour earlier, and it had only a couple of buildings with FOR SALE signs in dark windows. Since then, he'd seen nothing but cacti, prairie dogs, and turkey vultures circling lazily above the roadkill that littered the highway. He wished he'd brought his taxidermy kit: he'd never had the chance to stuff a vulture, let alone a prairie dog.

Mercifully, Tony spied a car approaching them across the hot sage and bitter brush, the sun glinting off the windshield as it bumped along the rutted road toward them on Route 66. It was the first car he'd seen in more than an hour. When the car was finally within about a hundred yards, he saw that it was the Arizona Highway Patrol and quickly pushed the coffee can out of sight under the front seat.

When the officer approached the car, he saw three hot and sweaty faces looking up at him.

"We're on our way to San Francisco!" Bonnie volunteered.

"Thought we'd see the Painted Desert on our way," Tony added.

"Painted Desert?" the cop said. "You missed that by about a hundred miles"—he pointed behind them—"that way." He looked inside the car. "Where's your water jug? Gotta have a water jug if you're going to drive these parts."

"Oh, I didn't know," Tony said. Then added lamely, "I'm from Boston."

The cop chuckled, pushing his hat back off his slick brow.

"Yep, I saw your plates. Don't see many folks from Massachusetts way out here. You better be careful in these parts. When people wander off into the desert, we usually only find a pile of bones, and not even that if the coyotes get there first." He pronounced it *KYE-oats*. Tony had never heard it said that way.

Tony peered into the desert; there was nothing but hot dust as far as the eye could see. Compared to crowded Boston and even Cape Cod, the desert felt like the moon—endless and anonymous and wild. It was indeed a place to get lost, or a place to lose something and, possibly, as the cop said, lose it forever. Once the car had cooled down, and with a water jug supplied by the officer, Tony and the girls continued down the hot highway.

What happened next remained a mystery for more than fifty years. Tony was back in Provincetown less than a week after he had left. He told

Avis that instead of driving Bonnie and Diane all the way to California as he had said he would, he had left them in Pennsylvania after the cops told him he couldn't cross state lines with a minor (Diane was sixteen). But then his story changed. Later, he told police he *had* driven them all the way to California and left them at their friend's mansion in Hayward, a small but wealthy farming community on the southern end of San Francisco Bay.

Neither story was ever confirmed by investigators or his own defense team. But regardless of where Tony "left" them, the two "groupies" who ran away from home seemed to evaporate into thin air.

The disappearance of Bonnie Williams and Diane Federoff caused barely a ripple of concern, even in their immediate families. Because both were "wild child" children of the sixties, Bonnie's mother and Diane's grandparents, with whom she had been sent to live, assumed the girls would return home when they were ready; worrying about their running away from home was one thing, but doing anything about it was futile.[3] They weren't the only girls who had vanished. The mid-1960s was a time of runaways, and the parents of itinerant teenagers came to expect sudden and unexplained absences. As the sexual revolution hit its stride and drug use among America's youth became rampant and routine, police took less and less interest in yet another kid running away from home. Across America, four thousand women and girls were reported missing, and police departments' phones were constantly ringing. Few of the reports were ever investigated, and some of the women never returned home. It wouldn't be until the infamous cases of Patricia Hearst, J. Paul Getty III and his severed ear sent with a ransom demand, and a millionaire's daughter buried alive with a tube to breathe through that missing women and children became news and police across the country finally took notice.

In short, the 1960s was a good time for anyone looking to find an aimless young woman in need of a friendly face.

Running away was a normal, even safe coming-of-age phenomenon for boys in America. But the growing number of runaway girls was alarming because, unlike the boys, the girls often turned up dead. The demographics of runaways also changed; whereas children from poorer neighborhoods, often orphans, ran away to find a better life and a regular meal, by the late sixties, it had become a middle-class problem. Churches began setting up runaway shelters to deal with the issue, and in the early 1970s, a nationwide hotline was established to better track the missing youth. But all of that came too late for Bonnie and Diane.

10

LIZA

I heard about Tony Costa weeks before I met him. I was seven that summer of 1966, when Mom got the job at the Royal Coachman and the three of us shared a single room on the first floor near the office. Louisa and I did our best to stay out of her hair, and whenever I could, I'd tag along behind Cecelia as she made her rounds through the rooms. If she wasn't humming some church hymn, she was talking about "my Tony."

"When my Tony gets back from his trip, I'll have him come over and meet you." "My Tony is a good man." "I raised my Tony by myself after his father died in the war." She didn't say what war, but I figured it was a long time ago and far away.

Cecelia talked about *her Tony* in a sort of low mumble, like a lobster boat idling at the pier, while she folded towels from the dryer or tucked hospital corners on the beds. I was happy to be out of my mother's reach, and happy to help Cecelia where I could—handing her little squares of soap for the dishes on the bathroom counters or gathering up the dirty linens from where guests had thrown them on the floor. She always thanked me with a smile or pat on the arm or even a hug. It was the hugs that I waited for most. She'd take me in her arms and hold me there as if she had nowhere else to go and nothing to do, as if she loved me. I'd seen Mom give Louisa a hug or two like that, but I'd never gotten one.

One day, as Cecelia and I were moving between rooms, a man drove up to the motel in a beat-up Oldsmobile. One of the many things Grampa Georgie had drilled into me was how to recognize the make of a car, and every time I got it right, I felt something close to pride and wished he were there to notice. I was standing by the linen cart with an armful of towels and stared as the man got out of the car and then smiled in my direction. He was tall and suntanned, with thick dark hair and straight white teeth. I was confused. I didn't know why a stranger would smile at me, but then he said, "Hi, Mother," and I realized Cecelia was right beside me. She stopped emptying towels from a large laundry bag and looked toward him. A look of worry momentarily flooded her face. Then, she gave her head a little shake and rushed past me, her arms open.

"Tony!" she said, throwing her arms around the man and kissing him on the cheek.

I hadn't seen many mothers throw their arms around their kids and kiss them, so I watched, my mouth open at the spectacle. But then I saw the man grimace and sort of shrink as he pushed Cecelia away. He reached up to wipe his cheek where her lipstick had left a red smear.

"I told you I don't like lipstick," he said.

"I like to look good for work," Cecelia said quietly.

She no longer seemed happy to see him. I wondered what had happened.

"You're back so soon. I thought you might find a job out there for a few months."

"I told you when I called from the road that things didn't work out and I decided to come back."

"But everything went okay, yes? No problems?" Cecelia said.

"Everything went fine, but I didn't end up taking the girls all the way to California," Tony said. "I left them in Pennsylvania instead, that's all." And before Cecelia could ask why, he volunteered, "They got bored with the ride, so I dropped them outside Philly. Where they wanted. It's where they wanted," he said again. "So here I am."

She seemed to think about that for a minute, then gave a little sniff.

"Well, Vinnie has been taking very good care of me with you away," she said, giving the bosom of her yellow sweater a little flick-flick-flick with her fingers, as if brushing off lint.

Tony laughed, but the laugh wasn't very nice.

"Yeah, I'm sure he did," Tony said.

Finally, Tony looked over Cecelia's shoulder and saw me standing there.

"And who's this?" he said. He smiled for the first time since getting out of the car, and I realized this Tony had a nice face.

Cecelia turned and also smiled. "Ah! This is Liza. My boss's girl and my little helper," she said, beckoning me over. "Liza, come say hello to my Tony."

I dropped my armload of towels onto the housekeeping cart and walked over, feeling my face burning with the attention both she and Tony focused on me. Not knowing what else to do, I put out my hand. With a little chuckle, Tony squatted down and took off his sunglasses. His eyes were brown like mine, and when he smiled, they smiled too. I watched my entire hand disappear into his large, tanned fingers.

"It's very nice to meet you, Liza. I hope to see you around, okay?"

All I was capable of was a nod into the front of my shirt.

"Okay, okay, enough of this," Cecelia said. "Liza and I have work to do."

Tony let go of my hand and stood up. When he did, I finally glanced up at him. He was looking toward the main door of the motel.

"Did you ask if there's any work around here for me?" he said. "I gotta find a job."

"Yes, I talked to Mrs. Becker about you. She runs the place most days. She's expecting you." Cecelia pointed toward the office.

Without another word, he strode off.

"It's good to have you back, Tony," Cecelia called after him. He didn't turn around.

As she and I walked back toward the linen closet, she shook her head gently.

"Ah, my Tony," she said.

11

TONY

Soon after Tony returned from his mysterious trip with Bonnie and Diane, he and Avis were fighting more than they were talking, and Tony moved out. It was the first, but it wouldn't be the last time he did. As she watched his car drive away from the apartment, she noticed a car with Indiana plates drive up. Twelve years after disappearing from her life, her father suddenly returned. She later wrote that having him walk back into her life was her "every-single-birthday-candle wish come true."[1]

For five days, Clinton "Johnny" Johnson reconnected with his daughter and got acquainted with his grandsons. A photo of their reunion showed a smiling Johnny, Avis, and her two boys and was made all the more poignant, as it would be their last. Johnny died two weeks later in a car accident back home in Indiana. He drove his car off the road, through his front yard and into a cornfield, where he was thrown free, but then the car rolled back on him, crushing him. He was forty-seven years old. The man Avis had mourned losing her entire life was now gone forever.

Even though Tony was working at the Royal Coachman, he still couldn't afford an apartment, so after he left Avis, he spent most nights sleeping out on the dunes or crashing on friends' couches. But when Johnny Johnson was killed in late July, Avis was grief-stricken and lonely, and she asked Tony to move back in with her and the boys.

It was hardly a joyful reconciliation; along with their ongoing money squabbles, their sex life remained stagnant. In fact, he recoiled from her embrace. It was as if "he was scared to touch me," she said later. Tony himself admitted that he feared what might happen if he did. And according to Avis, he rarely touched her again, and when he did it was often by force. On one of those occasions, he told her, "You're my wife and I want to fuck you," threw her to the bed and took her violently. She didn't think of it as rape because "I was his wife,"[2] and in 1966 women couldn't charge their husbands with sexual assault.*

By this time, Tony was regularly taking the sedative Solacen along with a variety of amphetamines by alternating handfuls. He was also experimenting with an ever-increasing array of street drugs—pot, hash, and even heroin and LSD. He told Avis he felt as if he were sitting outside himself, observing "Tony" from a distance.

Once, when she asked him, "Do you remember the time—?" he shut her off. She realized he never wanted to answer questions about what he did or where he'd been.[3]

"No, I don't want to talk about that: that wasn't me; that was someone else."[4] He looked upon himself as totally removed, separate from *that* Tony; it fascinated him more than it repulsed or scared him, and he set out to learn as much as he could about his favorite subject: Tony Costa. He read books on astrology, witchcraft, Buddhism, and the various psychotropic drugs he now took like aspirin. He also shared his self-observations and his growing feelings of darkness with friends.

Over a few beers one night at Fo'csle, he told a buddy that he thought of doing "really bad things, really horrible, terrible things."

The friend shrugged it off. "Yeah, Tony. We all feel like that sometimes."

Tony erupted in anger, something he rarely revealed to anyone but Avis. "You don't understand," he said, slamming his beer on the table as he rose to leave. "Nobody understands!"

---

* Spousal rape wouldn't become a crime in all fifty states until 1993. Even so, it remains very difficult to prove a lack of sexual consent within a marriage.

12

LIZA

Mom had the kind of looks that stopped people in the street. Even when she was a baby, strangers told Nana that they'd "never seen such a pretty child!" I don't think Nana, a plain, stern woman, ever forgave her for it. As Mom grew up, those beautiful baby looks matured into a sexuality so animal it was almost feral. She even smelled different from other moms— earthy, like warm topsoil.

Grampa Georgie called her a real piece of work. She had curly, shoulder-length blond hair that she "tipped" even blonder and later wore in a stiff beehive. She had freckles sprinkled across a button nose, a pretty smile, and bright blue eyes that blazed, especially when she was angry, which by the time I came along seemed like most of the time. She loved to laugh, but usually at the expense of others, and pulling a good prank on someone made her day. On top of everything else, her body resembled that of Marilyn Monroe's—curvy with *big boobs*. She warned me I'd probably end up with *big boobs* too, and that if I wasn't careful I could also end up with a *fat ass* like hers. The *dreaded Noonan ass*, she called it. She said she'd inherited hers from Grampa Georgie's mother and her mother before her. It was the only thing about her appearance Mom hated. Everything else worked just fine for her. In spite of her *dreaded fat ass* (and as I would later learn, maybe *because* of it) men seemed to line up at her door, waiting their turn to ask her out. Even I could see there was something wild and raw about her that men wanted, but it frightened me.

=======

That spring, after we had returned to West Bridgewater, Mom had found a new boyfriend, Tom, her boss, who was the principal of Stoughton High School, where she taught. Tom asked her to go on a date the minute he heard she'd gotten a divorce. Even though she loved the attention from the good-looking, well-educated principal, she had said no; he was married, and she didn't date married men. But Tom kept trying. Finally, he came to Mom with tears in his eyes and horrible news: his wife was dying of cancer. Doctors didn't think she'd last another month, six weeks tops. Soon after that, Mom gave in, and Tom became her secret boyfriend. He was not, however, a secret around our house. After he'd show up, she'd put us to bed, sometimes at three in the afternoon, pulling the curtains and telling us it was nighttime and to stop complaining and go to sleep. A few times, when I tried to get out of the room to go to the bathroom in the night, I'd find the door was locked, and I'd lie awake worried that if I fell back asleep, I'd pee the bed. A few times I did, and in the morning I had to rush to get the sheets in the machine before she found out.

That summer on the Cape, Mom waited for Tom's wife to die. I imagined Tom at his big house in Stoughton, carefully instructing the nurses in white starched uniforms how to take good care of his wife while he was at the beach, getting some air as she insisted he do, and then gently kissing her dried-up old forehead and tiptoeing out of the darkened room. *Poor old, dying Mrs. Tom*, I thought. I wondered if she knew my mother was counting the hours until she died and that Tom didn't spend any time at the beach getting fresh air.

As soon as Mom saw Tom's car speeding up the RC's driveway, she would put on her favorite pink lipstick, send us to Auntie and Uncle Hank's apartment above the office, grab a bucket of ice, a bottle of rum and a handful of little bottles of Coca-Cola, and head to the motel's most expensive room by the pool with Tom in tow.

Some nights when she knew she wouldn't be returning to our room, she'd send us home with Cecelia. Those were good nights because Tony would usually show up and Cecelia would cook us all dinner. Sometimes it was American chop suey, and sometimes it was what she called a Portuguese special, and she'd put a steaming bowl of sausages and pasta on the table. It didn't matter what Cecelia cooked; the fact that she cooked at all made it special. Mom taught cooking in her home ec class but was usually too busy to cook for us at home and instead opened a can of something and heated it up on the stove—that was Mom's idea of dinner.

Other nights, Mom left us with a couple of nuts who worked at the Royal Coachman, Mark and Debbie. Debbie's eyes were usually half-closed, and Mark's were so red they looked like they must hurt. They would drive us around town in Mom's car with the windows wide-open, screaming "FUCK YOU! NO, FUCK *YOU!*" at each other, swerving across the road and slamming on the brakes so hard Louisa and I would fly forward, hit the back of the front seat, and land on the floor in a heap. They always had a six-pack of beer on the seat between them and threw the empties out the window as they drove along. Mom told us littering was what bums did, but I didn't say anything. The last thing in the world I wanted to do was make Mark or Debbie any more mad than they already were. One time when we were driving home from doing errands in Hyannis on the Mid-Cape Highway, Debbie got so mad she screamed, "I hate you! FUCK YOU!" and reached over and grabbed the wheel, giving it a hard yank.

"WHAT THE FUCK?" Mark yelled as he tried to right the wheel, but it was too late. The car veered off the road, and when the tires hit the sand in the grassy median, it flipped over once before coming to a stop upside down in the grass, the wheels still spinning above us. I don't remember much after that, except that Mom was glad none of us got killed, and she told Debbie not to worry about it—she was ready for a new car anyway.

I never told Mom about the beer.

13

LIZA

I was standing with Mom near the wooden trash bins at the back of the motel when I saw Tony's Oldsmobile drive up. Nancy Sinatra's hit, "These Boots Are Made for Walkin'" was blaring through the open windows. As he pulled into a parking space, he switched off the radio.

"Hey there, Little Liza!" he called to me, and waved.

Little Liza. The only other person who ever called me that had been my great-grandmother, Nana Newquist. But she said it "Lil' Liza" and with a thick Swedish accent. After church every Sunday we'd go over to her house and she'd greet me at the back door with a sugar cube sitting in an inch of coffee. "Hey, Lil' Liza! Ready for a cuppa with your nana?" I loved hearing it again, from Tony. Little Liza.

I was about to wave back when Mom said, "Who the hell is *that*?" My hand froze at my side.

"It's Tony," I said. "Cecelia's son. I met him the other day."

She looked at me, doubting whether I was telling the truth, but before she could speak, Tony walked over and put his hand out to Mom.

"Hi, I'm Tony Costa, Cecelia's son. Joan said she had some work around the motel for me today."

I gave Mom a *See? I told you so* look, but she ignored it. Mom took his hand, her eyes suddenly bright, a little smile turning up the corners of her mouth.

"Well, *hello*, Tony. I can't imagine why we haven't met before. I'm Betty, the head of housekeeping."

"Hello, Betty. Nice to meet you," Tony said.

"Your mother is one hell of a hard worker," Mom said.

Tony nodded. "Yeah. I wish she'd clean *my* house!" They both laughed. Then he turned to me. "Hey there, Liza. Nice to see you again."

I felt myself blush under my tan.

"What's Joan got you doing today?" Mom said.

"I think she needs a load of trash taken to the dump." Tony looked over at me. "Hey, why don't I take Liza here for the ride?"

Tony looked at me and grinned. Like any man who was nice to me, he reminded me of Grampa Georgie and of my dad—tall, gentle, suntanned, and for some reason eager to have me around when no one else seemed to be.

"Great. Take her sister too, would you? They've been underfoot all day. I could use the break," Mom said, and went back to the office. Seemed she'd had enough of chatting up Tony.

I felt like reaching out so my fingers would once again disappear into his large, warm hand. But I didn't dare. It wasn't so much that he would slap my hand away—somehow, I knew he wouldn't. It was that Mom would.

I ran to get Louisa, and soon we were sitting in the cab of the Royal Coachman's utility truck with Tony, headed down the driveway with a load of the motel's trash. Turning around in the seat, I saw Mom standing in the office door, watching. I put my hand up to wave, but before I could, she turned and disappeared into the motel.

Out of the corner of my eye, I looked over at Tony. His face was angular, with strong bones that came to a point at a dimpled chin. His skin was smooth and dark, his teeth were white and really straight, and he wore his thick, black hair parted on the side with a clump hanging down over one eye. He had on granny glasses, which made him look smart even though they slipped down his nose all the time, and he kept pushing them back up and giving them a little adjustment with his thumb and forefinger. He sniffed a lot, as if he had allergies or a cold, through a nose that was just a bit too large for his face. I liked the way he looked.

I sat back and smiled; I felt so grown up sitting next to him on the seat, our legs almost touching. We drove the long way through town, up Route 6A and then onto Bradford Street.

As we neared the Dairy Land in the west end of town, Tony said, "Hey, girls, either of you like ice cream?"

Louisa and I both squealed "YES!" and in the next breath added, "Chocolate is our favorite!"

He laughed at our simultaneous glee and turned into Dairy Land.

"You two wait here. I'll just be a sec."

We watched him walk up to the window and lean in to give his order to the girl inside.

"Maybe he'll get us a double scoop!" Louisa said.

I gave her a hard pinch, and she shrank into the door on her side of the front seat.

"Shut up! And don't be greedy," I said. "If you get all greedy, he may never let us ride with him again."

She whimpered quietly but didn't say another word. She knew better than to challenge me if I was in one of my moods. Like Mom, I had my share, and a lot of them were directed at Louisa. Whereas I was covered in painful, unsightly eczema, Louisa had flawless olive skin that looked as if it had been poured smoothly over her bones. Whereas my hair was so curly combs got stuck in its tangle, hers was thick and wavy, almost luxuriant, and softly framed her face and deep brown eyes. And whereas I didn't even have a nickname, besides references to Dumbo and Bambi, hers was Brown Bear, for all her adorable beauty. And I made her suffer for it.

When Tony returned a minute or two later, he handed us our cones through the window. Then he climbed in and we drove back onto Route 6, heading to the Provincetown dump. As we drove out of town, Tony turned on the radio, switching through the channels until he found a song he liked: "(You're My) Soul and Inspiration."

"Yes!" he said, turning up the radio and singing along to the chorus: "'Without you, baby, what good am I?'" I knew the words by heart but

didn't dare join in. Mom always yelled at me that I "ruined" songs by singing aloud to them.

We drove along, the summer air rushing around us, each of us trying
to finish our ice cream before it melted all over the place. I was as happy
as I'd been since I realized the RC had an Olympic-size swimming pool.

Soon, Tony was a familiar face around the RC, loading the pickup with
trash, fixing a leaky toilet, or helping move large appliances and furniture. He was big and strong and did a lot of the jobs around the motel
no one else seemed able to. I heard one of the guys at the front desk say,
"Tony could pick you up and throw you out that window, if he wanted to."
(I didn't know why he'd ever want to do such a thing and didn't ask.)

Louisa and I would watch for him to arrive at the motel so we could
ride along on his errands. Most days we weren't disappointed. Auntie
would call out, "Here comes Tony!" and we'd run to meet him as he drove
in or rode his bike up to the motel. We became his regular companions
as he made the rounds to the town dumps in Provincetown and Truro
with the bed of the RC's truck piled high with trash. Within a few blocks
of leaving the motel, there would be a flock of seagulls following us, and
whenever we hit a bump, loose papers and other scraps of junk flew out
and down the road behind us. Unless it was raining, we drove with the
windows down, Louisa's and my hair flying around our faces and getting
stuck in the ice cream on our cheeks and chins. The truck radio was always
on. Tony told me he loved Top Ten music, and the summer of 1966 music
didn't disappoint: the Beatles and the Beach Boys and the Rolling Stones
and the Supremes and the Lovin' Spoonful and the Righteous Brothers
and the Mamas and the Papas (although whenever "Monday, Monday"
came on, he'd switch stations with a quick jerk of the dial) and Johnny
Rivers, who sang my favorite song, "Poor Side of Town."

Driving around with Tony at the wheel, the windows down and the
radio volume up just about as far as it would go, I felt like every eye of
Provincetown was on us as we passed. No matter what the errand was, as

soon as Tony jangled his keys in our direction, Louisa and I would bound to the truck like puppies, excited just to drive through town with him, and sometimes, if he had time, he'd push us on the swing set next to the Dairy Land. I loved that he never seemed to be in a rush or eager to get rid of us. Unlike every other adult in our lives, he seemed to like just being with us.

Tony talked a lot about his father, a war hero, he said, who'd drowned while saving the life of another sailor in someplace called *New Ginnie*. He told us that his *real* father had been a lot smarter than his *stupid stepfather* and how he wished and wished his mother had never married the *lowlife jerk* and how Tony's half brother was just as *stupid*. (I was glad I didn't have one of those.) But when he asked about our father and what he was like, I told him we didn't have one either because it was easier than the truth.

In spite of his occasional visits, Dad remained a stranger to me. When Mom slammed the door on him and threw him out of her life, she pretty much threw him out of ours as well. I would tell people I didn't have a father because I couldn't explain things I didn't understand. I was sad and ashamed. Nobody else's parents in the Irish Catholic neighborhood where we grew up had divorced. None.

Tony nodded and reached over with his free hand to give my leg a sympathetic squeeze and a pat-pat-pat. I looked at his fingers touching my thigh. I tried to remember if I'd ever seen a man's hand on my leg before.

Tony was different. Unlike Mom and Grampa Georgie and even Cecelia, he didn't smell of liquor, he didn't swear, and he never seemed to shout or get angry. When Grampa Georgie drove, he was always yelling at somebody: "What an *asshole*" or "Light's not gonna get any greener, buddy!" But Tony never yelled at the car in front of us or pounded on the steering wheel. Instead, he told stories and asked us about school and living at the RC and our house in West Bridgewater. And he sang along with whatever song was playing on the radio. After a few times riding with him, I finally dared ask if I could sing along too, and he laughed and said, "Sure!" like he really meant it. And he was thoughtful. Whenever he'd light one of his Parliaments while it was raining and the window wasn't already open, he'd make sure to open it a crack so the smoke wouldn't fill the truck. He was really good at blowing smoke rings, and I'd poke their holes with my finger before they disappeared. Once I asked him if he would let me try, and he just laughed.

"No way, kiddo! You're too young to smoke! Maybe in a few years, if you still want to try it."

"Oh, I will!" I assured him, feeling happy and grown up.

Whenever he took us on his errands, he would buy me and Louisa some sort of sweet treat, Lorna Doones, which he said were the best cookies in the world, or our other favorite, orange Popsicles, even though we made a mess. Just when the syrup was about to drip on the seats, he'd reach over and wipe the drips off our bare legs before they got the seat all sticky. Then he'd pull out a roll of paper towels and help us clean our hands of syrup. He was funny that way; he didn't like messes of any kind and would always be wiping things clean, even when they weren't dirty, like the handles of his tools, the bed of the truck, or the steering wheel. It was as if he could never get anything quite clean enough.

Sometimes Tony drove us all the way out of town to the Pine Grove Cemetery on the edge of the woods in Truro. He said he liked to go there and think because it was quiet and peaceful and with two babies at home he needed a lot of quiet and peace. Even the sound of too much change in his pockets could drive him nuts. He loved his sons, of course, but he really, really wanted a daughter, he said, maybe two so they'd be sisters, like me and Louisa. We'd walk through the rows of old tombstones, some of them so worn by time and the weather that you couldn't see the name of who was underneath our feet. If it was raining, we just sat in the truck—Tony smoking his cigarettes—and watched the hawks and crows fly through the scrub oak and pitch pines, their squawks piercing the otherwise silent woods around us. Now and then Tony would forget the time and we'd be gone until almost dark. I wanted to ask if his wife and babies missed him, but I didn't dare. I had met Avis a couple of times, and she seemed nice, even if she and the kids all looked sad and like they could use a hot bath. On extra-special nights, Tony would take me and Louisa out for a drive to Race Point Beach, where the air was cooler and the crowds were gone, leaving the parking lot and the sand dunes empty and quiet. It was almost like our own private beach without another person in sight. He also liked to stop at the salvage yard, even if it was closed for the day; Tony somehow knew how to get in. Some evenings we wouldn't get home until after sunset, hungry and tired and ready for bed. Mom didn't seem to mind, or even much notice.

14

THE PROVINCE LANDS

The Pilgrims called it the Province Lands. Most Americans and even many Cape Codders don't know that the Pilgrims first landed not at Plymouth but at Provincetown. They spent a frigid winter trying to survive but just over half of the 132 passengers and crew aboard the *Mayflower* died from scurvy, pneumonia, and tuberculosis, as well as at least one drowning—that of Dorothy Bradford, the future governor's wife, who either fell or jumped off the *Mayflower* and died in the icy waters of Provincetown Harbor. In the spring, the Pilgrims decided the tip of Cape Cod was too inhospitable, and most of them set sail across the bay for Plymouth, where they finally settled for good.

Life was hard for those who remained in Provincetown, particularly after they denuded the land of its old forests, leaving it a moonscape of marshes and sand, sand that blew across the barren land in the incessant wind. And while whaling was also grueling work, at least there were a lot of them. Until the mid-1800s, whales were so plentiful in the waters off Provincetown that one could be harpooned from the beach. Immigrants, particularly fishermen from Portugal and the Azores, flocked to its bountiful shores.

By the turn of the twentieth century, the quaint fishing village had been discovered by the likes of Charles Webster Hawthorne and Edward Hopper, Eugene O'Neill and Edna St. Vincent Millay, who painted and wrote famous works in little shacks that dotted the sand dunes less than a mile from Commercial Street. When they and their fellow writers and artists arrived, most of them fleeing the heat and stench of New York and Boston summers, they found a quiet, sleepy downtown with unpaved streets and small shops and cottages so close together that residents knew when their neighbors were cooking bacon for breakfast. The artists came for the promise of another cloudless day and a mirror-flat bay smelling of sun-warmed sand, seagrass, rose hips, and bayberries. But mostly they came for the quality of the sunlight, said to be the best in the world for artists.

But Provincetown's bucolic reputation for tranquil beauty and social tolerance had a dark and violent underside. In the early 1920s, the KKK burned a cross on the lawn of St. Peter the Apostle Catholic Church because it embraced the ever-increasing immigrant population—ironic, since a huge percentage of the population *was* immigrants. Nonetheless, the angry minority let its hatred be seen and heard. Mercifully, the town rallied to defend the church and its Portuguese immigrants, and the KKK left and went searching for more xenophobic brethren.

In those days, more than sixty narrow wooden wharves stretched out into the sheltered bay. Deep-sea fishing was then and remains one of the world's most dangerous occupations, and when fishermen came home after months at sea with the holds of their ships finally full, they would kneel on a wharf, bending to kiss its rough planks, and thank God that they had made it back from the roiling Atlantic one more time.

By the 1960s, Provincetown had been discovered by the world beyond the artist community. Norman Mailer described it to Jackie Kennedy as "the Wild West of the East." From Memorial Day to Labor Day, its two main thoroughfares, long since paved, were swarming with bicycles, Volkswagen Beetles covered with peace-sign decals, Harley-Davidson motorcycles ridden by tattooed men in leather vests, their long hair under WWII army-green helmets, and crowded family station wagons, with striped beach chairs tied to the tops, all headed to the end of MacMillan Wharf or the beach. Souvenir shops, stores dedicated to selling only leather or penny candy or beach umbrellas, had all but replaced the fishmongers, Portuguese bakeries, and dusty bookstores. From end to end, the air around Commercial Street smelled of burnt sugar from the cotton candy and candied apples sold out of many storefronts. It smelled of fried clams and grilled hot dogs from John's Footlong. It smelled of suntan oil and stale sweat, and when a bikini-clad girl on a bicycle or in a camper van full of teenagers passed, it smelled of patchouli oil and marijuana.

The Beatles' first hit, "Love Me Do," could be heard in the streets. Hippies clad in hip-hugger bell-bottoms and leather sandals danced. Closeted homosexuals, far from America's mainstream and its judgmental eyes, could finally and literally come out of their closets and front doors to a new and delicious freedom. For many, Provincetown offered a refuge from the ignorant and bigoted thinking that young straight men had to "watch out" for gay men. Even the trusted newsman Mike Wallace warned America on a 1967 episode of *CBS Reports* that an otherwise "normal-looking man" could attempt to befriend you on the street only to try to turn you into a homosexual.[1] But in Provincetown, the weird and eccentric were celebrated, not persecuted. This was twenty years before the AIDS epidemic decimated the gay community, a time when the worst that people feared from indiscriminate sex was a hangover and a penicillin shot.

No matter how hard some of the locals pushed back against the tide, the country's old and young, Black and White, artists and bohemians, hippies and homosexuals, flooded into Provincetown and changed it forever. Unlike other seaside resort areas, Provincetown historically had not had a huge social divide between the locals and the summer people. Its celebration of the iconoclast allowed for all classes to sit at the same table; it was not unusual to have the local girl who waited on you at lunch be sitting next to you at Tennessee Williams's dinner party that night. Here, the people who wore IZOD polo shirts and Lilly Pulitzer skirts and those who wore flannel work shirts and blue jeans shiny with dirt and grease sat elbow to elbow at the Atlantic House's happy hour bar.

It was on those streets that Tony Costa roamed, encountering Provincetown at its bohemian best—from Divine in her full drag queen glory to the aging Judy Garland, the pied piper to a parade of gay men. He watched men strut down Commercial Street in Speedo bathing suits and women wearing what were called "cunt ticklers"—skirts so short their pubis showed. And he often frequented "the Benches" outside town hall, a favorite gathering place of local teenagers known as the Meat Rack, where easy drugs and a quick blowjob were for the asking—all within just feet of the elementary school and the police station, the latter of which was housed in the basement of the town hall. There was Prescott Townsend, a Boston Brahmin and one of the nation's first gay activists, who rode the streets and beaches on a motorcycle handing out gay liberation material and who let random youth stay in his house for thirty-five cents a night. And always, there were artists and writers and performers, washing dishes and cleaning fish at the Cold Storage by day in order to pay for a drink or hit of LSD that night. When those starving artists couldn't afford to buy drinks, they'd go to Piggy's or the Atlantic House and wait for other patrons to hit the dance floor so they could slip over to the vacated table and drink their beers and finish off their half-eaten hamburgers.

Tony looked like just another stoned loner seeking an escape and his next thrill. Many nights he'd stop by his mother's apartment for dinner and to do laundry, but he craved solitude and silence. So he walked, often all night, finding his rare moments of peace and calm.

15

TONY

Tony Costa considered himself more than just an intellectual; he considered himself a superior mind. He visited the public library so often that Alice Joseph, the librarian, knew him by name and would hold books aside that she hoped he'd enjoy. He requested volumes on law, psychology, Eastern religion, as well as taxidermy and anatomy.

They'd sit quietly and talk about books and current events. He seemed to know so much about so many topics. He often boasted that he was going to become a doctor, having realized how "easy" it was to perform operations like an appendectomy or even an abortion. He also seemed determined to "better" himself. She'd find him laboriously copying words and their variations from a thesaurus into a notebook he always carried with him, as if for a later quiz. A plump and somewhat dowdy woman, Alice enjoyed the polite young man's visits. But too many times he'd come with a pack of his friends, friends Alice wished would stay outside. They were too loud, too rude, and unfortunately too unwashed; she always felt as if she needed to check the books they touched for any unsightly stains or grimy fingerprints or for pages that had been torn out. These friends were also years younger than Tony, which she found troubling, and he passed out Juicy Fruit gum to them, as if they were his children. It was almost as if he were grooming them for something. She even heard one of the boys call him Lord Antone and Sire something, and it unsettled her. The entire ragtag group sported odd nicknames: Snowman, Weed, Romulus, Sunshine, Boots, Fluff, Speed, Fingers, Cookie, Bubbles, Shag, Snow. She would watch as Tony and his strange pack left the library, shaking her head, wondering why a man of Tony's intelligence and, well, his warmth would want to hang out with such a bad lot.

Sometimes he would come to the library with a sweet teenager named Susan Perry, a petite girl with brown eyes and light brown hair who was known as a bit of a tomboy but who otherwise didn't stand out from the crowd. The librarian felt sorry for her. Town gossip had it that Susan's mother was an alcoholic who would sit in her easy chair from sunup to sundown chain-smoking unfiltered Pall Malls and drinking beer after beer, occasionally staggering out to her front porch to yell at mischievous boys who dared each other to knock on her door before running away laughing. Susan's parents had recently divorced, and her father had gained custody of the six children who still lived at home (the eldest daughter had recently gotten married and moved out).

Albert Perry was something of a living legend in town, owning and operating one of Provincetown's oldest and best-known fishing boats, the *Jennie B.* Like every captain up and down the Eastern Seaboard, Perry was gone to sea for weeks at a time, leaving his second-oldest child, Susan, in charge of the brood. Barely sixteen when this burden was placed upon her, Susan could only have been overwhelmed and resentful at having to raise five children by herself with just the meager allowance her father left for food while he was at sea.

Alice Joseph anxiously watched Susan and the boys she hung around with. She could see that the girl craved attention and affection, which she often found with the wrong crowd, particularly after she dropped out of high school in her junior year. But Susan had dreams and got a job as a maid at the big Royal Coachman motel out on Beach Point in order to earn money to go to the 1968 Olympics in Mexico City. Alice hoped Susan would make it out of Provincetown, and until then, she trusted that the girl had found in Tony a friend who treated her well.

16

TONY

Christmas 1966 and New Year's came and went. Avis was once again pregnant, this time with their third baby. As her belly grew, everyone around her, especially Tony, hoped this baby would be a girl. Avis just hoped the baby was healthy.

In March 1967, Tony went back to Dr. Callis's office complaining of recurrent stomach pain and ongoing depression; Avis was eight months pregnant and exhausted, money was typically tight, and they were once again fighting all the time. Along with more Solacen, Callis prescribed a newly approved drug, Aventyl, for depression. It's doubtful whether Callis read the warning label: *Side effects include hallucinations, mania, severe abdominal pain, persistent heartburn, water retention, and decreased sexual ability.* In giving Tony Aventyl, Callis was throwing gasoline on Tony's already smoldering fires—both physical and emotional. Used sometimes for chronic bedwetting, Aventyl was eventually found to have no real effect in combating depression. And as if all those drugs were not enough, he also gave Tony meprobamate, yet another tranquilizer. For that, Callis didn't bother writing a prescription; he just gave Tony a handful of samples from his desk drawer. Regardless of the wild side effects that so many concurrent drugs may have had on Tony, it's safe to say that no one was watching his accelerating symptoms or monitoring the effect of so many drugs. In fact, antidepressants and antianxiety medications were new to the psychopharmaceutical market, and overseeing of their efficacy was rare.

Tony also got prescriptions from their regular family physician,

Dr. Daniel Hiebert, for a laundry list of ailments, some fabricated, some real. Most bothersome and persistent were gastritis and urethritis, the latter a painful inflammation of the urethra, often caused by sexually transmitted diseases. But it hardly mattered to Hiebert if Tony's ailments were real or imagined: Hiebert was in his late seventies, with tired, watery eyes and stooped shoulders, and was known to fall asleep during patient consultations. He had been practicing medicine in Provincetown since 1919 and had delivered most of the townspeople, including Avis's mother, as well as many of her and Tony's relatives. Through the years, Hiebert had witnessed any innocence the old fishing village once held disappear into the new world of rock and roll, psychedelic drugs, gay pride, free love, and flower power. Rather than fight the changing tides, he seemed to embrace them. Around town, people called him Dr. Feelgood[1] because he handed out diet pills like candy and even left free samples in his mailbox of the notorious amphetamine "Black Beauty," which resembled today's Adderall and was taken off the market in 1998, in part because it was absurdly prone to abuse.

Among Hiebert's patients was the up-and-coming avant-garde artist John Waters, who at six foot one and 130 pounds hardly qualified for diet pills—but he got them anyway, so many that he was able to sell the surplus for rent money and to help finance his latest theatrical project. Waters became a one-man dispensary who rode up and down Commercial Street on a bicycle selling the extra pills Hiebert had given him.[2]

Like John Waters, Tony Costa had no problem filling his pockets with drugs from both Hiebert and Callis. And as if those supplies weren't enough, Tony began visiting the Boston Common, a burgeoning drug scene that, by the mid-1960s, was becoming the city's own Haight-Ashbury. During those turbulent years, anti-war protestors and civil rights activists often camped out on the Common for days, and drugs of all kinds flowed through the makeshift tent city. Like Waters, Tony began selling drugs he bought on the Common and didn't consume himself to many of Provincetown's worst users, running a sideline business in amphetamines, barbiturates, antidepressants, tranquilizers, and painkillers, as well as marijuana, hash, and LSD.

Tony was one of Provincetown's first drug dealers and soon became its biggest and its only year-round dealer. Some of his steadier customers, many of them barely teenagers, began following him like a guru, calling him Lord Antone, Sire of All Things True, and Antone of Rome—monikers that started as a joke during high school because he told them wild tales of believing himself to be the reincarnation of a medieval Greek warlord who rode around in a chariot and beheaded every opponent in his path. But the joke became serious, at least to him, and he flaunted himself around town like the second coming of Christ. In fact, he called the boys his disciples and the girls his "kid chicks." He also became the kids' "go-to guy" when any of them overdosed; he had stolen a copy of *The Physicians' Desk Reference*, a catalog of every drug on the market, their side effects, and their overdose antidotes, and touted himself as knowledgeable as an MD when it came to pharmaceuticals.

Later, a member of his defense team asked him, "Tony, was it like you were a drug pusher?"

"It wasn't 'like,'" Tony said. "I *was*."

17

LIZA

A couple of weeks before Easter 1967, Mom had two late-night visitors come to our back door in West Bridgewater. From my room I heard the banging and then Mom clumping down the stairs to answer the door. I leaped out of bed and ran to the window so I could hear the conversation below.

Mom flipped on the outside light and opened the door. Her boyfriend, Tom, and a tall brunette stood on the stoop.

"Tom? What's going on? Who is this?" she said, but she had to have already known, right? I knew, and I was only eight.

"I'm his *wife*," Mrs. Tom said. Her voice was hard and angry.

"His *wife*? But he told me you had cancer and were dying!" I almost felt bad for Mom. In my whole life, I'd never heard her sound so scared.

"Do I *look* like I'm dying?" Mrs. Tom asked.

And I could have added, *You don't sound like it either.*

So that was the end of Tom, and with him Mom's hope that he would be the one to take care of her—happily ever after.

"Boy, it's a good thing I don't own a gun," was the last thing I ever heard her say about Tom.

After her breakup with Tom, Mom decided she needed a road trip, so she and Auntie announced they were taking us all to Jekyll Island, Georgia, for Easter vacation. The two mothers and all four kids crammed into Auntie's station wagon for the thousand-mile drive south. We hadn't been on Jekyll Island a full day before things unraveled.

After dinner our first night, the mothers headed to the Beachview Motel's porch with their drinks and two men they'd met at the pool. With Louisa and Gail already asleep in the room next door, Mom plunked me and Geoff in front of the TV, another one of her favorite babysitters, to keep us out of trouble.

By this time, I had become an expert at making myself "feel good." It could have started with my uncle Ulle, Nana Noonan's brother, insisting I sit in his lap when I didn't want to while we worked on his jigsaw puzzle. I'd have to suffer his lingering embraces and his breath, hot and rotten against my neck, as he rubbed himself against me. But most likely it started because I was an eavesdropper, listening in on the adult conversations around me, hoping to solve my biggest mystery: Why did my mother seem to hate me so much? So I started listening and snooping, going through her bureau drawers, digging into the back of her closet opening boxes, running my fingers through her silky dresses and wool skirts.

One day, I crawled under her double bed and found a shoebox of letters, held together with a rubber band. They were love letters, and they were from Tom. I had never heard some of the words, and certainly never in letters to my mother. I didn't know what sex was, but its language was fascinating—*nipples, ass, cunt, dick, prick, fuck, suck*—actually, lots of fucking and sucking—and how he wanted to be hard inside her, whatever that meant. I knew finding and reading the letters was wrong, but even without knowing what they were all about, reading them made me tingle between my legs in a way that was as exciting as it was frightening. I returned to those letters every time I was alone in the house, to feel that tingle. One day while reading them for the umpteenth time, I put my fingers down the front of my shorts and rubbed my fingers around until a great, hot roar moved through my body that was as powerful and wonderful as anything I'd ever felt. It was magic, but it also felt dangerous, and I knew I could never, ever tell anyone. Because along with the explosive roar that I now seemed to crave came shame. I was as bad as my mother always told me I was. I was a liar who kept secrets, and now I was dirty. Maybe there really *was* something wrong with me.

Still, that tickling, tingling sensation came back to me when I saw Geoff pull his pants down getting ready for bed, revealing the tiny bump of his little-boy penis through his white underpants. Ashamed and excited, I decided I wanted to see him naked.

"Let's get in the tub together," I said.

Geoff agreed to play the game, pulled his underpants down, swung one leg and then the other over the edge of the tub, and lay down. I quickly undressed, got in, and lay down next to him. Not quite sure what to do next but excited by my grown-up daring, I put my arms around him and gave him a long Cecelia hug.

"What in *hell* is going on?"

Mom and Auntie stood at the bathroom door, their eyes huge in their heads and their mouths open in shock. I jumped up, and Mom threw a towel at me while Geoff remained in the tub, dazed.

"Liza wanted to take a bath," Geoff said, his now-worried eyes looking from mother to mother.

"Oh my God!" Auntie said, and fell to her knees on the floor, reaching into the tub and stroking Geoff's head and chest, making sure I hadn't bitten him or something worse.

"Get out of that fucking tub, *now*," Mom growled, and without waiting for me to move grabbed my arm and dragged me naked out of the tub, out of Auntie's hotel room, and out onto the motel's balcony, where everyone stopped what they were doing to watch the spectacle while I tried desperately to hold the towel against my bare body. Finally, she threw me into our room next door and stepped in after me, slamming the door behind her with such force the map of the hotel on the back fell to the floor. Louisa woke up with a small cry but immediately knew not to ask what had happened. She pulled the covers up to her chin, watching us, her eyes huge and wild with fear.

"*What* the *fuck* were you doing?" Mom screamed, her face inches from mine. Her breath was sour, and her beehive hairdo was coming apart and falling over her face. "What were you doing in the tub with Geoff? What are you, some kind of a pervert?"

Pervert. I'd heard the word but always thought it meant sad, old men who hung out near our school or at the package store on a Saturday morning. Sad, lonely, nasty old men like the guy who lived down the street from us whose shades were always drawn and whose house needed a coat of paint. Now my mother thought *I* was a pervert. Maybe she was right. Maybe I was. A pervert. The word washed through me, filling me with shame. I was only eight years old, but already I was bad and I was disgusting.

"I only wanted—"

"Shut *up!*" she screamed. "Just shut the fuck up. I can't stand to look at you. Get into bed and don't say another word. You disgust me."

I slipped between the sheets of the rollaway cot and turned to the wall, staring at the pattern of the wallpaper, my heart pounding and my shame coursing through me in a great, hot flood.

In the morning, the six of us piled into the car to drive straight back to West Bridgewater. Mom drove and she was so eager to get going that she pushed but didn't latch my door closed, and when she pulled out of the parking lot she took a corner hard enough that the door flew open and I fell out of the car and hit the pavement. I didn't make a sound, but Louisa and the other kids screamed, and Mom slammed on the brakes. Everyone jumped out of the car and came over to where I lay in the driveway. I was wearing only my bathing suit, and gravel was imbedded in my stomach, arms, and legs.

"You're fine," Mom said. "We just need to rinse you off somewhere." Looking around her, she spied the swimming pool on the other side of the hedges. "Come on, we'll put you in the pool."

Knowing how much the chlorine stung my eyes, I hung back.

"Move! We have to get on the road," she said, pulling me up and across the driveway. "Haven't you made enough trouble for one damn trip?" she said, bending low to say it right in my ear through her clenched teeth. When we got to the pool, she said, "Good thing you already have your suit on. Now get in."

I walked slowly down the stairs, feeling the first burn as the water hit the raw scrapes on my legs and knees. I hesitated on the last stair but again heard "Get *in*," and I did, up to my neck while holding on to the edge of the pool as the water burned through the abrasions covering my body. I bit my lip against the tears but knew if I cried it would only make her angrier.

"Okay. That's enough. Get in the car," she said, lighting a cigarette while she waited.

I made feeble swipes at my arms and stomach, but it hurt too much to rub any harder, so most of the little stones stayed right where they were, stuck in my skin. She threw me a towel, and I wrapped it around me and walked back to the car. No one said much as we all climbed back in. This time, Mom slammed my door and pushed the lock down before she got in behind the wheel and started out.

It seemed like we drove in near silence for the entire thousand miles home. Crouched in the back seat behind Auntie, I sat awake the whole ride and watched the passing road signs all day and then the headlights all night, twirling my hair and scratching at my eczema until it bled.

A few days later, Auntie called Mom to tell her that she didn't want me playing with Gail or Geoff and "exposing them to things they shouldn't be exposed to."

"Are you happy now?" Mom yelled at me when she got off the phone. "I'm probably gonna lose my job at the Royal Coachman because of you. She doesn't want you around her kids! She wants to protect them, from *you*! Fabulous. Just fabulous."

She should talk, with those creepy letters from Tom under her bed, I thought. But still, I became nearly mute, feeling the hot shame wash over me, again and again, and seeing Mom's face, twisted in revulsion. At me, her daughter. *There is definitely something wrong with me*, I thought. *How can I be so repulsive?*

18

TONY

Back in Provincetown, the streets were starting to fill with young people looking for summer jobs in the cafés and motels, and hippies looking for cheap, if not free, places to crash for the season. Shopkeepers were ordering tourist trinkets and beach gear, and hotels and motels were unshuttering their doors and windows, sweeping out the dust and hanging their VACANCY signs. Tony and Avis's new baby, Nichole, was already three months old. Avis knew exactly when the girl had been conceived because except for a single coitus in August, she and Tony never had sex anymore. Nichole was their last. So, between the two small boys, a new infant, and Tony's ongoing inability to hold a job, they now had no money *and* no marriage. Near the end of her rope, Avis again threw him out of the apartment. He wasn't doing her or the kids any good with his hand-wringing angst.

With his duffel bag over his shoulder, Tony went from one friend's couch to another's. His half brother, Vinnie, had returned from the army after being drafted two years before, and the two of them spent many afternoons on Cecelia's couch, not doing much of anything.[1] It was the start of the Summer of Love, and Tony took advantage of an ample number of women's beds and the flood of drugs in the streets. Along with Callis's prescribed antidepressants, Tony was taking heavier drugs, including LSD. When the song "White Rabbit" was released in June, it became an anthem, and everywhere Tony and his minions met, they played the song over and over.

When the first warmth of summer hit the Cape, Tony decided to plant several marijuana plants in what he called his "garden" in the Truro woods near the lovers' lane where he and Avis had driven to have their early, forbidden sex. As the little shoots started poking out of the soil, Tony enjoyed showing the plants, and a stash of drugs he kept buried there, to his much-younger friends who looked up to him in a way Avis no longer did. His coterie of teenagers, his stash of pills, and his marijuana helped mask his ever-increasing feelings of inferiority; by surrounding himself with idolizing acolytes who needed a hero, he could feel more in control, sophisticated, confident, and, of course, more intelligent.

Finally, Tony ran out of couches and beds and again knocked on Joan Becker's door at the Royal Coachman, asking for work. Unlike other employers around town, she had never been disappointed with Tony's work and gave him a full-time job, telling him he could stay in staff housing. That afternoon, Tony moved into a tiny, pine-paneled cottage at the edge of the property's parking lot.

Once settled, Tony piled his bedside table with books on criminal psychology, Transcendental Meditation, and psychoneurosis as he continued to intellectualize the roots of his own dark demons. With typical grandiosity, he seemed to think he could cure himself of whatever was wrong with him. But no matter how many books he read and how many times he read them, he found no peace. He continued taking an ever-increasing number and mixture of drugs. Even though he had a job at the Royal Coachman, he spent most of his off-hours hanging out on the Benches or walking the dunes. His stomach continued to be a cauldron of acid indigestion; he lost more than ten pounds, dropping to around 165, and he continued to battle a chronic case of urethritis.

Tony got up each morning and greeted his reflection in the cottage's cracked bathroom mirror, saying, "Good morning, you fucked-up world."[2] In some weird variation of Oscar Wilde's *The Picture of Dorian Gray*, Tony Costa found it harder and harder to look in the mirror because he wouldn't recognize himself in his reflection. Rather, he began to see "Him," an ominous alter ego, staring back.[3]

Joan Becker, somehow oblivious to Tony's condition, sent her seven-year-old son, Geoff, to the cottage every morning to get him out of bed and off to work. Some days, Geoff had to knock and call his name for five or even ten minutes before Tony finally came to the door. Like Liza had the summer before, it was now young Geoff's turn to idolize Tony, hanging on his every word and shadowing him as he fixed things at the motel and drove to the dump in the motel's utility truck. But Tony's mood had darkened, and instead of the entertaining handyman he had been, that summer he complained about all the people who had done him wrong and how he just couldn't catch a *fucking* break. Geoff had never heard the word before, and while it made him a bit uneasy, he considered Tony a great guy. His bad language made the boy feel grown up.

After work, Tony frequently rode his bicycle downtown and stopped in at Adams Pharmacy on Commercial Street for a hot drink. One of the few things he still enjoyed doing was dunking his Lorna Doones into a cup of tea and listening to the counter ladies' gossip. It helped soothe his churning stomach. As he settled himself onto a stool, he looked over at a slender young woman with long, brown hair who was putting away the sample perfume bottles and closing down her station at the cosmetics counter. She looked like a prettier version of Avis, with straight white teeth and beautiful eyes that even from twenty feet Tony could see were bright green. He leaned over the counter and whispered to Ethel Ross, one of the waitresses.

"Hey, Ethel, who's that?" he said.

Ethel looked over at the young woman.

"Christine Gallant. She's new. She's a Fall River girl." Ethel gave Tony a sly smile. "But you be careful, Tony. We hear she's Raul Matta's."

Tony smiled back at Ethel as she refilled his teacup with more hot water. "I can handle Raul."

"Yeah, sure you can, Tony." She shook her head and walked away.

Christine Gallant was a pretty nineteen-year-old from a once-thriving mill town in southeastern Massachusetts that was known for its drugs, boarded-up cotton mills, and seasonal fishermen barely able to eke a living out of the sea. Christine had left Fall River and moved to Provincetown right after she graduated high school and found the summer job at the pharmacy. Her on-again, off-again relationship with Matta was stormy. Matta, a brooding, darkly handsome man, was also married and reportedly abusive toward both his wife and Christine. Dr. Callis had treated Matta for syphilis and said the man "screwed anything that moved." According to several friends of both Tony and Christine, Matta had forced her to get an abortion when she became pregnant with his child. With abortion still illegal in the 1960s, a friend of Matta's was rumored to have performed the procedure, which nearly killed Christine when she hemorrhaged afterward. Even if the rumors were only partly true, theirs wasn't a storybook romance.

Tony watched Christine put away the last of the display items on her counter and give it a wipe with a white cloth. She then disappeared into the back of the pharmacy where the employees kept their coats. Tony called her "the most beautiful girl" he'd ever seen, "with eyes that burn with an inner fire."[4]

Several days later, Tony was strolling up Commercial Street when he saw Christine duck into Molly Malone Cook's bookstore. He quickly crossed the street and walked into the store a few moments after her. Looking around, he saw her standing in the stacks, searching the book spines for a title. Tony, pretending to also search through the books, positioned himself to gently bump into her as she inched along the shelves.

"Oh! Sorry!" Christine said, jumping back.

"No, it was my fault," Tony said, putting out his hand. "I'm Tony Costa. You new here? I haven't seen you around town before." She took his hand.

"Hi. I'm Christine. I just moved here to work for the summer."

"Groovy. I've lived here my whole life. Let me know if you need a tour guide," he said, offering her his best smile. The two exchanged small talk until Christine said she'd better be getting to work.

"I'll see you around," she said.

"Definitely," Tony said. "You'll *definitely* be seeing me around."

On the days that Tony didn't have work, or when he would skip out on a job entirely, he'd walk the entire length of Commercial Street and then across the causeway out to the Long Point Light, over five miles from the Royal Coachman to the tip of Cape Cod, chin tucked to his chest and his hands shoved deep in his pockets, deaf to the raucous summer scene around him. One day as he walked through the downtown, a flyer was thrust at him.

"Eat it, read it, and *come!*" a woman said, her voice loud and singsong.

He looked up. Two people stood there, a woman and a person—Tony wasn't sure if it was a guy or girl—who carried the pamphlets and wore some wild costume with feathers and so much makeup it was impossible to discern his or her gender. If Tony had introduced himself, he would have met John Waters and Mary Vivian Pearce promoting their newest film, *Eat Your Makeup*.

Then, the woman, dressed like a Jean Harlow drag queen, handed him a candy lipstick.

"Just *come!*" she repeated, and laughed, then the two characters continued on down Commercial Street.

Tony watched them go, thinking what a lot of locals were thinking during the late 1960s: *Jeez. What a pair of knuckleheads.* But at least they weren't as bad as the guy who had accosted Tony on the beach, riding a motorcycle in nothing but a G-string and handing out what looked like homosexual pornography. Tony was relieved to see that the man was handing out his "fag" literature to everyone on the beach, not singling Tony out.

When his marijuana plants had finally gotten large enough to harvest, Tony took Marsha, one of his "kid chicks," out to his garden in the woods to get high. Marsha liked both Avis and Tony and on occasion would look after their children. Tony told her he always appreciated having company out to the woods because he got "creeped out" going alone. Along with his pipe and matches, he brought a bow and arrow. If Marsha thought it odd that he would bring a bow and arrow to smoke dope in the woods, she never mentioned it to police or to Cory Devereaux in the many conversations they had about the incident in the years to come.[5] As Marsha was walking ahead of Tony through the trees, she suddenly felt something hit the back of her coat with a dull thud. Turning around, she saw an arrow lying on the ground. Tony ran over, profusely apologizing for "accidentally" hitting her, claiming he'd aimed at something else but that the arrow had ricocheted off a tree and hit her square in the back by mistake. He offered to take her to Dr. Hiebert, but she said she was okay and just wanted to go home. Marsha had had enough of Tony Costa for one day.

19

LIZA

Mom was right; Auntie did not invite us back to the Royal Coachman for the summer. Mom was plenty pissed, and embarrassed, but she didn't wallow in it. Instead, every night after dinner she pulled out the want ads, poured herself a rum and Coke, and settled into a kitchen chair to look for summer work. No matter what or where, she knew she wanted a job that would allow her to swing on the Cape again for the summer. I had just finished second grade and was proud of my reading skills, so I would help her browse the ads. I was eager to help, especially since I'd been the one who got her fired from the RC. It didn't take her long to find a job, and as soon as school was out and her car was packed, we headed down Route 24 with her singing along to "Ruby Tuesday" blasting on the radio. This time she'd be cocktail waitressing at the Wequassett Inn in Harwich, about thirty miles south of Provincetown.

Our summer location may have changed, but Mom's revolving door of admirers didn't. I'd developed a rating system for them from one to ten. That summer's list included a round, little Jewish man who sat at the bar all night and left her a whopping $500 tip for her "incredible service" of putting drinks in front of him (he got a five on the scale for the tip alone), and a loud, fat, tough-talking lawyer from Boston named Al. Even though I was only eight years old, I knew a creep when I met one, and Al was a creep. He drove a bright red Cadillac with a white ragtop. Even on the hottest days he wore the same gray leisure suit, white leather loafers, and a shirt with a too-tight collar that made his flushed and fleshy neck bulge over the edge.

On especially hot days, it looked as though his head was going to pop right off his shoulders. And he always seemed to have his fat hands and fingers all over Mom, even while he was driving. She'd wrap her beehive in a scarf and scooch over into the middle of the front seat so that his fat arm could drape around her shoulders. Louisa and I would make faces at him from the back seat. If we made too much noise or asked too many questions, Al would open his glove compartment and throw Twizzlers over his shoulder at us. We called him the Candy Man, and gave him a boyfriend rating of two. (He would have ranked a zero, but we liked the Twizzlers.)

I wondered why Mom couldn't find herself a ten, like Tony.

That summer, Mom rented a tiny cottage in Brewster because, unlike the RC, the Wequassett didn't provide staff housing for women with children. The cottage had two beds, and Mom and Louisa slept in one bed and I slept in the other with Maggie, a sixteen-year-old student from Mom's home ec class at Stoughton High School she'd brought along to look after us. There were no closets, so we all hung our clothes and towels from hooks and nails pounded into the pine paneling. The place had a little kitchenette with a fridge that fit under the counter and a propane stovetop, although I don't remember ever cooking much of anything on it besides SpaghettiOs and hot dogs.

Maggie reminded me of Cecelia: short, round, and fleshy, with black hair and warm blue eyes. Black Irish, Mom called her. Maggie was a step up from the ragtag collection of oddballs Mom had look after us in Provincetown, but she was a tad distracted. On a day while she was napping, I almost drowned. Louisa and I were swimming by ourselves in a pond near the Wequassett, when I got trapped under an inflatable rubber boat. No matter how hard I tried to push it off me, it wouldn't budge. Finally, I took a gulp of air from the air pocket around my head, dove deep, and swam free of the boat. I came up gasping, swam to the shore, and crawled to the beach, where I lay on my stomach in the sand, choking and catching my breath. No one noticed because we were alone at the pond.

I missed Provincetown. I missed swimming in the RC pool and riding my bike to the Penney Patch, the penny candy store in town. I missed Cecelia and the cozy RC laundry room and playing with Geoff and Gail. I even missed all the thick seaweed on the beach in front of the Royal Coachman. But more than anything I missed riding around town in the truck with Tony and feeling like I belonged somewhere.

Then one hot August day, my prayers were answered.

"Pack a bag," Mom announced. "I have two days off, so we're goin' to P'town." She was as happy as I'd seen her all summer. So was I. I wondered if Auntie was still mad at me, and even though I had a nervous stomach worrying what she'd say when she saw me, I didn't dare ask Mom about it and ruin her good mood.

Louisa and I already had our bathing suits on, so all I had to pack were jacks, marbles, my Fred Flintstone puppet, and my pajamas; all Louisa packed was some Wrigley's Spearmint gum. We jumped into the back seat of Mom's used Ford convertible and tapped our knees together, waiting for her to get ready.

Provincetown at last! I thought.

Mom started the car, wrapped a soft, yellow silk scarf around her hair, put the top down, and finally pulled out onto Route 6 headed north. She turned up the radio and sang all the way.

The music and her happy mood allowed me to relax into the back seat. There was no doubt my mother had a date that night. Date nights were the only times we saw her that happy.

As we pulled into the RC driveway, Mom took her best pink lipstick out of her pocketbook and applied it perfectly before she even stopped the car.

"Okay," she said to me as she turned off the engine. "Take your bag up to Auntie's. And for God's sake, don't do or say anything stupid."

I got out of the car, and the first person I saw was Tony, sitting in the RC's truck with Geoff riding shotgun. I waved to both of them, and Tony got out and came over. As he approached, he put a piece of Juicy Fruit gum in his mouth and handed me the rest of the pack.

"Wow, you're not Little Liza anymore! You're almost all grown up!" he said, leaning up against the side of the car to light a cigarette. He winked at Mom, and she smiled. He looked back at me. "Where ya been this summer, kiddo? Can't believe it's been a year since I've seen you!"

I smiled and nodded, unable to talk through the wad of gum I was struggling to chew, and without thinking, I pulled my hair over my Dumbo ears, even though Tony never said anything mean about them sticking out. Instead, he always said something nice about my wild, curly hair or new bathing suit or how tan my legs were getting. Tony was one of the few grown-ups who never yelled at me, never called me *difficult* or *fresh* or a *nightmare* or a *whole hell of a lotta trouble*. Instead, he'd push his glasses up his nose and say, "You sure are gonna be a pretty chick when you grow up."

I had to look away because my cheeks always turned bright red when anyone said anything nice about me, especially when it was Tony.

"Geoff and I were just heading out to the dump. Wanna come along?" he said, looking at Mom for her approval.

"Please, please, please can we go?" I said.

She looked down at me and then up at Tony. Just then, Auntie strode through the office door and joined us in the parking lot. She was all dressed up in a striped dress, and she was wearing fake eyelashes and a lot more makeup than I'd never seen her wear in the middle of the day. Her thick, tanned feet looked like they were trying to squeeze out of her high-heel sandals.

"I missed you, girlfriend," she said, giving Mom a quick hug.

"Me too," Mom said.

Auntie looked at me and gave me a little smile. I didn't know how, but everything seemed to be all right.

"Looks like you ladies are ready to hit the town," Tony said.

"Finally!" Mom said. "I couldn't wait to get back to P'town. Harwich is Deadsville!"

Mom and Auntie laughed. Tony didn't.

"Mummy, can we go with Tony?" I said, hoping she hadn't forgotten his invitation.

Mom and Joan looked at each other.

"Hey, Tony, can you take all four?" Auntie said. "I'll throw a little something extra in your paycheck if you've got room in the truck."

"Sure thing. Louisa and Gail can sit on Geoff and Liza's laps, right, guys?"

"Sure!" I said. "There's plenty of room." Although I wasn't at all sure there was. I just knew I wanted to go wherever he wanted to take us.

"Okay then," Tony said. "It's settled. Liza, why don't you go find Gail, and we'll be off."

I ran toward Auntie and Uncle Hank's apartment to get Gail before anyone could change their mind.

We drove out of the RC, the five of us crammed onto the front seat, and drove slowly through town with the radio on, past the Lobster Pot and John's Footlong. The summer traffic thinned as we neared the west end. Louisa had somehow squeezed on the seat between me and Geoff, who held Gail half on his lap and half on the armrest of the passenger door. I was close enough to Tony to smell his cologne. He told me once it was very fancy stuff his wife always gave him—English Leather. I looked over at him just as he looked at me.

"You're never gonna ever wear makeup or lipstick, are you?" he said. "Because you're already such a cute chick without it. I always tell Avis: makeup and lipstick only make a good girl look like a bad girl."

I thought about Mom's thick pink lipstick and heavy blue eye shadow and Auntie's fake eyelashes and heavy rouge, and I wondered if he thought they were bad girls.

I moved the wad of Juicy Fruit to the side of my mouth. "Nope," I said. "I'm never going to wear it."

"Promise?" Tony said, looking at me so long I got nervous, because he wasn't watching the road.

"Yes, I promise, Tony."

On the radio, Tommy James and the Shondells were singing their hit

"Hanky Panky," and Tony sang along. We all joined in for the chorus, and I threw in a shimmy with my shoulders like I'd seen the girls do on American Bandstand.

My baby does the hanky panky . . .

Tony laughed. "How do you know all the words?" He looked at me like I was the smartest girl in the class. I felt my cheeks go red again.

"I know the words to all the songs," I said, and I did. My mother's favorites that summer were "The Girl from Ipanema," "A Whiter Shade of Pale," and "Wild Thing," which she would turn up as high as the volume would go and sing along with the chorus while the palm of her hand hit the steering wheel with the beat.

I looked over at Tony again, who caught my glance and winked at me as the song came to an end, and he started flipping through the stations to find another he liked. It was always hard to find a good song on the radio in Provincetown. Only a few stations came in clearly, and only one or two of them played music, so you were always turning the dial all the way one way and back again through the static until something good came through.

Later that evening, exhausted from the sun and swimming and full of ice cream and hot dogs, Louisa, Geoff, Gail, and I climbed the stairs to Auntie's apartment and fell into the bunk beds, a tangle of sticky hands and sandy arms and legs.

It felt so good to be home.

20

TONY

By the end of the summer, Tony had had quite enough of hauling garbage, repairing broken lamps and windows, and unclogging toilets at the Royal Coachman. He begged Avis for yet another reconciliation, and her response was less than open-armed; she warned him, "If you leave us one more time, Tony, I'm through."[1] He promised he had learned his lesson and wouldn't leave them again; he would find reliable work and settle down. Somewhat appeased, Avis agreed, so Tony left his grim cottage at the RC and once more returned to live with her and the children. In mid-September they rented a tiny cottage on Shank Painter Road from David Raboy, an assistant professor at Rhode Island College who summered on the Cape and then rented the cottage out during the winter months.

As had been the case in their earlier apartments, Tony and Avis's "pad" became a gathering place for young people to hang out, drink, and do drugs. Many of the kids were Avis's girlfriends from childhood. Those girls had watched Avis become a bride and then a mother before she turned fifteen. Now at eighteen, the girls envied what they perceived as Avis's life of freedom as an adult with a handsome husband and her own apartment. Although one of them thought Tony odd and that "everything that came out of his mouth was just strange," the young woman never said it out loud to anyone at the time. She even thought there was something slightly sinister about him. But, he was a grown-up, and his strangeness was made "cool" by his being older. It didn't hurt that he also sold or gave most of them drugs. So, strange or not, they clamored to be with him.

In October, with the departure of the last of the summer population, Tony lost the few handyman jobs he had around town. To make matters worse, Avis had a pregnancy scare from one of their rare copulations and it rattled them both. They couldn't afford the three children they had; a fourth would have been disastrous. Besides, she often felt as if she already had a fourth child in Tony, who teetered on a knife's edge, swinging wildly between manic energy and lethargy so profound he could barely get out of bed. When, during a particularly bad argument, he hauled off and whacked the back of her head, he was as stunned as she was.

When he wasn't looking for work or walking the dunes, Tony busied himself with finishing a partially framed room in the basement of their Shank Painter apartment for his "art projects." The room was partitioned off from the rest of the basement, and when he finished putting up plywood walls, he put two padlocks on the door. He spent untold hours in his private "studio" but never had any artwork to show for it.

He also spent a lot of his time pursuing Christine Gallant, who had moved to Hyannis with her sister after the summer job at Adams Pharmacy ended. She came to Provincetown often to visit Raul Matta, but she would also see a fair amount of Tony, who listened patiently as she bemoaned that Matta was still very much married. Like so many other young women in Tony's circle, Christine had a sad and sordid history with men and with drugs, an escalating habit Tony was only too happy to supply. She often called the Shank Painter apartment looking for Tony and would instead talk to Avis, who, for her part, didn't mind that another woman was calling her husband. "[Tony and I] were just living together by then," Avis later said. "I didn't care what he was doing."[2]

As November loomed, Tony finally found a job in New York City. He was hired on a trial basis as a clerk at Emery freight company near John F. Kennedy International Airport; if after forty-five days it worked out, he would be brought on full-time. Avis wasn't wild about the prospect of leaving Provincetown and moving to New York, but the money was good, and if he got the full-time job, the plan was for her and the kids to follow as soon as Tony got situated. "Despite it all," Avis said, "I think we both really wanted to make it work."[3]

When Tony left for New York, Sarah Cook, Avis's aunt, who was actually only a couple of years older than Avis and more like a sister, moved in to help her with the children. Along with most of Avis's relatives, Sarah didn't like or trust Tony and watched him come and go through the late fall of 1967 with a growing sense of unease. She observed that he was strung out all the time and his drug use was making him even odder and more volatile. Sarah didn't hold back.

"He's insane, and he's going to kill you," she warned Avis. "You have to leave him. One day he's going to flip out and kill somebody, and I don't want it to be you."[4]

21

TONY

It was a surprise to almost nobody, least of all Avis and her family, when Tony lost the job in New York. After his forty-five-day trial period ended, he was fired. By the time he returned home to Provincetown, he had fashioned a story that his and several other employees' jobs had become "redundant," and he was no longer needed. Back in Provincetown, it was the same old Tony saga: no job, no money, but plenty of drugs. Again, Sarah warned Avis, "Don't take him back. Don't do it. You'll be sorry." But Avis did take him back, and soon they were fighting around the clock.

"We were having a lot of hassles over money because we owed so much money to so many people," Avis later said.

Finally, they decided to officially separate. Avis hoped it would jolt him into getting a real job and supporting his family. Tony did what he always did; he looked for an escape. He couldn't find work now that the tourist season was officially over, and he had already burned just about every bridge with the few people who hired help during the winter. As the bitter winds of another cold, gray January began to blow, Tony knew he had to get out of town. Then, a buddy, Ronnie Enos, told Tony he was headed out west to visit his mother in Arizona, and the two decided to hit the road. A week later they drove out of town, leaving Avis standing in the driveway, once again abandoned and with a baby on her hip.

As she watched the car disappear, Avis decided she'd finally had enough. With Sarah's urging, Avis filed for divorce, citing Tony's cruel and abusive behavior.

"In those days you had to have a reason," she said.

She was nineteen years old, had three children under the age of six to feed and clothe, and she didn't know whether she'd be able to pay the next month's rent. Tony left for San Francisco with $450 in his wallet, nearly $3,500 in today's value. He left Avis $80.

Before Tony and Ronnie left town, they stopped at Dr. Hiebert's for a supply of amphetamines so they could drive to California without stopping. As they left Provincetown, they passed a road sign at the terminus of Route 6 that read, BISHOP, CALIFORNIA, 3,205 MILES.

Ronnie rolled down the window and raised his fist: "'California, here we come!'" he sang into the cold January air.

"I hate that song," Tony said. "Roll up the window, it's fucking freezing out there."

Fueled by two coffee cans full of amphetamines, Tony and Ronnie drove nearly straight through, traveling on I-80 the entire way, from its beginning in New Jersey to its terminus in San Francisco. Their only stop was in Chapel, Nebraska, nineteen hundred miles from Provincetown, where they napped, showered, and within hours got back on the road. When they made it to San Francisco, they headed straight to Haight-Ashbury, where two sisters from Provincetown had an apartment on Oak Street. They also met up with another Provincetown local, Matt Russe, who had gone AWOL from the army. Russe had a well-earned reputation as a bully; he once sided with his pit bull after it bit a child. By the time he turned fourteen, he and his equally delinquent older brother already had rap sheets that included petty larceny, breaking and entering, and assault with a deadly weapon.

"The Russe boys had their territory long before there was such a thing as gangs," Avis said.[1]

After four days in San Francisco, Tony and Ronnie found their own apartment and Tony spent all but his last five dollars on rent. It was a squalid dive on Haight Street, furnished with little more than stained mattresses on the floor; dirty, chipped dishes in the sink, and a soiled, torn sheet on the front window. Nevertheless, he wrote Avis that "a new life" had begun for him now that he had found his "kind of people at last." And indeed, Tony once again gathered a coterie of Provincetown transplants—Ronnie, Matt, and a handful of others.

With the San Francisco newspapers on strike, there were no want ads to comb through, so Tony and the Provincetown gang used the strike as an excuse to remain unemployed. Most days he and his flock hung around hustling for spare change and doing whatever drugs they could round up, including heroin, which was plentiful and often free on Hippie Hill in Golden Gate Park.

They'd been in the apartment less than a week when Tony, Matt, and Ronnie tried to crash a party upstairs in their building, but the host threw them out, telling them, "Get lost, neighbor. You weren't invited." They returned downstairs, and soon there was a knock at the door. Tony opened the door to a short young woman with brown eyes and long, brown hair smiling up at him. She reminded Tony of Avis. Her name was Barbara Spalding, and she had come downstairs from the party to apologize for the host.

"Greg is very rude. He shouldn't talk like that to strangers from out of town," she said. "I knew by your accents that you weren't from California."

Tony invited her in, and no sooner had she crossed the threshold than Matt Russe dropped his pants and mooned the woman. She screamed and ran from the apartment. Tony went after her and caught up to her on the stairs.

"Listen, Barbara," Tony explained, "Matt is always clowning around. He doesn't mean any harm. It's just his foolishness."

They stood together on the stairs, and after they chatted awhile, Tony offered, "How about a date? You can tell me about Haight-Ashbury, and I'll tell you what Provincetown is really like."

She told him she had a little boy and would have to bring him along, and they agreed to meet at the Golden Gate Park the next day.

It was only a matter of days before Tony moved into Barbara's even dingier room in a communal apartment on McAllister Street with her and her two-year-old son, Bobby. She had divorced Bobby's father five months before and was living off the welfare payments for her son. And now, so was Tony.

"I loved that kid," Tony later said.[2]

And maybe he did. But he didn't seem to care that the two-year-old boy was witness to his and Barbara's drug use. One of their highs of choice was a "match head," in which methamphetamines are mixed with red phosphorous. They also did whatever speed, LSD, hash, and heroin they could find. One night they mixed a possibly tainted dose of methamphetamines with alcohol and then shot it up. Barbara immediately went into convulsions.

"Get me to a hospital," she begged. "I'm dying."

Tony took her to the nearby San Francisco General Hospital, where they rushed her to the ER. He outweighed Barbara by as much as seventy pounds, and so fared better, but he too was given Librium to come down from the drugs and soon recovered. In the middle of their near-fatal overdoses, the hospital filled with other casualties: it was February 19, the night of the Haight-Ashbury riots. While Tony waited seven hours for Barbara to stabilize, he did what he had once done with Peter when Avis overdosed on chloral hydrate: he walked the halls with Bobby on his shoulders and sat while the boy napped in his lap. All around the hospital and the city beyond, the sirens screamed.

The overdose didn't stop or even slow their profligate drug use. With Bobby in tow, he and Barbara made almost daily rounds to the various hippie hangouts and communes in and around Golden State Park. Through it all, Tony wrote letters to Avis about how carefree and wondrous Haight-Ashbury was, much like one describes a childhood of pony rides and playing street hockey with their friends until Mom called them home at sunset.

A few days after his and Barbara's overdoses, Tony received word that the Provincetown police had a warrant out for his arrest for nonsupport of Avis and the three children. He also learned that Avis had filed for divorce. The papers had been delivered to his mother's apartment on Conant Street in Provincetown.

The news shook Tony. While he and Avis had agreed to a separation, no one had talked about a divorce. Sure, they'd had countless arguments, separations, reconciliations, and betrayals, but he never imagined a life without her. She was his true north. Stronger than he and decidedly a better parent to the children, Avis had been his one constant in life, the one person he always knew he could count on when his chips got low. But now she'd done the unthinkable; she'd abandoned him, just like Cecelia had abandoned him in marrying Joseph Bonaviri and having another son. Confident that he could talk Avis out of the divorce, he decided to head back to the Cape to "clear things up" with her and the police.

Tony called his mother and told her to tell Vinnie to wire him money for a plane ticket home. Even though he used a friend's American Airlines student ID for a reduced fare, the ticket still cost $75 ($554 in today's money) and it was $75 he didn't have.[3] Vinnie wired the money, and at the end of February, Tony flew home. Later, when asked why he left his car in San Francisco, he told authorities he gave it to Barbara. However, months later it was found on McAllister Street where he left it, covered in parking tickets. Barbara had apparently never touched it.

22

LIZA

I think it was right after I turned nine that I first started asking God for a new family. Unfortunately, I got what I asked for. Dad again reappeared, this time with a very pregnant wife and her three-year-old daughter. Mom couldn't wait to send us off to Dad's dreary apartment in Middleborough for the weekend; she positively giggled as she watched us walk out to his car, our feet and overnight bags dragging down the front walk.

Louisa and I spent the weekend sitting on the couch watching television and eating tuna fish sandwiches and Cheetos, not knowing where to wipe our orange fingers and trying to keep Holly Berry, Louisa's puppy that she'd gotten for Christmas, from peeing on the carpet. When we got back to West Bridgewater Sunday night, I knelt by my bed and told God he'd made a mistake; I'd asked for a new *family*, not a new mother. I had enough trouble with the one I had.

As the summer of 1968 approached, I was finishing up third grade and Mom was getting restless. She didn't want to cocktail waitress at the Wequassett again. One summer working nights in a bar with its sloppy drinkers and their meat hook hands all over her were enough. She pulled out the want ads and sat at the kitchen table poring through them, looking for a job in a motel or restaurant in Provincetown, or at least nearer to it than "Deadsville" Harwich.

Then, John Atwood, who owned the Royal Coachman with Uncle Hank, called to tell her that the motel across the street was for sale and might be within her means. But Mom had no means. Dad never did send any money, and she earned just enough at her home ec job to keep food on our table. So she went to Grampa Georgie and begged him to finance the $50,000 purchase. (Among all the things single women were prevented from doing in the 1960s was obtaining a mortgage.) While Grampa Georgie was never what you might call generous, he knew a good investment when he saw one, so he agreed to cosign the loan and gave her the down payment. She was thrilled. Not only would it get her back to Provincetown; it would enable her to quit her job at Stoughton High School and never again have to face Tom or the other teachers' ugly whispers that followed her when she walked through the halls.

As usual, we started packing.

23

TONY

The day after he flew back from California, Tony was arraigned for non-support and placed on probation with the condition that he pay Avis $40 a week—$10 for each child and herself. But nothing had changed; Tony's construction jobs were few and far between, and when he did find work he failed to keep it. Again, Avis and the children received almost nothing from him. His only steady source of income was dealing drugs, and that of course was unknown to the welfare department.

Tony's life became even more quarrelsome when Avis started hanging around with another of Provincetown's drug dealers, John Joseph "Jay" Von Utter, a summer kid from Greenwich, Connecticut, who could always be counted on to supply the locals with LSD, speed, and marijuana. While Tony was angered by what he saw as Avis's betrayal with Von Utter, the Provincetown police chief saw an opportunity.

Respected and feared throughout the Outer Cape, Chief Francis "Cheney" Marshall was a bearish man with a powerful, raspy voice, steel-blue eyes, and a military-style crew cut that fit like a tight cap on his skull. Ambitious and savvy, he had run Provincetown for thirty-four years like his own private fiefdom. In 1960, when homosexuals were considered "subversives" and were a target of law enforcement nationwide, Marshall, with the encouragement of Father Duarte at St. Peter the Apostle Catholic Church, required background checks on restaurant employees in an attempt to weed out any with a prior arrest for sodomy. As the 1960s wore on and the town's good-time atmosphere inspired an influx of vagrant hippie youth and their drugs, "Marshall law," as his detractors and supporters alike called it, helped hold Provincetown in one piece.

Part of that Marshall law was a pilot task force the attorney general of Massachusetts had formed in January 1968 to help combat the nation's ever-increasing drug scene. The AG had put Marshall in charge of the Outer Cape area. And while it had lessened the availability of some drugs, Jay Von Utter, the "Connecticut punk" who was hanging around Avis, had been able to keep LSD, marijuana, and an assortment of uppers and downers flowing into town. Marshall needed an impressive arrest to prove that he and the drug task force were doing their jobs, and the Von Utter kid was a perfect patsy: he wasn't from the area; he was a spoiled rich kid who drove around town in a two-door sedan with JJVU vanity plates; and, except for his drug customers, he had few friends among the locals. What the chief needed to nail Von Utter was someone who knew enough about the drug scene in Provincetown to know when Von Utter was next coming to town with a load to sell. Provincetown police sergeant James "Jimmy" Meads told Marshall he knew just the guy, a man born to be a snitch— Tony Costa. Marshall, however, was reluctant to use him.

"That guy is a pig on drugs. He'll take anything," he told Meads.

Nonetheless, Marshall needed his bust and finally agreed to use Tony in the sting. For his part, Tony was all too willing to see Avis's suitor get taken away in cuffs.

The warrant was issued, and on Monday, March 19, 1968, when Von Utter drove up Route 6, Jimmy Meads and two other police officers were sitting in their cruiser at the Provincetown line waiting for him. When the officers saw Von Utter's car pass, they quietly tailed him to the Mayflower Café on Commercial Street, where he stopped for lunch. When Von Utter opened the car door, the officers surrounded him, served the warrant, and opened up the wheel covers. There they found LSD and marijuana, just where Tony said it would be.

With Von Utter's arrest, Marshall got his big break and eighteen months later was promoted to chief of narcotics at the state police barracks in West Yarmouth, a job he held until his retirement in 1975.

For Tony, the arrest was a turning point in the wrong direction. His already troubled reputation around Provincetown now had an even darker stain: snitch. While the locals may not have liked Jay Von Utter all that much, they certainly didn't want to see him get arrested, particularly given that he had supplied them with drugs. Then, when word got out that Tony had been the police's rat, many of his old friends never trusted him again, and several of his employers realized that in order for him to squeal on Von Utter, he too must have been involved with drugs coming into and out of Provincetown.

Tony had always struggled with paranoia, a phobia only made worse by his drug use. But when Provincetown started to buzz with talk of his being a stool pigeon, his periodic anxiety became permanent, and everywhere he went he thought he heard murmured voices talking about him.

Soon after the drug bust, Tony started frequenting the Pilgrim Club, which had moved from Commercial Street to Shank Painter Road, conveniently close to the cottage he and Avis had rented the fall before. She refused to let him move back in, but he hung out at the club in order to keep an eye on her, any new boyfriends, and the endless stream of kids who seemed to constantly come and go from her apartment.

One day, over a game of pool at the club, he saw Sydney Monzon waiting on tables. He'd seen her before on the Benches in front of town hall, but this time he went over and introduced himself. Sydney was a tiny young woman, barely five feet tall and exceptionally pretty, with almond-shaped eyes, full lips, long dark hair, and a mysterious, sultry air. She looked like a Cherokee princess, almost regal in her bearing. Her boss at the restaurant where she had worked during high school said she moved "like a little cricket" from table to table, charming her customers and employer.

Always planning her future far from the constraints of Cape Cod, Sydney had been something of a shy loner in school and usually had at least one part-time job, sometimes two. Once she graduated, and away from home and on her own, she was known to be somewhat "kooky, wild, and up for anything."[1] Like Tony, she complained that the Cape was provincial and boring. She dreamed of becoming an airline stewardess or joining the

Peace Corps—she wanted to see the world, and in the turbulent days of the Vietnam War and its protests, she told people she hoped to work for peace. She had graduated from Nauset Regional High in June 1967 and bought a car with money she had saved from her various jobs. Soon after graduation, she packed up the car and with a friend drove to San Francisco, proudly announcing she was going to become a flower child and "work for peace, one way or the other." After three months loafing around Haight-Ashbury, she decided she'd had enough and drove to Canada, then south to visit one of her brothers, and then flew to the Bahamas for a short time before finally returning to Cape Cod in January 1968.

By the time she got home, she was hooked on speed and thin to the point of being gaunt; some friends even suspected she was sick. While some thought she had picked up her drug habits in the hash dens of San Francisco, her sister later told investigators, "Sydney didn't learn anything about drugs in Haight-Ashbury. She already knew." She revealed to friends that her drug use was an effort to suppress some "sorrow in her past,"[2] a "shattering memory of a childhood sexual experience which left an [entrenched] psychic scar."[3] Whatever that "shattering memory" was, she suffered horrific nightmares and panic attacks and was on medication for chronic heart palpitations. Perhaps the drugs *were* her best escape.

Once back on the Cape, she rented a room in the apartment of a friend, Roland Salvador. While many suspected that he was bisexual, if not gay, Sydney told a friend that she hoped by living with Roland, and caring for him and his home, she could turn him away from any latent homosexuality.

Her sister, Linda, who was a short-order cook at the Pilgrim Club, got Sydney the job waitressing there most afternoons and evenings. Sydney settled back into life on the Cape and, like everybody else, waited for the tourist season and its bigger tippers to return. Then, on a slow afternoon at the club, she met a man playing pool—Tony Costa.

Linda, as well as Roland and his brother, David, warned Sydney to steer clear of Tony. A friend, Bob Anthony, described Tony as being "always a click off." Indeed. According to one member of the circle, Tony snacked on

Milk-Bone dog biscuits and ate his cooked peas one by one with a pair of tweezers. But more than being known as an oddball, he was now infamous as the snitch in the Von Utter drug bust.

"I was between the devil and the deep blue sea on that one," Tony later boasted of his role in the arrest.[4]

Linda, for one, didn't want her sister caught in the middle. She and a few of their friends may also have tried to warn Sydney off Tony because he was carrying on with three other women at the time. But, at nearly twenty-four, Tony must have seemed like a man of the world to Sydney, filling her head with tall tales (most of them lies) about all the exotic places he'd been and those he was planning to visit. Despite her friends' best efforts at thwarting a relationship, Sydney and Tony soon were often seen riding their bikes together or holding hands walking up and down the streets of Provincetown.

In April, after two and a half years of giving Tony handfuls of drugs, Dr. Callis finally wearied of his demanding, strung-out patient. (He had also begun to worry that the rumors around town of Tony's excessive drug use as well as his drug dealing were true.) Callis gave him a final supply of Solacen and told Tony he would no longer see him as a patient, which of course meant no more easy supply of drugs. After a few weeks of being cut off, Tony's cache was running low. Almost a month to the day after the doctor's rebuff, Tony took matters into his own hands and robbed Callis's office in Wellfleet.

He chose a miserable night for his burglary; the rain was coming down in sheets, and visibility on the roads was reduced to yards. Without a car of his own, he asked Sydney if she could borrow Roland's, to which she had access when Roland was at work. Tony promised her a share of the loot, and she agreed. On the night of May 17, she picked him up at the Crown & Anchor Inn, where he was staying for free in exchange for working to get the inn open for the season. They drove through the rain to Callis's office in Wellfleet, where it took Tony only twenty seconds to pick the lock.

"It's easy," he boasted. "Once you know how the tumblers work in Yale locks, you're home."[5]

After he broke into the office, it took him only another five minutes to load an oversize Kalmar Village motel pillowcase full of drugs.

Dr. Callis and Tony later made separate lists of the stolen drugs, and they were wildly divergent; Callis was most likely protecting himself by underreporting the scope and amount of drugs he had stored in his office, and Tony was most likely inflating his résumé. Callis's list totaled drugs worth a few hundred dollars; Tony said his take was more than $5,000 in drugs (nearly $36,500 in today's money).

Regardless of its actual size, Tony was elated with his haul and quickly buried it in two stashes—the one in the Truro woods and another behind the Provincetown dump. Callis immediately fingered Tony for the heist, but when police failed to find any of the drugs in his Crown & Anchor room, they couldn't arrest him. The ease of the robbery only fed his urge for more. With Callis refusing to see him, Tony returned to his family doctor, Dr. Hiebert, eager to keep his cache as fat as possible. On one visit to the office, he noticed the doctor's medical bag just sitting on the back seat of his car parked on Commercial Street. Tony casually opened the car door, took the bag, and kept walking. When he was a safe distance, he ducked into a narrow alley, undid the buckles, and looked inside the bag. He saw an assortment of drugs and surgical tools, among them syringes, needles, scissors, and a scalpel. He carefully lifted the scalpel out of the bag, examining the sharp blade in the light.

Sydney was excited about her new day job at the A&P in Provincetown because, along with working nights at the Pilgrim Club, she would be able to save money more quickly for her next adventure. This time, she told her mother, when she had enough saved, she was going to Europe.

Friday, May 24, Sydney cashed her paycheck from the A&P, put ten dollars of it in her pocket and deposited the rest in the bank. Later that afternoon, her sister, Linda, was walking home from work when she saw Sydney standing in the street at the top of Watson Court, visibly distraught. She saw that Sydney was having a heated conversation with someone in a parked car. Sydney called to Linda that she needed to talk to her, but Linda waved her off, saying she didn't have time right then; she would catch her later. She saw Sydney get into the car and watched it drive away. Linda came back in an hour to talk to her sister, but Sydney was gone.

The next day, Sydney's bicycle was spotted leaning up against the A&P's employee entrance, but she had failed to show up for work. A week went by, and Sydney was still nowhere to be seen. Linda later told investigators that because she suspected her disappearance might have had to do with her drug use, she waited three weeks before accepting that something was terribly wrong. She finally called her mother in Eastham and said that Sydney was missing. On June 14, a missing person's report was filed with the Provincetown police. When they interviewed Linda, police asked her who was driving the car that she had seen Sydney get into. As if considering it for the first time, she told them, "Well, I think it was Tony Costa."

Tony would later claim that Sydney went to Europe early. "I never gave it a second thought," Tony said. "Hippies are like that; here today, somewhere else tomorrow."[6]

24

LIZA

As soon as school let out for the summer, Mom quit her home ec job. She loaded the car with just about everything we owned, and we headed to Provincetown, this time for good. She told Grampa Georgie to put our house on the market; she was *done with West Bridgewater, finally!*

I was ecstatic. For years, I had dreamed of moving to Provincetown permanently and becoming a local. I had always wanted to belong somewhere, anywhere, and after our first summer in Provincetown, I wanted it to be *there.* To be part of that close-knit community, part of Cecelia and Tony's people, who seemed to like me and would probably welcome me into their family. To live downtown in a small, shingled house overlooking the wharves. I wanted to be one of the cool kids, the townies, many of whom worked at the Royal Coachman as maids and groundskeepers. To stroll Commercial Street, my arms linked with other girls, wearing tank tops and cutoff blue-jean shorts, flirting with the boys who rode by on their bicycles. To sit on the Benches and laugh at the drag queens, stoned hippies, and tacky tourists. To eat hot dogs and french fries and hot fudge before going to the beach and working on our tans. I wanted it all, and now that we would be living full-time in Provincetown, I hoped I had a chance of getting it.

Mom's new motel, the Bayberry Bend Motel and Cottages, had seven rooms and eight cottages, all tucked by the side of Route 6A and across the street from the Royal Coachman. When we got there, the first thing she did was hang out the wooden VACANCY sign and tack a HELP WANTED sign in the front window. She was in business.

The three of us moved into number nine, one of the small motel rooms next to the office. It had a double bed for Mom and bunk beds for me and Louisa, leaving just enough room for us to move between the beds if we scuttled sideways.

One of Mom's first hires was a chambermaid, Sally, a sixteen-year-old girl from Truro who along with cleaning rooms worked the front desk and looked after me and Louisa. In exchange for those added duties, Mom gave her free room and board, so number nine got even more crowded when Sally moved in with us. Louisa slept in Mom's double bed with her, and Sally slept on the top bunk.

During those years, and particularly those summers, Mom loved to go dancing at the clubs, as many nights as she could get away, except Sunday, because the blue laws made it illegal to dance in a bar on Sunday. Most nights, she'd come home in the early hours of the morning and I'd be wakened by her tiptoeing into our room, her shadow moving across the wall, her shoes and sometimes her clothes in her arms.

One day, I asked her whom she danced with, and she said, "Whoever. There's always somebody who wants to dance at the Pilgrim Club." Then she hesitated and smiled at herself in the mirror as she applied her lipstick before adding, "With me."

On the weekends, Fat Al the Candy Man sometimes drove down from Boston, renting one of the cottages and watching television in his T-shirt all day until Mom was able to leave for the night. Louisa and I spent those weekend nights with Sally and her boyfriend at the Wellfleet Drive-In, where we'd see half of Provincetown in the line to get popcorn while *The Parent Trap* loomed on the big screen. (I loved Hayley Mills and, watching the film, wondered if I too could get my parents back together.)

When Sally was busy or had the day off and Mom needed someone to keep an eye on us, she would ask one of the motel guests, Bob Stranger, to look after us in exchange for a slightly reduced rent. Bob, who rented cottage two for the entire summer, was a frail, pale little man who loved the place. He even brought his own piece of artwork he hung on the wall. It was a poster he'd found at one of the shops on Commercial Street of a fancy lace bra with the words *I just bought a Living Bra and I don't know what to feed it* written under the cups. Bob had a Chihuahua named Duke, and he kept mostly to himself, rarely venturing beyond the grounds. He always seemed to be hiding from something, or someone, looking furtively over his shoulder or hurrying back to his cottage in little geisha steps whenever a car drove into the driveway. Every morning before it got too hot and the sun got too bright, he walked Duke around the motel's tiny lawn, and the whole time Duke would bark as if being attacked by coyotes. Bob, smoking a really long, slim cigarette and wearing large, dark sunglasses reminiscent of Jackie Kennedy, a loosely tied white terry-cloth robe, and penny loafers with no socks, would mutter, "Cool it, Duke. Just cool it." Mom had a rare soft spot for Bob, and every couple of weeks, she would return from the A&P and hand me a box of Kotex.

"Take these to Bob."

"What does he need *these* for?" I asked the first time it happened, turning the box over in my hands.

She laughed and said, "He likes to wear them. They make him feel more feminine," as if that answered my question.

I walked to his cottage with the blue box tucked under my arm and knocked on his door, embarrassed and worried that I might be interrupting something but not sure of what that something would be, maybe just his privacy, or a nap. With Duke scratching at the door and barking his ear-piercing bark, Bob came to the screen door and looked at me standing there with the box of Kotex in my hand. I don't know who was more uncomfortable. Probably Bob. He didn't say a word, just opened the door wide enough to reach out and take the box from me. He whispered, "Thank you, Honey," gave me a little smile, pushed Duke out of the way with his foot, and shut the door quietly.

Every time I saw Bob after that, I tried not to wonder if he was wearing a Kotex pad.

Even though Mom often stayed out late, she took the business of running Bayberry Bend very seriously and was always the first to wake up, getting out of bed at 5:00 a.m. like she'd pole-vaulted off the mattress. Whatever else she wasn't, she was a hard worker, even at fifteen when she waitressed at the Howard Johnson's off the old Route 6 in Buzzards Bay. She never actually made us breakfast; she poured cereal. But in running a motel, she was as good, sometimes better, than the help she hired. She could fix broken lamps, unplug clogged pipes, replace torn screens and cracked windowpanes, and did her fair share of scrubbing toilets, making beds, and mopping floors. By six in the morning, she was mowing the lawn or watering the bushes or brushing sand off the patio or deadheading the geraniums. Always something. Always moving. That's what I remember most clearly: my mother in motion.

The minute Louisa and I got out of bed, she'd put us to work. We got really good at tucking hospital corners on the beds, folding sheets and towels, scrubbing tile until it gleamed, and sweeping the sand out of the rooms and cottages. We would giggle whenever we found used condoms and gag when we had to clean pubic hair out of the drains. (It was very different from head hair and we knew what it was, even though we didn't have any yet.) And when we cleaned the toilets, we fought for the one pair of rubber gloves without holes in them. Mom also showed us how to do some small repairs—like tighten screws in a door hinge or hammer down a loose floorboard. And then there was relighting the gas pilots.

The cottages had little kitchens with old propane stoves that would constantly go out, spreading the smell of gas. Bob's in particular seemed to go out all the time, and he'd stand at his cottage door and call, "Betty! Pilot's out again!" and one of us would go over.

"God knows what he's doing in there," Mom muttered. It happened that often.

Bob was afraid to relight it himself, so Mom taught me how to do it. I'd lie flat on the floor, open the bottom drawer where the pilot was, reach in with a lit match, and relight it. When I did it right, there was a little *poof* as the gas reignited. I got pretty good at draining the line of gas before striking the match, but one time I screwed up and a pocket of gas exploded in my face. Bob, who had been standing at a safe distance with a yapping Duke in his arms, dropped the terrified dog and came rushing over.

"Oh, Christ! Are you okay?" he said, helping me up. "Where's your mom?"

He brushed off my legs and inspected my face for any cuts, then took me outside for fresh air.

Mom said she never heard a thing.

25

TONY

With the 1968 summer season and its jacked-up rents about to start, Avis once again packed up the three children and moved out of the cottage on Shank Painter Road and into an even more cramped apartment on Commercial Street. When David Raboy arrived at the cottages to get them ready for his summer clientele, he was surprised to see that a room had been built in the corner of the basement and the door had two padlocks on it, even though he hadn't been asked permission for the construction. Looking around, he found a large screwdriver and broke off each lock, then opened the door. The room was empty. A thin beam of light filtered through the dust and shone on a rough table, built into the wall. Walking over, he saw that several papers had fallen behind it. He reached down and pulled up a 24-by-36-inch piece of poster board covered with what looked to be images cut from magazines. Peering closely, Raboy felt his stomach lurch when he recognized what he saw: female body parts, most of them breasts and genitalia, taped together in hideous caricatures of the human form. Disgusted and unaware that he was looking at potential evidence, he threw it in the garbage so that no one would have to "experience the same revulsion I did."[1]

Meanwhile, Tony was as depressed and anxious as his friends had ever seen him. And along with getting high every day, he was also getting religion and would incessantly expound on his theological beliefs, writing one friend, "If the Apostle Paul had the willpower to live with a woman and refrain from sex, then everyone should have to."[2]

By early June, his malaise had morphed into irritation. Everywhere he went the police seemed to follow him. He'd be riding his bike through town or sitting on the Benches with a group of his "kid chicks," and the police would approach him, asking questions about Sydney. When had he last seen her? Where were they driving when they'd been seen leaving town on Route 6? Did he have any idea where she might have gone? Her sister, Linda, said she had seen Sydney crying before she got in Tony's car—what was that about?

In the days after her disappearance, Tony kept to his story. How was *he* supposed to know what happened to Sydney Monzon? He barely knew the girl. And that's what he told them, over and over, until he finally decided he needed to get out of town for a while. His job at the Crown & Anchor was done, and they needed him to move out so they could rent his room to tourists. Even if they hadn't needed his room, they were ready to throw him out because he always seemed to have an unsavory group of teenagers hanging around, smoking dope, doing drugs, and coming and going at all hours causing a scene. The police had even shown up to search his room for drugs. The owner of the Crown & Anchor had had enough.

One day while Tony was hanging out on the Benches, he met Sandy, a young woman whom everybody called Croakie. She had been encouraging him to clean up his act and get a real job. She thought him drop-dead gorgeous and a real charmer with a lot of potential, and she was determined to be the woman to get him on the straight and narrow.

Tony was always looking for a way to get out of town and away from his obligations, but this time, he seemed a little more frantic about it because the cops were harassing him about Sydney's disappearance. By mid-June, Avis observed "it seemed as if he had to stay stoned to remain calm." She always knew when he was high because "when he wasn't stoned he was just impossible to be around. For one thing, he had a bad temper. And he'd wring his hands and bite his fingernails. I don't think he could stand to be around himself when he was straight. I'd say, 'Jesus Christ, Tony, will you go get stoned? I can't stand it; smoke or do something. Just go get stoned!' "[3]

In early July, Croakie heard of a construction job with a company near where she worked in Dedham, a suburb south of Boston. Tony got the job, and before leaving Provincetown, he and a couple of friends robbed Bob Murray's Pharmacy in Wellfleet, just to make sure he'd have the drugs he needed on the job while he was away from his usual haunts. While one friend drove the getaway car and another set fire to some brush by the side of the road to distract police, Tony easily picked the lock and walked away with another pillowcase full of narcotics and morphine substitutes, as well as a fat supply of hypodermic needles.[4] By this point, Tony, by his own account, had begun to shoot up morphine and heroin.[5]

He also bought a .22-caliber revolver from one of his young followers, Cory Devereaux, the same kid who five years before had most likely stood as an altar boy at Tony and Avis's wedding. Cory had recently stolen the gun from his grandmother in West Virginia. Tony told Cory he needed it for protection after the Provincetown police had let it be known that he had been their snitch in the Jay Von Utter arrest in March. In addition to the police, Tony was increasingly paranoid that a so-called "organization" was after him for undercutting their drug-dealing business on Cape Cod. As always, Tony's woes were somebody else's fault.

He felt he had a target on his back.

26

LIZA

Bayberry Bend sat on the far side of the road from the beach. The *wrong* side. It didn't have a swimming pool, shuffleboard court, soda machine, or any of the other fun extras at the Royal Coachman. It also didn't have Cecelia. So when Louisa and I weren't cleaning rooms or helping with the laundry at Bayberry Bend, we'd wait around for Geoff or Gail to invite us to come over to play. Mom forbade us to go uninvited because, she said, "It wasn't anyone else's job to watch a bunch of kids." But I was nine years old that summer and the oldest, and I didn't feel like a kid anymore. When they didn't call us over, Louisa and I would sit on the brick wall out front of the Bayberry Bend and count the cars coming down the RC driveway. When we saw someone we knew heading into town, we'd wave and ask them for a ride to Commercial Street. Once in town we'd go to the Penney Patch for candy or to a spin art place, where a machine splattered paint onto a T-shirt. Of course, my favorite ride into town was still with Tony.

One day in the middle of June, Sally was busy cleaning a room, so I covered the front desk while Mom ran a quick errand. Someone had left a copy of the *Provincetown Banner* on the desk, and in big bold letters the headline read, MISSING EASTHAM GIRL, 19, REPORTED TO POLICE. Most times the *Banner* just reported on missing dogs, not missing girls, so I opened the paper and read the story about how a pretty young girl suddenly disappeared into thin air. I wondered how that happened. Where did she go? Why didn't she tell her parents where she was? Why didn't she just call from wherever she'd gone? And why did she leave her bike behind at the A&P? But mostly I wondered—*If girls can just disappear into thin air, could it happen to me too?*

As I read the article a second time, a car pulled up, its tires scrunching across the crushed white seashells in the driveway. A tall man got out and came into the office. He jangled his car keys in one hand while he pushed his sunglasses onto his head. I didn't like him. Right away I could see he was in a hurry and that was somehow my fault.

"Can I help you?" I asked in my most grown-up voice.

"Yeah. You got a room available?"

I glanced at the clock on the wall: ten o'clock—too early for checking in. People were always stopping at the Bayberry Bend to look at the rooms, make a future reservation, or see if they could bargain Mom down in the price. Sitting at the south end of Provincetown, it was among the first cheap motels travelers came upon as they crossed the town line. Mom could spot the hagglers a mile away, but I was new to the game.

I grabbed a key from the pegboard and walked the man down to number twelve, unlocked the door, and followed him into the room. Just as I thought, he was in a hurry. He walked into the room and checked out his unshaven face in the bathroom mirror, giving it a slow stroke along the jawline. He turned to me, showed his mouthful of dirty yellow teeth, and said, "I'll take it."

I told him he'd have to wait for my mother to get back from town before he could check in but that it shouldn't be more than a few minutes. Besides, I told him, it was still morning and long before check-ins were allowed anyway. He didn't like that.

"Forget it!" he said. "Who does business like that?"

He pushed past me and slammed out the door, his shoes crunching across the driveway. He got in his car and gunned it onto Route 6A, oyster shells flying in his wake.

Walking back to the office, I felt something I never had felt before in Provincetown—fear. Fear of this man and his noisy keys, fear for the pretty young girl who'd gone missing, and fear of Mom when she learned I'd let a customer get away.

On a really hot July day, Louisa and I were playing with our marbles in the Bayberry Bend parking lot when we saw Tony ride his bike up the Royal Coachman driveway and then head into the motel. I hadn't seen him in a couple of weeks, so I pocketed the marbles, quickly swiping one of Louisa's favorites when she wasn't looking, and went to the Bayberry office. Sally was sitting behind the front desk, her feet propped up on the counter and a portable fan blowing on her, reading a paperback—*Valley of the Dolls.* I tried to picture what an entire valley would look like covered in Barbies and baby dolls and why anyone would read a book about it.

"Hey, Sally! Tony just rode up to the RC. Can we go over and see him?"

"Okay," she said, not looking up from the book. "Be careful crossing the street, and don't be too long. Your mom is due back in a couple hours."

I held Louisa's hand waiting for the traffic on 6A to ease, then we ran across the road and found Tony out back at the dumpsters, loading up the truck.

"Hey, Tony! Where you been?" I asked.

"I got a job near Boston," he said, throwing a bag of garbage in the truck. "I'm just down here to check on things and pick up some odd jobs here and there."

I didn't really care where he had been, only that he was back and headed out in the truck. "You going to the dump? Can we go with you?" I said, hopping up and down with excitement.

"Sure." He reached in his pocket. "Here's ten cents. Grab yourselves a couple of Popsicles before we head out."

I took the two nickels, and Louisa and I ran to the ice cream cooler by the pool. I saw Cecelia moving between rooms with an armload of towels and gave her a wave. She nodded and smiled and disappeared into one of the rooms. I put the money in the machine, reached in, and rooted around in the frosty air until I found two orange Popsicles, then slammed the lid shut. We both tore the paper off and started back to the truck, but we hadn't gone ten feet when they were already melting down our hands and arms.

It was hotter and more humid than usual, even for Cape Cod in the summer. Everything on the Cape was always damp—our cereal was soggy, our crackers were limp, and our bathing suits and beach towels never dried out completely; within a few days of the summer's start, they smelled moldy and stayed that way.

"Whoa," Tony said, seeing the orange syrup all over our faces and hands. "Can't get in the truck all sticky. Here, let me clean you up."

He tore off two paper towels, and with one in each hand began wiping gently at our faces. We both stood, faces raised to him, while he dabbed at our cheeks and chins, occasionally moistening the paper towels with the tip of his tongue.

"Now hold out your hands," he said, and then he carefully wiped each of our fingers until he was satisfied there was no syrup left on them.

"Okay! Nice and clean. Now you can get in the truck."

We clambered up and sat happily back against the seat, feeling the hot vinyl through our shirts and against our bare legs, as he climbed in after us and started the engine. "We're off!" he said, reaching down to turn on the radio.

At the dump, he emptied the motel's garbage from the truck and swept the bed clean of remaining scraps and dirt.

"Can you keep a secret?" he asked as he climbed back into the truck.

"What kind of secret? Another Popsicle?" Louisa said, bouncing up and down on the seat.

I pinched her hard and gave her a stern look as a silent warning to not say something stupid and make him change his mind about sharing his secret.

"Ouch! Whaddya do that for?" she said, rubbing her leg where a little red welt was rising.

"I'm a good secret keeper," I said, ignoring her and turning back to Tony. "Timmy Johnson says I'm the best secret keeper in third grade. What's *your* secret?"

Tony reached over and pulled free a curl of my hair that had gotten stuck to my cheek. I tried not to blush but could feel my cheeks getting hot. He put his hand back on the steering wheel.

"It's something I've got in the woods, out by the cemetery. I only show it to my *closest* pals and chicks. Wanna see it?"

Louisa and I both nodded so eagerly Tony laughed. "You look like a couple of bobblehead dolls," he said.

I loved it when Tony laughed.

We left the dump, and instead of turning right and heading toward the Royal Coachman, we sped up Route 6 toward Truro and onto a back road I'd never been on before. I looked at Tony to make sure he knew where he was going. He caught my glance, reached over, patted my knee, and smiled. I smiled back. When the road came to a dead end, I thought he must have gotten lost and wondered how he was going to turn the truck around in so small a space. But instead of slowing down, he revved the engine and drove down a small embankment, which put us on a dirt path, invisible from the road we had been on.

"Wow! You really know your way around these woods," I said.

Tony smiled. "I sure do."

We drove slowly, the pickup rocking on the rutted path. When we hit a big pothole, it sent both Louisa and me flying off the long bench seat, nearly hitting our heads on the roof.

"Hold on, kiddos!" Tony laughed, wrestling the long gearshift back and forth, knocking into my left leg when he did. The pickup pitched and groaned as he ground it into a lower gear.

I looked at Louisa to make sure she was okay. She was, but I could see she was sweating from the heat and wished Tony hadn't interrupted our game of marbles to take us on a hot, bumpy drive through the woods. She was seven that summer and had developed a nervous habit of rubbing her fingertips together, as if she were spreading pinches of salt on her food with both hands. As we drove along, her fingers were fluttering away in her lap. I reached into my pocket and pulled out her favorite marble and handed it to her. She didn't even get mad that I had stolen it; she just smiled and began rolling it in her fingers.

The air inside the truck was thick and had only gotten thicker once we left the highway. I'd never been into woods so deep I couldn't see through the trees; they blocked all direct sunlight, and in some places their branches scraped the truck's doors. It felt as if we were rocking through a tunnel of green straw. I'd been surrounded by water and salt and sand and seagulls for so long, it took me a few moments to realize how odd it was to be in a place without any sign of the ocean. And there were no tourists, no motel guests, no beachcombers—no one. We were alone with Tony. A special adventure.

"It's hot in here," Louisa complained from her side of the truck's seat. I narrowed my eyes at her and clenched my teeth like Mom always did.

"Shut up!" I hissed.

"Don't worry, we're almost there," Tony said, and sure enough, a few bumps later he stopped the truck in a small opening in the thicket of trees and turned off the engine.

"Is this where the secret is?" I asked, twisting around, trying to see something. But there were only trees.

"Come on, I'll show you," Tony said, opening his door and pocketing the keys. He got out and held the door open so I could slide across the seat and hop down. Then he reached into the cab and picked up Louisa under her arms, swinging her out and placing her feet on the ground.

Tony led us through the woods, holding branches aside so we wouldn't get hit in the face as they snapped back into place. I looked up through the trees and could just barely see a patch of blue through the canopy of green.

So the sky is still up there somewhere, I thought.

We came to a clearing in the woods, about the size of the RC's pool, and Tony stopped.

"Here it is!"

I looked at where he was pointing, but all I saw was a small patch of dirt, a mound, really, with a few scraggly plants sticking out the top of it and a bunch of pine needles and leaves.

"I'm hot," Louisa said, by now almost crying.

I ignored her.

"What is it?" I asked, not wanting to insult him by asking, "Is that *it*?"

"It's my secret garden!" He grinned.

I knew gardens, and this didn't look like one. Grampa Georgie, now *he* knew about gardens, and because he taught me, so did I. For the very first time since I'd met him, I felt a little sorry for Tony. I couldn't understand why he thought these shriveled stalks were something to show off.

"It's really nice," I lied.

"Where's the surprise?" Louisa asked, wiping sweat from her brow. I think she was still hoping for another Popsicle.

Tony knelt in the dirt and pulled a couple of tiny weeds from the base of one of the plants, then picked off a couple of the larger leaves and stuffed them in his breast pocket.

"What did you plant?" I asked.

He put his finger to his lips. "*That's* what we have to keep secret!" Tony said, his smile so big and his mouth so wide I could see his back teeth. I couldn't help smiling too. I liked that he trusted me.

"Wait here," he said, and stood up. He walked over to a big pine tree at the edge of the clearing, squatted down, dug around with his fingers, and pulled something out of the dirt. But then he seemed to change his mind and quickly reburied it. I couldn't see what it was, but when he walked back over to where we stood, his head hung down so that his chin almost touched his chest. He looked so unhappy.

"It was my father's," he said. "It's one of the only things I have of his."

"What was it?" I said, looking back toward the tree.

Tony just shook his head. "Nothing."

Louisa shifted from foot to foot as if she had to pee, while I stood still, waiting for what was next. I hoped he'd turn toward the truck and tell us it was time to get back home. I wanted to get out of there and back on the main road, where I could smell the ocean and feel the breeze, where I could take a deep breath. But he didn't seem to want to leave.

"Come here," he said, walking over to another mound of dirt. "I'll show you a better secret. I've got lots of them. Come a little closer."

I thought we were already close enough, so I didn't move. Tony looked at me and slowly smiled. He seemed to be over his sadness. "Come on," he said, waving us closer. "I won't bite."

Suddenly I felt nervous flutters in my stomach. Without thinking why, I reached down and took Louisa's hand, and we took a step closer. The ground felt soft under my feet, squishy almost. I looked down, and I could see that unlike the earth around it, this little garden had freshly dug dirt and all the leaves and pine needles had been swept off it.

This was the first time an adventure with Tony was becoming less and less fun. In fact, I was done with the garden. I wanted to go home. But Tony wasn't ready to leave.

"I just love it out here," he said, sitting back on a pile of leaves. "Sometimes I wish I could live out here, near my garden."

"But why do you keep it way out here?" I said. "Why not closer to town, or behind the Royal Coachman? There's plenty of room there for a garden."

Tony sat back on his heels and chuckled.

"Oh, no," he said. "I need this garden to be secret. I don't want anyone but my best cats and chicks to know where it is."

"But couldn't it be a secret in town?"

"You ask a lot of questions."

"My mom says that too," I said. Suddenly, and for the first time, I was irritated with Tony. There was something about his expression, kind of a half smile, that wasn't very nice.

"Let's go, okay?" I said, stepping away from his little garden and pulling Louisa with me.

Tony stood up, brushing the dirt off his hands. "I promise I'll tell you why it's a secret when you're a little bit older. Until then, don't tell anybody about it, okay? I can trust you, can't I, Liza?" He reached out his hand for a shake.

I felt a rush of heat go through me as he took my hand in his. "Yes. I promise not to tell anyone. She won't either," I said, nodding at Louisa.

He gave my hand a little squeeze and a shake. "You're a good girl," he said. "I've always liked you."

I bit my lip and lowered my head so he couldn't see me blush.

27

TONY

By August, Tony could breathe a sigh of relief. His job at Starline Construction was going well; he had worked there for nearly two months, a record for him, and he was finally out of Provincetown. But while he was working steadily for one of the first times in his life, his old bad habits refused to die, and his girlfriend Croakie realized he had no intention of growing up and giving up his drug dealing and use. As with most of his girlfriends, Tony had resisted having sexual intercourse with her, preferring instead to lie naked in bed, comforted by the warm body next to his. Avis later said that he preferred to just sleep with a woman because it helped soothe his terrifying dreams and even-worse violent imaginings. If Tony was "actually balling a chick," Avis could immediately tell because he would find fault with the woman and soon think of ways to "get rid of her."[1]

True to this pattern, soon after he and Croakie finally had sex sometime in late August, they broke up.

With Croakie out of the picture, Tony filled the Dedham apartment with his harem of Provincetown teenagers, girls and boys, all eager for a place to drink beer, do drugs, and have sex, away from the watchful eyes of Provincetown, where everybody knew everybody else's business. When Tony or one of the kids wanted to try a drug they didn't have on hand, they'd take the bus into Boston and score something on the Common.

One weekend, the Provincetown group brought along Susan Perry, the rebellious and insecure girl about whom the librarian, Alice Joseph, had worried. Alice's concerns proved well-founded. After a year of raising her five younger siblings while her father was at sea, Susan had had enough and in July 1968 quit school and left home. She was not yet eighteen. Her father's response was "good riddance." At first, she stayed in staff housing at the Royal Coachman, where she worked as a chambermaid, but the arrangement didn't last long. In her rebellion, she had gained a reputation as a "wild kid" with "round heels" who'd go with any boy just to feel fleeting moments of being wanted and liked. But her friends believed that she slept wherever and with whomever she needed to in order to survive. Hoping that Tony might finally be a safe haven, Susan approached him to ask if she could crash at his apartment.

She found him in the small kitchen making dinner: peanut butter on Ritz crackers.

"Gee, I feel kinda bad barging in on you like this," Susan said, looking up at him as she nibbled the edge of a cracker.

"It's okay with me," he said. "You'll just have to share my bed, I guess." Then, giving her his best smile, added, "You are like a little kid chick. Stay here with Sire and you will learn."[2]

Susan was thrilled.

Later, when he wrote of the exchange, Tony's pious vanity was never more apparent: "You mustn't feel funny," he reportedly told Susan. "Too many live for themselves, but I live for God and my fellow man."[3]

As they talked, Susan told him that she had finally run away from home, even though "my father said if I left home to never return." She hoped she would never have to. Unlike Tony's more steady girlfriends, Susan and Tony had sex that first night, after which she told a girlfriend, "I hope Tony will like me now."

In the morning, Tony went to work and she got nosy, poking through his drawers and closets, looking for evidence of another girlfriend. Instead, she found the .22-caliber revolver he had bought from Cory Devereaux in the bedside table. She carefully put it back, wondering why on Earth Tony would need a gun.

28

LIZA

One Saturday toward the end of the summer, Tony came back into town and Auntie asked him to run a load of the RC's trash to the dump. Always on the lookout, I ran across the street when I saw him and asked if I could go along. Louisa was taking a rare nap, so I was on my own. Soon he and I were headed toward town. As he drove, he reached across my knees to push in the cigarette lighter, and when it popped out, he lit a cigarette, smiled, and handed it to me. After three summers of my begging, he said now that I was going to be ten soon I was old enough to learn how to smoke. I took the cigarette from his fingers, took a huge drag the way my mother always did, and coughed so hard I nearly threw up. Tony patted my back and laughed. He took the cigarette out of my fingers, and I watched him slowly place it between his lips. He looked up, caught me staring at his lips, and smiled.

"Hey, did I ever show you the oldest gravestone out in the Pine Grove Cemetery?" he said.

"No! How old is it?"

"So old you can't even read the date. But at least one hundred, one hundred and fifty years. Let's go take a look. Your mom isn't expecting you back, is she?"

"Nope!" I said, almost chirping I was so happy.

When we got to the cemetery there wasn't much to see. As Tony had said, the stone was old and rounded, and whatever words had once been carved into it were all but erased.

"It's erosion from the wind and rain," Tony said, standing next to me. "Pretty cool, huh?"

"How do you know this is the oldest one?" I asked, waving my arm at the rows of tombstones all around us.

"Oh, I've been coming out here since I was a kid, like you," he said, his fingers running lightly across the stone. "I've even slept out here."

"Really? Isn't it scary?" I asked, looking at the small mounds in front of the graves and suddenly picturing old dead Joe Rose from my grandfather's funeral parlor in the ground at my feet. "Aren't you afraid sleeping with all these dead people under you?"

Tony put his head back, filled his lungs with air, and slowly exhaled.

"Nope. I love it." He looked down at me. "Maybe it's just something you have to get used to."

As we drove back into town, Tony talked pretty much nonstop, telling me stories I wasn't supposed to tell anyone else. About how he might be moving to California soon, and how he'd once driven there in thirty-six hours straight without stopping and then turned right around and came home, thanks to his special vitamins. He talked without a break, more to himself than to me, the subjects rambling all over the place, while he chewed his fingernails and gum at the same time—covering subjects from his lousy stepfather, to rotten Avis, who was a lousy mother who never took baths, to his kids, who always seemed to be sick and dirty and crying, to his stupid boss, who didn't understand that he sometimes stayed up all night worrying about the kids and couldn't get to work on time. He got so wrapped up in his stories that he pulled out his comb and instead of combing his hair, he ran it across his arm back and forth, hard enough to leave deep scratches. I wondered if he had eczema like me.

"Tony, does your arm itch?" I asked. He looked down at the red scratches; some had little droplets of blood in them. He quickly put the comb back in his pocket and brushed at his arm, streaking the blood with his hand.

"Shit," he said. "Blood totally freaks me out. I must have got a mosquito bite." He spit on his finger and quickly wiped away the blood.

29

TONY

Tony was scheduled to work through Friday of Labor Day weekend, so Susan Perry left Tony's Dedham apartment and took the bus to Provincetown on her own. She left him a note saying that she'd be back on Monday with more of her things. Once in Provincetown and wanting to avoid running into her father, whom she had not spoken to since leaving home in July, she asked two girlfriends to go to her house and pack some of her meager belongings.

Susan spent much of the weekend sleeping on the beach in the rain, doing drugs, and looking around town for Tony, but she didn't find him; he was holed up with Christine Gallant, the pretty woman from Fall River.

Tony and Christine spent the weekend stoned to the gills on LSD and barbiturates, with some Thorazine here and there to bring them down when they'd taken too much speed. They reportedly professed their love for each other and Tony went one step further, telling people they were to be married. The weekend ended abruptly when Christine's mother drove up to Provincetown and took her daughter back to Fall River, and Tony returned to Dedham. Christine was scheduled to move to New York City the next day.

Disappointed at missing Tony in Provincetown, Susan returned to Dedham on Tuesday, September 3. The next day, her girlfriends brought her the green army duffel bag of clothes she'd wanted. They all went to the Boston Common, where they scored some drugs before returning to Tony's apartment. Since her friends had to be back in Provincetown for school the next day, they headed home in the early evening. As their car pulled out of the driveway, Susan and Tony stood on his front porch waving goodbye. Susan had her arms around his neck, kissing him.[1] They never saw her again.

Two days later, Tony himself left Dedham and headed back to Provincetown. He was "going like hell,"[2] heading north on Route 6 in Truro, when he got pulled over by state trooper Edgar Thomas Gunnery because his muffler was loud enough to cause a disturbance. Tony got out of his car and walked toward Gunnery, something Gunnery thought odd and a sure sign the driver didn't want police to look inside his car.

"Evening, Officer," Tony said, putting out his hand and giving Gunnery his best Eddie Haskell smile as the officer approached him.

Gunnery's instinct told him the guy was hiding something, but he didn't have a warrant or just cause to search the car, so he gave Tony a warning to get the muffler fixed and sent him on his way.

"That kid's a real smoothie," Gunnery said to himself as he walked back to his cruiser.

After Tony got back to Provincetown, he borrowed a car with a less noisy muffler and several tools, including a shovel, from a friend's parents. When he returned the car, the tools and shovel were missing and the car was full of sand. Tony never accounted for either.

30

LIZA

A few days after Labor Day, Mom and Joan decided they needed to have one last "fun run" to Hyannis before the end of the summer season, to shop and linger over martinis after a long and lazy lunch of fried clams and coleslaw at Baxter's Fish N' Chips on the wharf. Louisa and I sat on the edge of her bed while she tried on one outfit after another, tossing the rejects into an ever-growing pile on the bed. She was in a rare good mood—happy and cheerful—and we both sat as still as we could, hoping it would last. After many combinations of clothes, Mom finally selected what she thought was the perfect outfit: a simple red skirt, a white cotton blouse with a Peter Pan collar, a checkered scarf around her neck, and a wide white leather belt tying it all together. She clipped big red plastic earrings onto her earlobes and pirouetted through the room checking herself out in the mirror over her dressing table. Satisfied, she sat down in front of the mirror and applied her trademark blue eye shadow, black eyeliner, black mascara, and a dab of rouge on each cheek. Then she picked up her lip liner and began drawing a careful pink line around her mouth.

"Girls, I know I've said this before," she said, her lips stretched taut over her teeth. "Do you remember what I told you is the most important piece of makeup?" Without waiting for our answer, she continued, filling in the pink boundary around her mouth with Yardley's "Pink Plus" lipstick as she spoke.

"Lip. Stick," she said, making it two distinct words and patting her lips together with a *smack smack smack*. "Because not only can you use it on your lips"—she then touched the lipstick tip to each cheek and gently smoothed the small pink smudges into her cheekbones—"you can also use it for rouge." She turned her head in the mirror this way and that, admiring the result.

"And, finally," she said, again pausing for effect before putting a tiny dab of it on the tip of her index finger and then putting the finger to her eyelids, "in a pinch you can use it, but only sparingly, as eye shadow."

Louisa and I exchanged a look, not at all sure of her all-makeup-in-one tutorial; I was just happy to be near her and not feel afraid.

"There!" she said, capping the lipstick with a satisfied click and throwing it into her pocketbook. She stood up with a final admiring glance in the mirror and put the pocketbook straps over her arm. "Okay! Joan should be here any minute, and then we are *outta here!*"

It was Sally's day off, and I knew Bob was feeling poorly (Mom had laughed that maybe it was his time of the month, which I didn't think was very nice), so I wondered who she was corralling into looking after us. Just then, she saw Tony heading out of the Royal Coachman with a load of garbage.

Bingo, I thought, and ran outside. He saw me and pulled into the Bayberry's driveway.

"Looks like you're dressed up for a night on the town," Tony said to Mom, "but it's only ten o'clock in the morning." He gave a short laugh that wasn't cheerful at all.

"Joan and I are headed to do some errands and have a little lunch in Hyannis," she said, tying the checkered scarf around her head. "Now that you're here, can you watch the kids for a few hours?"

He didn't answer her immediately, and I was worried he'd say no, that he was busy or that he just didn't want to. He sure didn't *seem* like he wanted to. But then he looked away from Mom and down at me and smiled.

"Sure, I'd be happy to. I always like company out to the dump. How long do you think you'll be?" he said.

"Oh, you know Joan and me! Once we get started on *errands*, we lose all track of time! But we should be back before suppertime."

Just then, Joan drove up in her bright yellow Karmann Ghia convertible, and Mom hopped in.

"Okay then! Thanks, Tony. You're a doll."

Tony muttered something, but I couldn't hear what.

"I gotta make a run to the dump. Let's go," he said.

I pushed Louisa up onto the truck, then climbed in after her, pressing her against the door so I could sit, as I always did, next to Tony. When we got to the dump, Louisa and I stayed in the truck while he threw the motel's trash into the open pit and then poked through a pile of old radios and televisions, looking for ones he thought he could sell. They appeared pretty broken and rusty to me, but occasionally he found one that looked brand-new, and I wondered why anyone would throw out a perfectly good TV. Tony never seemed surprised at finding the shiny, clean radios and televisions; he just wrapped them in an old blanket he kept folded under the front seat and placed them carefully in the back of the truck.

After he was done digging around, he got back in the truck and started the engine.

The seagulls were swarming above us; their caws were so loud Tony had to lean toward me to be heard. He lit a cigarette while he focused on the bumpy road out of the dump.

"Do you know what seagulls eat?" Tony said.

"I dunno," I said. "Maybe garbage?"

He blew a string of perfect smoke rings before answering.

"That and a lot more. Especially fish. Watch 'em sometime. They fly just above the ocean's surface and then use their claws to reach down and grab their dinner right out of the water. It's wild."

He downshifted the truck, and it lurched. I grabbed for the dashboard to keep from being thrown off the front seat. Louisa lunged for the armrest near her. He didn't seem to notice the rough ride.

"Did you know a seagull can eat an entire rabbit, whole?" he said.

I wondered how he knew such a thing, but I didn't ask.

"I've got to check on my stuff in the woods, okay?"

"Sure," I said, knowing Mom wouldn't be home for hours.

Once again, we headed down to Truro, but instead of entering the woods on the dead-end road off Route 6, Tony drove around and approached his secret garden through the cemetery at the other end. He drove past a few rows of tombstones and stopped the truck at the edge of the cemetery. He told me we were going to walk from there. He seemed anxious. I got out, told Louisa to stay put, and followed him to the woods. As we approached the clearing, which I now knew the kids called lovers' lane, I smelled something like burning leaves and could hear music filtering toward us. Then I saw that there was a party going on. There were two VW buses with flower power decals on them parked in the clearing, and a bunch of kids not much older than I was stood around smoking cigarettes and drinking beer. The air was hot and clammy in the woods. Someone had made a sort-of lean-to, so I had some shade out of the sun. It was a good thing, because Tony told me to stay with the kids while he disappeared into the woods.

He was gone a long time.

31

TONY

Tony never again stepped foot in Dedham. He didn't even bother to call his boss at Starline Construction; he just didn't show up for work. Instead, he returned to Provincetown, landing on Vinnie and his girlfriend's couch. Often "inconsolable," Tony offered no explanation for his dark mood and he spent the next couple of weeks stoned to near oblivion.[1] When he walked the streets of Provincetown, they felt deserted now that Labor Day had come and gone and nearly all the tourists and summer people had left.

The silence seemed to unnerve Tony. He took a handful of Nembutal to quiet the voices in his head, voices that became screams in the empty streets. "You promised . . . you promised!" one of them cried.[2] But the drugs didn't work; the voices only got louder, so he did something he hadn't for a long, long time. He went to confession at St. Peter's. He needed penance. He needed salvation. He needed forgiveness. His only hope, he thought, was to confess his sins and emerge absolved. Totally absolved. That sounded right. But when he got to the church, a group of faithful parishioners was practicing the ancient ritual of walking the stations of the cross, and their shuffling feet across the stone floor of the sanctuary sounded to him like a chorus of those accusatory voices. Tony looked around, expecting to see angry faces looking at him, their shouts of defamation echoing through the pews. But all he saw were the bowed heads of the pious, and he fled, unforgiven.[3]

Later that day, he was walking down Commercial Street and saw Davy Joseph, one of Susan's friends who'd crashed in the Dedham apartment the week before.

"Hey, Tony," Davy said. "How's Sue?"

Tony shrugged. "I dunno. She's gone. Just took off for Mexico with a bunch of druggies. But she left this," Tony said, and reached into the front pocket of his white corduroy jeans. He pulled out a ring and handed it to Davy. "She said to give it to you."

It was a class ring that Susan had finagled out of a boy she'd been hoping to date, but it held no sentimental value for either Susan or Davy.

Davy held it out on his flat, open palm and looked up at Tony. "I don't want this. Why would she want *me* to have it?"

Tony shrugged again. "No idea, Davy. Gotta run. See ya," he said as he walked away, heading toward the west end of town. Dave stood in the street, still looking at the ring.

When asked, Tony told Susan's friends what he had told Davy—that she "had split for Mexico" with some "cats" she'd done drugs with on the Boston Common. He offered nothing more, and no one asked. She had become so estranged from her family that her parents didn't even report her as missing. And so, the sad girl who so desperately wanted to find love simply vanished, and no one seemed to notice, or much care.

With Tony out of the Dedham apartment, Cecelia told Vinnie to go and clean the place, but not simply to empty out the refrigerator and sweep the floor. He was sent primarily to retrieve Tony's gun from the bedside table as well as check what condition Tony had left the apartment in. Vinnie did as he was told.[4]

32

LIZA

Now that we were going to be living on the Cape full-time, Mom did two things to get us ready for our new life. First, she enrolled me and Louisa in the Provincetown elementary school, and then she gave away Louisa's puppy, Holly Berry, to a friend of Auntie's. Mom said the dog would probably get hit by a car anyway, so better to give her away before that happened.

"People who live on busy streets shouldn't have dogs," was all she would say as we drove away from the new owners' house and Louisa sat, inconsolable and sobbing, in the back seat. I guess Mom never thought of putting up a fence.

Provincetown was building a new grade school that wasn't finished yet, so at the beginning of the school year they put us in the basement of the high school. Right after school started, I saw Tony talking with some high school kids on the playground and waved to him. He finished up his conversation, stuffed something in his pocket, and came over to where I was watching some of the kids play dodgeball.

"Hey, Tony, what are you doing here? At school, I mean," I said.

He looked over his shoulder, then back at me. "Aw, nothing. Just checking in with some cats and chicks of mine."

Tony was a grown-up, and I thought it was strange that he had friends still in high school, but I didn't say anything. I was the new kid in my class and hadn't made any friends yet, so I was just happy to see a friendly, familiar face.

=======

Toward the end of October, Louisa had her first Holy Communion. Mom broke her own rule and attended the mass, and Dad said he'd come down for it too and then take us all to lunch. I spent the entire mass turning around in my pew, looking at the door, waiting for him to show up, until Mom pinched my ear and told me to sit still and behave. I settled in and watched the parade of little girls in their miniature white bride dresses and veils float down the aisle to Father Duarte, who put the holy host in their tiny mouths. They looked like baby birds in a nest—little pink open mouths raised up to Father Duarte. *Body of Christ, amen.* I knew it by heart and looked around the church, bored. Tony's son Peter, who was two years younger than Louisa, sat in a nearby pew with Cecelia, looking just as bored as I was.

After the mass, we sat on the front steps of the church, waiting for Dad. Peter and Cecelia were also there, I supposed waiting for Tony, but he had been a no-show for the service. Same as Dad.

"He's such an *asshole*," Mom said to no one in particular as she paced in front of the church, smoking her little cigars, one after another.

It was a chilly day, and even though Louisa and I were dressed in our best Sunday wool coats and little gloves, we got colder and colder sitting on the stone steps as the wind picked up. I had a wool hat on, but Louisa refused to take off her white veil, so she was even colder. Below us on the sidewalk, Mom stomped back and forth, muttering.

After about a half an hour, Cecelia and Peter stood up and she brushed off the seat of his pants.

"Well, we better head home," she said, bowing her head against the cold and wincing a little as she walked Peter down the steps. I never knew who they'd been waiting for, but if it was Tony, he was nowhere in sight.

Mom nodded at them and continued her pacing. Whenever a car approached from down the street, she stopped and squinted at it until she saw that it wasn't Dad and started pacing again. Finally, she stopped in front of us, her hands on her hips, blocking the sun and what little heat it offered.

"It's noon. C'mon, get up off those steps. He's not coming. *Obviously.*" Then to herself she added, "I shoulda fucking *known* he wouldn't show. *Asshole.*" She grabbed Louisa's hand and pulled her down the steps. Louisa stumbled after her, her free hand trying desperately to hold her veil on her head. I followed them down the stairs and across the church's parking lot to Mom's car, the only one still there.

"Get in," she said, fishing the keys out of her purse. When we had closed the doors behind us, she put the key in the ignition and started the engine, giving one last look toward the church and down the empty street. She gritted her teeth, revealing her famous fangs, then banged the steering wheel with both hands. "Shithead!"

She put the car in gear and it lurched forward, its tires squealing as she accelerated out of the parking lot and through the narrow streets and toward the Bayberry Bend.

Louisa and I hung on to our doors, trying to avoid sliding all over the back seat as Mom took most corners on two wheels. Louisa quietly cried and used her free arm to wipe her nose on the sleeve of her coat. It was a beautiful coat, light blue wool with pearl buttons that Mom had sewn herself. I worried Mom would yell at her to stop wiping her snot all over the coat, that she would ruin it. But Mom didn't yell. She didn't even look at us. She just drove, her knuckles white on the steering wheel. Under my coat, I could feel my arms start to itch.

That night for dinner, she plunked plates of cold canned spinach and barely boiled hot dogs in front of me and Louisa. We looked at the thin green water leaking toward the hot dog and then up at her. She stood over us, a drink in one hand, a cigarette in the other.

"What?" she said. "Not good enough for my little princesses?"

I knew I should keep my mouth shut, but I was afraid if I tried to eat what was on the plate, I'd throw it right back up and then she'd be even more mad.

"Could we have some ketchup?"

She looked at me, and I watched her eyes narrow into a danger-ous squint. She slowly opened the fridge and pulled out the ketchup bottle. Then, while holding the cigarette between her teeth, she poured the ketchup until it covered my hot dog and spinach and just about the entire plate. When the bottle was almost empty, she slammed it down on the table, hard enough to make my glass of milk jump.

"There you go, *Little Liza*, just like you requested. Is there anything I can get you, Your Highness?"

I shook my head but didn't dare speak or look up at her; tears were dripping onto the red mess, and I knew my crying would only make it worse.

"Okay, then. You sit there until you've finished every last bite. Food costs money, you know." She stormed out of the tiny efficiency kitchen by the office.

But I couldn't finish dinner; I couldn't even start it. Long after Louisa had finished hers and gone to our room, I sat at the table waiting for it to get late enough for Mom to have gone to sleep, before I dared get up and go to bed.

In the morning, my plate was where I'd left it. The ketchup had congealed into something resembling a red Frisbee—hard and almost plastic-looking, with the lump of the hot dog and spinach underneath. That was breakfast. She called from the front desk when she saw I was up, "We don't waste food. Children are starving in Biafra."

Wherever Biafra was, I wished I could send them my hot dog.

In all my memories of my mother, I have only one that is tender. It was when she would read *The Wind in the Willows* to us at night. She would settle in on Louisa's bed, and I'd lie on mine and watch her chest rise and fall with her breath, her voice husky and soft at the same time. As she got into the story, I would cross over to Louisa's bed and lie at the foot, slowly inching up to them as far as I dared, hoping she wouldn't notice. But as soon as I got close, Mom would look over the edge of the book, nudging me with her leg, and say, "Go back in your own bed. There's not enough room for you over here." I'd scramble back and pull the covers up to my neck, waiting for her to continue. When she finished a chapter, she'd snap the book shut, get up, turn out the light, and tiptoe out of the room, closing the door with a soft *click*.

I cherished that moment like an old photograph and would pull it out when she was particularly angry at me, which felt like just about all the time. Most of the attention she paid me was with the back of her hand. By far the worst punishments came when she suspected me of lying.

She told me Dad had spent some time in a VA hospital where he was diagnosed as a pathological liar. True or not, it allowed Mom to forever dismiss him as a bad man and father. It also seemed to make her watch for telltale signs of the same pathology in me. I wouldn't know it then, but I think she could have been more afraid than angry.

"You're just like your father," she would say as she slapped me, some-times hard enough to leave a mark. "A stinking *liar.*"

I wondered why she wasn't worried about Louisa being a "stinking liar" as well. Just me.

33

TONY

On the twenty-fourth of September, 1968, Provincetown patrolman James Cook pulled up behind Tony on Commercial Street and told him there was once again a warrant out for his arrest for nonsupport of Avis and the children. He was handcuffed and arrested on the spot, taken in the police cruiser to the Barnstable County House of Correction, known locally as simply the Barnstable County Jail, locked up, and sentenced to serve six months; his arraignment was scheduled for March 18, 1969.

While in jail, Tony had a lot of time to think, and he spent most of it worried—not that people would ask what had happened to Susan Perry but that he might lose Christine Gallant during his long incarceration. In the letters he wrote from jail, he berated the one person he felt was responsible: Avis. *After all, she ratted me out about the child support and landed me in jail, hadn't she?*

Actually, she hadn't. And when she wrote back, she told him so. According to the law, Tony was to have paid his $40 a week for child support to the Provincetown Division of Child Guardianship (today's Department of Children and Families), which in turn would have doled it out to Avis. But Tony never paid the money, and the department, ever watchful for cheats and scofflaws, put out the warrant for his arrest. To Tony, it was just another instance of his not being able to catch a break.

Wild with anxiety and missing his easy access to the bucket of drugs he'd been taking for nearly three years, Tony wrote Avis ugly and angry letters, in which he again insulted her judgment and her looks.

She replied, "I think you have often assured me my exterior will never be beautiful. I accepted that long ago."[1]

Tony once told Paula Hoernig, a friend of Susan Perry's and one of his teenage followers, "One must never compliment a woman because it goes straight to their head."[2]

He also wrote Avis letters in which he detailed her alleged drug use, hoping the jail censors would read it and arrest *her* for child abuse and neglect. He didn't stop there. In an eerie innuendo, he threatened to cut her up "into little pieces." For what supposed transgression, he didn't say. With that, Avis had had enough and responded with a threat of her own regarding *his* drug use and dealing: "There is much too much evidence and too many witnesses and people against you already. . . . If you persist in hassling me I may have to revert to something that turns my stomach to even conceive of. It gets pretty cold in federal prison, I hear. Sorry, but that's where it's at."[3]

When he wasn't harassing Avis, he obsessed over his drug caches in the Truro woods and the Provincetown dump. And he had every reason to worry; never one to keep his cards close to his vest, he had bragged to his less-than-savory followers about the amount and variety of drugs in both places. They helped themselves, selling what they didn't use. There was actually a measure of honor among these thieves, who put aside some of their "earnings" and gave the money to Tony when he was released from jail.

During the drug bust of Jay Von Utter, Tony had developed a friendship of sorts with Sergeant Jimmy Meads. Now sitting behind bars, Tony asked Meads to plead his case for an early release. Meads complied and went one step further, personally guaranteeing that Tony would show up for his trial. The court agreed to let him out, and Tony was released on November 8, nearly four and a half months ahead of schedule, and apparently without paying any bail, all thanks to Jimmy Meads.

Once out of jail, Tony went straight to Avis and asked her and her boyfriend, Jon Doeringer, to drive him to the bus station in Hyannis, where he bought a ticket and headed to New York to visit Christine. They spent that weekend and the weekend after that getting high on a bagful of pills Tony had brought from the remaining supply in his two caches. Whether those weekends were heavenly or hellish, after them Christine wrote her friend Martha Henrique in Provincetown that she was going to marry Raul Matta, her problematic lover, now that he had finally agreed to get a divorce.

Martha was confused; Tony had been telling people all over town that he and Christine were going to get married. But now, Christine was writing that Tony "freaked her out" because of his intensity. Further, and according to one of Christine's friends from Provincetown as well as phone records obtained later, she called Raul in Florida three times on Friday, November 22, and told him she thought Tony Costa was going to kill her.[4] Perhaps she used the phrase colloquially, as in, "When he hears that we are engaged he's going to kill me!" But perhaps she also used it literally, as in, "I am afraid for my life." Whatever her tone, Raul was concerned enough that he immediately left Florida, where he had found work during the Cape's off-season, and headed to New York City. But Tony got there first, arriving around noon the following day, Saturday, November 23. When he got to Christine's apartment, she told him she was finally getting married to Raul.

It's not known how Tony took the news, but given that he described her as "everything I was looking for in a woman. She was me. She was myself,"[5] probably not well. What is known is that they took some of the drugs Tony always brought with him, but this time, instead of the 30 milligram Nembutal pills Christine normally took, Tony gave her pills over three times as strong—100 milligram. Then in the early afternoon, Tony left her apartment alone and went to visit her friend Primotivo Africa, an artist in the Village, to score some marijuana. When Primo asked where Christine was, Tony replied, "She's sick," but offered no more information. Tony stayed for an hour at Africa's and then went straight to the Port Authority station and took a bus back to Cape Cod. When he got to the Hyannis terminal, he once again called Avis and asked her and Doeringer to come and drive him back to Provincetown. When they dropped him off, Tony told

Avis that if she was asked, she was to tell people he came back from New York a week earlier than he actually had. She didn't ask why.[6]

When Christine's roommate, Cynthia Savidge, returned to the apartment Sunday night, she found Christine's naked body kneeling facedown in a half-filled bathtub, a bruise on her shoulder and three cigarette burns on her chest. Police determined she'd been dead approximately thirty-six to forty-eight hours; the cause was recorded as "asphyxiation due to drowning."

The New York City associate medical examiner, Dr. Michael Baden, officially ruled Christine's death a "possible suicide" because he found a "large amount of barbiturates in stomach and brain."[7] When questioned later about the case, he said he couldn't remember having made a determination about the bruise or the cigarette burns and what role they may have played in connection with her death. But he added that in 1968 it was common practice to put someone in a tub of cold water to shock them out of a potential overdose of barbiturates.[8]

Back in Provincetown, Tony told anyone who would listen that Christine was suicidal and that she had made repeated threats because "she couldn't live without me." Avis echoed his suicide story, claiming that during the weekend before Christine's death, when she was visiting Tony in Provincetown, Christine had had a bad acid trip and told Avis that she needed to "shed the flesh."[9] Tony also claimed that he received a postcard mailed just hours before her death in which she apologized for killing herself; but he never produced the note to investigators. Tony also hypothesized that Christine could have been a victim of violence, presumably at Raul's hand. "She knew my life and she had been threatened because of it," he said,[10] although he never explained what that meant or why she would be threatened because of his actions.

According to homicide detectives, kneeling facedown in the tub would have been an unusual choice for suicide for the simple reason that it's physically awkward and uncomfortable; most who die from true suicides by overdose take a lethal amount of sleeping pills, lie flat in a warm tub filled to just below the jawline, and once they've passed out, they slowly sink under the water.

Rather, when all things are considered in Christine's case—her relationship with Tony, her growing concern about Tony's intensifying behavior, her reported impending marriage to Raul, and Tony's abrupt departure from New York the same day he had arrived—the more likely scenario is that whether accidentally or intentionally, Tony gave her three times the normal dosage of Nembutal and she passed out. Then, perhaps as Baden explained, Tony put her into a half-filled tub of cold water to revive her. When it didn't work and she died, he left the apartment and fled back to Cape Cod.

In later evaluations, it was suggested by Dr. Harold Williams, one of the many psychiatrists who examined Tony, that by putting her body in water, Tony felt he was cleansing her of her "sins." Among those sins, in Tony's thinking, was rejecting his affections in favor of Raul Matta. In addition, those same psychiatrists speculated that he used the cigarette burns to symbolically mutilate Christine, perhaps even brand her as "his."

Beyond all the speculation, the facts remain: Christine Gallant died sometime Saturday, November 23, from a monstrous dose of Nembutal, naked and kneeling facedown in her tub with fresh cigarette burns and a bruise on her body.

Once again, Tony Costa was the last known person to see a young woman alive.

34

LIZA

As the fall deepened on Cape Cod, Provincetown and the Bayberry Bend emptied of tourists, and Mom found herself bored and alone, if you don't count Louisa and me. All of her summer friends and beaus had gone back to their homes in the city, and she felt isolated and restless. So she called an old college buddy who lived near Hyannis and asked, "Do you know any single men you could set me up with?"

In fact, her friend did, but with a caveat: "His ex-wife once told me he's not the kind of guy you'd want to marry."

Mom didn't ask why, and she didn't care. She wanted to go out to dinner with a man who'd compliment her *and* pick up the check. Within a week, she had a date with Ron Sloan.

She and Ron agreed to meet in a parking lot on Route 6 in Wellfleet after he dropped his two children off with their grandparents, who lived nearby. From there, they drove together in his convertible Thunderbird to the Captain's Table that overlooked the harbor in Hyannis. It was an old Yankee institution with dark paneling, faded paintings of clipper ships in rough seas, hard wooden chairs, and little pots of port-wine cheese and crackers on the table. Ron ordered a gin gimlet. After a lifetime of drinking rum and Cokes, Mom said she'd have the same. Gin felt like a step up. Stronger. Cleaner. More mature. And most important—classier. When, during dessert that night, Ron reached across the table and held her hand, she was hooked—to him, to the sophisticated gimlets, and to the life he seemed to offer.

Ron watched her across the table thinking she was different from any woman he'd ever met. Until the day he died he told the story of their ride that night back to the parking lot in Wellfleet. It was well after 1:00 a.m. when they arrived at her car. He turned off his engine, and they sat talking. Then, she reached into her pocketbook, pulled out a cigarillo, and lit it. They kissed, lightly and briefly; she thanked him, and got out of the car. He watched her walk to her car, start the engine, and put the top down. As she backed out of the lot, he could hear the song on her radio: "Harper Valley P.T.A." She waved to him as she pulled onto the highway, the smoke from the little cigar trailing behind, and disappeared down the dark road to Provincetown. He said any woman who would smoke a cigarillo, never mind on a first date, couldn't be all bad.

Mom moved in her typical fashion—fast. The morning after that first date, she called Grampa Georgie and told him to take our house in West Bridgewater off the market. She was leaving the Cape and moving back to be closer to Ron, who lived in Newton, just west of Boston. She was not going to let her big fish get away. This was her chance to live the way she had always wanted to live and to have the things she had always wanted to have. Life with Ron promised so many of the things she had craved— normality, respect, a fancy house in the suburbs, and perhaps most of all, a really big diamond ring that everyone, everywhere she went, would see.

For one of the first times in her life, Mom was happy, or at least a little less miserable and angry than she always appeared to be.

In mid-November, she drained the Bayberry Bend pipes, shuttered the windows, put the lawn furniture in the storage shed, and closed the motel. Before I knew what hit me, I was taking my seat in Ms. Johnson's fourth-grade classroom at the Rose L. MacDonald School in West Bridgewater, and Provincetown was once again a memory.

35

TONY

Christine Gallant's funeral was scheduled for the Friday after Thanksgiving, and again Tony asked Avis and Jon Doeringer for a ride, this time to Fall River so he could attend. It was becoming enough of a routine that Doeringer would later post on Facebook[1] a long essay describing the time period titled "Driving Tony Costa."

Tony claimed he had been asked by Christine's mother to be a pallbearer, something that galled her friends because they knew he was probably the last person to see her alive and could very well have had something to do with her death. According to one friend, some of Christine's family members "never got over" his presence at the funeral.[2] Tony smoked dope in the back seat all the way to Fall River, and the next day he returned to Provincetown, still stoned and openly distraught.

With nowhere else to go, he crashed on various friends' couches until he got a room at the White Wind Inn on Commercial Street. In his bathroom, friends saw that he kept a quart-size mason jar jammed with "bennies" and that he was taking as many as ten at a time hoping to drown out whatever convoluted emotions he felt over Christine and her death. He refused to let anyone hug, console, or even touch him, and if they tried, he violently jerked away.

Strung out more than he was sober, he nevertheless made the rounds, applying at the few hotels and motels that would remain open through the winter, trying to find work that would help pay his child support. But he had burned nearly every bridge in town by routinely not showing up for work or by being so stoned when he did that his work was shoddy at best. Nearly all of his old employers wanted nothing to do with him. Then Tony remembered there was new construction starting at the Royal Coachman. So he hitched out to Beach Point where John Atwood, who was overseeing the work, was desperate for carpenters in order to meet a May deadline. Atwood hired him, even though the job foreman, Roger Nunes, wasn't so sure.

"That kid is trouble," he told Atwood. "Mark my words."

Meanwhile, Tony continued his downward spiral. Word got back to Avis that Tony might be trying to kill himself with an overdose "like Christine," and she went to visit him at White Wind. She climbed up the fire escape on the back of the building to Tony's room carrying an early Christmas gift, a bottle of English Leather, and sat him down, hoping to talk him off the proverbial cliff.

"What have I got to live for?" he said, his voice a squeaky whine.

"Well, you have your children," she said. "They need you."

Tony seemed to get better and went to see his kids more regularly as he tried to pull himself out of the depression. But more often than visiting his kids, he drove out to the woods to tap into his drug supply, usually with one or more of his young followers in tow. His entourage ranged in age from fifteen to nineteen, and each helped themselves to drugs from a jar measuring a foot high and five inches across, "filled to the brim" with pills.

A few days before Christmas Tony was driving out to the woods when he decided to get his mother a Christmas tree. He pulled over when he spied the perfect tree. One of his "kid chicks" in the car wondered how in the world he was going to just run up and get the tree. She soon had her question answered; Tony had an ax and a handsaw in his trunk. He always did. He was a carpenter, after all. He never knew when he might need his tools.

As Christmas approached, his landlord at White Wind told him he would have to move out; like he had at the Crown & Anchor, Tony had brought too many drugs and too many "freaks" in and out of the place at all hours of the day and night. He had no place to go, so he asked Avis if he could move in with her. With three children and now a live-in boyfriend sharing her one-bedroom apartment, Avis asked Donna and Woody Candish, who lived in the downstairs apartment, if Tony could crash on their couch. Even though theirs was a small one-bedroom apartment, the Candishes agreed. Not only did Donna know and like Avis, but the three kids were frequent visitors at Donna and Woody's apartment and would often come downstairs for their evening baths. Donna had always thought Tony to be fastidiously clean and polite to a fault, so they agreed to his moving in but told him he would have to leave when their baby was born in mid-January.

Tony was the perfect roommate; quiet, neat, and nearly absent. He'd get up in the morning and head out, either to work or to roam the streets. He never ate a meal with them. And while he rarely "hung out" at the apartment, he occasionally would have a couple of his followers over who'd sit at the kitchen table high on drugs. One day, Donna watched the head of one young man fall right to the table, passed out. Another time, as Tony and his small entourage were leaving, he invited a very pregnant Donna to come along.

"We're going to the woods in Truro," Tony said. "Why don't you come? We go and rap and shoot arrows."

Donna demurred, saying she'd rather just stick around the apartment. But the invitation "gave me a funny feeling," she said later.

On New Year's Eve, Woody and Donna threw a party, and as Donna was making herself a cup of tea in the kitchen, Tony came in and sat on the counter. He asked her, "If I could give you anything in the world that you wanted, anything, would you sell your soul?"

Startled by the odd question, Donna paused, stirring her tea. She looked at him and what she saw stayed clear in her memory for the next fifty years. There was track lighting behind Tony's head that backlit him, shadowing his already dark face and exaggerating his pointed eyebrows.

"He looked evil, like the devil," Donna later said. "I'll never forget that face. I'll take it to my grave."

She took a deep breath.

"No, Tony, I never would. Things are just things in the world, but your soul is all you have."

Tony looked stricken, then put his head in his hands, and wept. Through his tears he said, "I have done three things in my life that I can never be forgiven for. Never. This lifetime is a forfeit for me."[3]

When Avis arrived at the party, he approached her, still weeping. She accused him of being drunk.

"No. No. You don't understand," he said. "I need prayers. Pray to God to forgive me. I need forgiveness. Only God can give me that."

She asked if this had something to do with Christine's death, and he said yes, but that there were two others. She didn't ask who they were.

"There isn't any forgiveness, no forgiveness for Tony," he said, slipping into the third person, then back. "I sold my soul to the devil. I can never atone."[4]

36

LIZA

When we returned home to West Bridgewater, we found that Nana and Grampa Georgie had moved away from their house next door. His red barn was empty, and the shades in the house were drawn. No one said anything about why, but I figured it had something to do with Grampa Georgie being in trouble. What if he had needed us to pick him up at the police station again and we had been far away in Provincetown? A few days after we got home, I was listening on the stairs above the phone and I finally got the story.

"My parents sold their house next door," Mom told Ron. "My father had to get out of town, I guess. So I can't go out tonight—I'm a little short on babysitters." She laughed as she exhaled her cigarillo smoke and took a sip of her gimlet. I ran back upstairs to bed.

Had to get out of town . . . I rolled the words over and over as I lay in my bed trying to fall asleep. I knew enough to know that if Grampa *had to get out of town* it couldn't have been good. I remembered all the nights Mom would haul us out of bed to go get Grampa Georgie out of the drunk tank. I could never tell whether she was scared or angry or both. I asked her once, "Are you angry, Mummy?"

"How many times do I have to tell you that children are to be seen and not heard?" She looked at me in the rearview mirror, her angry face reduced to a rectangle and filtered through cigar smoke. "Huh? How many times?"

I never said another word on those trips, but I remember the darkness, the low hum of the radio, the skidding sound of the tires as my mother took a left onto North Elm Street and headed to the station. I always pretended to be asleep. It was safer that way. After she collected him from the station, she'd open the car door and I'd feel a gust of cold, crisp air. Then, when my grandfather stumbled into the front seat, the peaty, acrid scent of liquor sometimes mixed with urine and vomit would fill the car.

"I'm sorry, honey," he'd mumble as Mom slammed the door. "I'm sorry."

"Shut up, Dad," she said. "Just shut the hell up." She only dared talk to him that way when he was drunk because she knew in the morning he wouldn't remember she'd sworn at him.

I'd hear his heavy breathing and smell his sour breath. It would drift into the back seat, and I'd have to swallow hard and breathe through my mouth in order to not be sick from the stink of him. Sometimes Mom could tell he was really, really drunk and would have us keep an eye on him for signs that he was about to puke, and we'd warn her so she could pull over before he was sick all over the front seat. Sometimes we fell asleep and missed his telltale gagging as the vomit rose up through his throat.

"God*damn* it, Dad!" Mom would yell as the stench of fresh vomit filled the car, and she'd slam on the brakes so he could finish in the gutter.

So when Grampa Georgie and Nana disappeared from next door without saying goodbye, it hurt me and I missed them, but I wasn't surprised. With him it was always something. Besides, nobody ever seemed to say goodbye.

Things improved when, one day after school, I saw a moving van and a big car pull up into Grampa and Nana's driveway. When the car stopped, the back doors flew open and four kids piled out. Right away I noticed the oldest boy, who was tall, slender, and had a head of dark curly hair. He kind of reminded me of Tony, only younger, about my age. I put on my jacket and ran over to say hello. As I got closer, he smiled.

"Hi," he said. "Do you live right there?"

He had green eyes and his voice was warm and gentle.

"Yes! I'm Liza."

"I'm Tex," he said, outstretching his hand.

That was all it took. I was hooked. Who had a name like Tex except some really great boy with a lot of adventures to share? Turned out I was right. His parents were Christian missionaries and had just moved back to the States from Brazil. I had no idea what a missionary was or where Brazil was, but it sounded so different and so far from West Bridgewater that I immediately put it on my list of travel destinations for when I grew up and got away from my mother.

Tex was patient and soft-spoken; I'd rarely met anyone who was both. Tex taught me to ride his horse, Vulcan, and to do a back handspring. The Summer Olympics had just happened in Mexico City, and after watching them I wanted to be a gymnast, even though I was already getting the *big boobs* my mother had warned me about and also towered over the itty-bitty girls I'd seen on television. Still, before the snow came that winter, Tex and I would practice doing cartwheels in the field for hours. I didn't know if I wanted to kiss him, but I knew he wanted to kiss me, and one day behind the red barn he did. It was quick and scratchy, with our teeth clicking together, but even so, it felt like we had gotten married.

We spent nearly every afternoon together, and quickly—maybe too quickly—he gave me his grandmother's ruby ring and asked me to go steady. When my mother saw it, she asked if I'd stolen it. I told her I hadn't, but she didn't believe me and made me march my "little ass over there and return it." Tex looked confused, and I think hurt, but he said he understood and tucked the ring in his pocket.

Louisa and I didn't see much of Mom in those days. She had demanded her home ec job back at Stoughton High, and they'd given it to her because of the shoebox of Tom's dirty letters, so days she was busy working and nights she was with Ron. She seemed happy. Ron fit her bill perfectly. He owned his own company, which sold chemicals to paint, rubber, and plastics firms, and half jokingly called himself a captain of industry. In Ron, my mother saw a man who could finally give her the financial security she craved. What I didn't see was love, not the kind I felt for Tex anyway. Mom liked to say that her favorite color was crystal, and finally, here was a man who could fill her cabinet with it. He bought her extravagant dinners in fancy restaurants, took her away on weekend trips where they stayed in expensive hotels in Newport, Rhode Island, and on Martha's Vineyard. He drove a flashy car and lived in a big house in the suburbs where he employed a full-time housekeeper to take care of his young daughter and son who lived with him. I didn't know kids could live with dads—we certainly didn't but given half a chance would have in a heartbeat.

I think Mom felt special and pampered in a way she never had before. With Ron, she might finally be able to get away from what she called the stink of West Bridgewater and all the gossip that still whispered through the Stoughton High teachers' lounge.

Right before Christmas, Ron and his kids came to West Bridgewater for the weekend. The four of us all bunked in Louisa's and my tiny room—his son and daughter in sleeping bags on the floor—while Mom and Ron slept in her bedroom. Louisa and I were used to random men spending the night with our mother, but this was the first time one of them brought his kids to sleep over as well. Mom got us a babysitter while they went out to dinner, and we stayed home and ate Swanson frozen dinners and watched *The Monkees* on television. Ron's daughter, Jill, was exactly my age, with the long, straight, light brown hair I always wanted. From the moment I saw her I wanted to be pretty like her. Ron's son, Danny, was a year younger than Louisa, and he had white-blond hair and both of his front teeth were missing. He said they'd been knocked out when he was hit by a car crossing a busy street near their mother's house.

Suddenly just crossing the street became another thing I worried about doing.

37

TONY

Donna Candish began having labor pains in early January, and she paced the floor of her living room, nervous and scared. Every hour on the hour she had the nagging pain. The baby wasn't due for two weeks, and she felt something was wrong. When Tony came into the apartment, he immediately calmed her down.

"You're fine, the baby is fine," he told her. "Don't worry. Avis has had three babies; this is totally normal."

And it was. Two weeks later, she went into actual labor, and Woody took her to Cape Cod Hospital to have their son. In the recovery room, she told Woody it was time for Tony to leave their small apartment and find his own place. It was January 16. Tony packed his meager belongings into a duffel bag and walked the empty streets of Provincetown looking for a room to rent. That same day, he spied a VACANCY sign in the window of the 5 Standish Street Guest House. He knocked on the door, and the landlady greeted him.

Patricia Morton was the daughter of the late *Atlantic Monthly* editor Charles Morton and was known around town as something of a kook who had taken her maiden name back after her divorce. She was known by everyone in town as Mrs. Morton. She had bulging, hyperthyroid eyes, jittery nerves, and, according to some of the town's louder gossips, gave a few of her male guests "special treatment." They said she dressed in too-tight clothes, revealing altogether too much of her backside and bosom for a forty-eight-year-old divorcée, and she wore too much rouge and lipstick, as if on her way to some long-ago prom. She had bought the two-story house in the center of town in 1963 and turned it into a rooming house. It had white clapboards with black shutters and faded striped awnings over the windows, and it sat almost on the street, where only a wobbly trellis fence separated the front door from the sidewalk. The building—its bones somewhat of a colonial revival Cape—was a hodgepodge of construction. In fact, it looked as if it had been assembled in parts, with windows and doors added here and there and porches stuck on the front and side almost as afterthoughts. With its peeling paint and shrouded windows, it appeared somewhat sinister. Inside it was even worse; its narrow, steep staircase and dark halls were painted a dull gray, and the floors were what Mrs. Morton called a "marine orange," to somehow impart both warmth and cool. The guest rooms all shared common baths, and the rooms rented for anywhere from $5 to $12 a night and slightly less by the week. She kept a keen eye on those coming and going and resisted renting to single men, fearing those same town gossips' wagging tongues, but she relented when Tony appeared on the doorstep looking for a room. She didn't know he had been thrown out of the White Wind, and of course he didn't volunteer the information. He turned on his infamous charm and offered to help Mrs. Morton with odd jobs that needed doing. She rented him the Bay Room, which she called her best room, overlooking Standish Street, at a reduced rate of just $20 a week. He moved in two days later.

On January 24, 1969, Tony returned to his garden in the Truro woods to "check on things." Even though it frightened him to go back in, it had nonetheless become routine. But what he saw as he approached the clearing that afternoon stopped him cold: a human hand was sticking out of the ground; its shallow grave had been disturbed, most likely by coyotes or foxes that roamed the woods.

Tony stared at the hand in shock and wonderment, almost as if it were a prop in some horror movie. But he knew it was very real because he had put it there. As he stood transfixed, looking at the hand, the sun broke through the trees and something sparkled on one of the white, clenched fingers. As he inched forward, he saw it was a diamond ring. He thought about taking it, but instead quickly pushed the hand back into the ground with his foot, covered it with some leaves, and raced back into town. When he ran into one of his "head chicks," Robin Nicholson, she later said he was "chalky white."[1] Something had frightened Tony, and he didn't frighten easily.

He didn't stay frightened for long. Instead, he returned to his Standish Street room, took a handful of pills from his mason jar, and got ready to go out for a beer. As he watched himself shave in the bathroom mirror he put his earlier horror out of his mind; now his only concern was how he was going to get his paycheck in the morning from the Royal Coachman down in North Truro. It was too cold to ride his bike, and he was again carless.

After drying off from his shower and pulling his turtleneck over his head, he heard a knock at the door. He opened it, and Mrs. Morton stood at the threshold with two young women, one striking with strong, almost masculine features, black hair, and heavy makeup around her dark eyes; the other was prettier with large blue eyes and light brown hair. Tony noted that the more attractive one had on too much lipstick.

"Hi, Antone," Mrs. Morton said. "These girls just checked in and are staying in number two upstairs for a couple of nights."

"Cool," Tony said, looking at the women. The darker woman looked familiar to him; he couldn't recall where he'd seen her, but he knew she'd been to Provincetown before.

Mrs. Morton continued. "I rented the other room upstairs to three fishermen who'll be painting the house, so it's rather crowded up there. Would you mind if the girls used the bathroom down here near your room?"

"Sure," Tony said, smiling at the girls. "I'm Tony." He stretched out his hand.

"Hey," they said back in unison, smiling at him.

"I'm Pat," the dark-haired woman said, taking his hand, "and this is Mary Anne." She indicated her friend with a wag of her left thumb. "We're up for the weekend from Providence."

Patricia Walsh and Mary Anne Wysocki had been friends since high school and had attended Rhode Island College together. Pat had graduated and now taught second grade at the Laurel Hill Elementary in Providence. She was a down-to-earth young woman who took her job as a teacher seriously and who enjoyed folk music; in December she had gone to a Judy Collins concert with friends. Mary Anne on the other hand struggled with her grades; she had earned only a 2.86 GPA her first semester at RIC and dropped out. For two years she had worked and saved enough money to return to college. She had one more year to go before she finally graduated, and she hoped to also become a teacher. The women told their parents that they were tired from their heavy workloads and needed a fun weekend away. Pat called in sick at the Laurel Hill school so that they could leave early on Friday morning and have a full two days on the Cape.

Tony helped the women bring their things in from the car—*Enough stuff for a month*, he thought.[2] The entire back seat and trunk of Pat's Volkswagen Beetle were full of small suitcases and clothes in shopping bags and on hangers. It took them three trips to move everything into the small room. When they were finished, they asked Tony if it was a good time for them to take their showers in the nearby bathroom.

"Groovy," Tony said. "I'm going out anyway."

When he left, the girls brought down what they needed for their showers, and while one used the bathroom, the other sat on Tony's bed, thumbing through his copy of Rowan and Martin's *Laugh-in* magazine and reading the funnier parts out loud through the partially open door. Then, because his room was warmer than theirs, they remained there to dress and dry their hair with Mary Anne's portable hair dryer before returning upstairs.

It was a cold night with temperatures in the teens, so Mrs. Morton climbed the two flights from her basement office apartment to check on the women and make sure they were warm enough. She found them sitting on the twin beds chatting, both wrapped with blankets around their shoulders. They thanked her for her concern and assured her they were fine.

"Girls, would you mind leaving your door open when you leave later?"

Mrs. Morton said. "It makes the heat circulate through the rooms better. Your things will be perfectly safe, I assure you."

"Sure," Pat said, and Mrs. Morton went on her way.

As the women talked and put on their makeup, another boarder popped his head in the door to introduce himself. Soon, they realized they had a mutual friend in Providence, and the three talked easily about what a small world it was. Around 7:00 p.m., the women headed to the Mayflower Cafe for dinner and then onto the Fo'csle for a few drinks.

During the dreary winter months, The Fo'csle provided a rare gathering spot for those whom Tony labeled as "bohemians, artists, writers, faggots, lesbians, young folk, and fishermen"[3] who stood around the juke box and "chatted merrily." Tony was one of the regulars who would sit at the bar and watch the crowd. That night, his friend Wolf Fissler joined him at the bar and bought him a beer. Tony had already had a glass of wine over dinner at his mother's, which was unusual for him, but he needed something to wash down her kale soup and grilled sardines, and the beer instantly went to his head. Around 9:00 p.m., he watched Pat and Mary Anne enter the place and sit at a table along the far wall, but he didn't approach them.

The bar was crowded, and Pat and Mary Anne were sitting alone until two women approached them and asked if they could share their table. Brenda Dreyer and Irene Hare, high school friends from Shrewsbury, Massachusetts, were also on a girls' weekend trip to Provincetown, and the four were soon comparing notes about boyfriends, makeup, work, and travel.

Tony watched the women from a distance, but he still made no attempt to say hello. He finished his beer and, feeling a little light-headed, asked Wolf to drop him off at 5 Standish Street. When Tony walked into his room, he found that Pat and Mary Anne had left a wet towel on the floor. *Slobs, just like Avis*, he thought.[4] Miffed because he felt he had generously allowed them to use his room only to find they had disrespected it, he decided they *owed* him a ride to the Royal Coachman in the morning to get his paycheck. He tore off a piece of brown paper from an A&P

grocery bag. On it he wrote, "Can you give me a ride to Truro in the morning?" and signed it "Tony." He went upstairs and into their open room. He tacked the note to the closet door and then returned to his room and smoked some hash.

Meanwhile, Pat and Mary Anne and their two new friends left the Fo'csle together and moved on to the Pilgrim Club, where they stayed until closing. The four women made plans to see each other again in March, when they all hoped to return to Provincetown. When they left the club, Brenda and Irene led Pat's VW through the dark streets back to 5 Standish Street, then watched as Pat and Mary Ann safely walked up the front stairs and waved from the door. Brenda and Irene waved back then drove away.

Standing behind the curtains in his front window, Tony watched Pat and Mary Anne enter the house, wondering where they had been until almost two o'clock in the morning.[5]

At around 9:30 the next morning, Tony was awoken by Pat and Mary Anne, who had found his note and agreed to take him to the Royal Coachman in Truro. They were anxious to give him his ride so that they could get back to town in time to meet up with a friend around lunchtime at the Fo'csle.

Tony's head ached, and he realized with a grimace he had a bit of a hangover and a sour stomach.

"I need to take a quick shower, okay? Give me half an hour."

Pat and Mary Anne asked him for a place to have breakfast, and he told them Wally's was one of the few restaurants still open in January. They returned to Standish Street shortly after 10:30 a.m., and then they and Tony headed out to the Royal Coachman so he could collect his paycheck.

Meanwhile, Mrs. Morton made her usual rounds through the house, removing the piece of brown paper from the women's closet door. She saw that it was a note from Tony asking for a ride to Truro. Having seen them all leave together, she figured it was old news, threw the note in the trash, and continued on through the house.

At the Royal Coachman, Roger Nunes had had enough of Tony Costa; Tony hadn't even bothered to show up to work for five days running. Nunes had a deadline to meet on the RC expansion, and he needed workers he could count on. He gave Tony's last paycheck to Jim "Zach" Zacharias, another worker with whom Tony occasionally carpooled, and said, "If you see Tony, give him this and tell him he's fired."

When Tony got to the motel, he went into the office, but Atwood told him that Roger had given his check to Zach.

"Roger's had enough, Tony. You're through. He needs reliable workers," Atwood told him.

Tony walked back out to the VW and got in. He asked Pat if she minded going back into town so that he could find Zach and get his check. Pat agreed, turned around, and drove toward downtown. They spotted Zach on his motorcycle turning onto Bradford Street. Tony waved him over and rolled down the window.

"Atwood says you have my paycheck."

Zach walked over to the car, leaned down to look in the window, and nodded at the two women; they both smiled back at him. They seemed happy and carefree, just glad to be out enjoying their day on the Cape. He handed Tony the check.

"Glad I saw you. Here's the check. But Roger says to tell you you're fired because you didn't show up for work. You're through at the RC, Tony."

"Yeah, I heard," Tony said. "Thanks." And he rolled up the window.

Jim Zacharias watched the VW drive off. He realized Tony had always creeped him out, and today was just another example of why. *Who were those women? Why hadn't Tony introduced them? And why in hell were they headed to Truro?*[6]

The last time he saw the car, it was headed toward Route 6. It was around noon on Saturday, January 25.

175

38

LIZA

The afternoon of January 25, Ron and his kids came for Louisa's eighth birthday party. Mom had decided to pull out all the stops and invited the whole neighborhood and all her friends and their daughters. It was more girls than we knew, and several more than we were actually friends with. Mom filled a piñata with candy, set up a pin the tail on the donkey and musical chairs, stacked a mound of presents two feet tall, and made a cake large enough to feed both Louisa's and my entire classes.

Nana came, but Grampa Georgie didn't. Nobody said why, but I heard Nana say he'd been fired from his job and had finally thrown away the last of his nips, for good this time. Whatever had happened, Nana sounded pleased by it all. I finally learned that when they sold their house, they had bought a trailer and now lived by the highway in nearby Kingston, Massachusetts. I think Grampa Georgie liked the idea of being able to hit the road at a moment's notice, house and all.

I sat with the other girls watching Louisa open her mountain of gifts and tried to smile and have a good time. But all I could see was Mom fawning over Louisa like she was her pet, smoothing her hair and plumping up her skirt for yet another photo while Ron looked on.

After I had ruined several family photos by sticking my tongue out, Mom stopped calling me over to be in any of the pictures.

When the party was all over, I helped Nana clear away the plates, put the last of the cake in the fridge, and start on the dishes. Mom and Ron had disappeared.

39

TONY

After Tony got his paycheck, Patricia Walsh didn't drop him off in town. Instead, the three of them headed to the Truro woods. Perhaps Pat mentioned her hobby of making gravestone etchings and Tony told her of the Pine Grove Cemetery's ancient headstones. Or perhaps he explained that he needed to "get something" from his drug cache and that it would only take a few more minutes. Whatever the reason, the three left Provincetown and headed out to Truro. On their way, they stopped at Dutra's general store off of Route 6, where the women bought a pack of Pall Mall cigarettes and a bottle of Chianti to share with Mary Anne's friend from Providence, Russell Norton, who was hitchhiking up from the bus station in Hyannis to join them for the rest of the weekend. Tony had already dropped a hit of acid and was starting to feel its effects; suddenly he thought "Carl," an alter ego who had appeared in one of his earlier LSD trips, was in the car with them, silently watching in the back seat. Tony would later try to finger Carl as responsible for what was to come.

What happened when they got to the woods near the cemetery can only be gleaned through comparing all the various sources of information—autopsy reports, fifty hours of interviews with Tony conducted by his defense team, transcripts from his nine polygraph tests, more than two dozen psychiatric evaluations, and finally Tony's diary and "factual novel" written in prison. And while Tony's writing contains the grandiose ramblings of what at least one psychiatrist would later call a delusional megalomaniac, if read with a careful and discerning eye and cross-referenced with other witnesses' testimony, certain details of the murders and their aftermath become clear.

It was a sunny and particularly mild January day. The women weren't dressed for a walk in the woods, but because it was a beautiful day, they may have decided to take a stroll rather than wait in the car for Tony to dig up his drugs. Regardless of why, once they were deep in the woods, they all got out and walked toward Tony's garden.

As they got farther away from the car and into the trees, the women may have balked, even insisted they turn back. Tony later made several references to Mary Anne being a "bitch" and laughing at him; she would have been unaware that her ridicule was triggering a killer's brain. Tony wrote that one of the tree trunks looked to him like a "gigantic wrist protruding from the ground. The top of the tree . . . appeared to be the hand and fingers of a colossal and fearfully gruesome skeleton."[1] Maybe as the three were walking along the dirt road, the partially decomposed hand had once again become exposed and was sticking out of its shallow grave. If this is what happened, then the rest falls into place. The women, now terrified at the sighting, probably started to run back to the car, and Tony's impulse was to stop them in their tracks. But perhaps simply having the women alone in the woods, his own private killing fields, triggered his murderous thirst.

Patricia had bruises on her neck consistent with strangulation from behind; she may even have lost consciousness. Tony then pulled out his .22 and shot her just below the left ear, severing her carotid artery and killing her instantly. Meanwhile, Mary Anne was running for her life. At the first blast, she may have looked back, horror registering as she saw her friend crumpled on the ground. She ran through the woods, tripping over the brush, downed limbs, and thorny vines that grabbed at her ankles. As she ran, Tony calmly walked behind her and took aim through the woods, fired, missed, fired again, missed again, and then, with his third shot, hit her in the back of the head.[2] He saw her tumble to the ground, headfirst, her boots kicking up leaves as she fell. He walked over to her and saw that she was still alive, perhaps even pleading for her life; the bullet had hit the base of her skull but not penetrated her brain. He moved closer, put the gun behind her left ear and shot her again. To his amazement, she still didn't die; she began making "gurgling" sounds that repulsed and terrified him. He tucked the gun in his belt, ran back to his cache, and pulled out his father's knife that he always kept buried at the base of the big pine tree. Holding it out in front of him like a sword, he walked back to where Mary Anne lay dying. She was still gurgling. *Damn, why won't she just die, already?* He knelt down and, using the blade of the knife, cut away her coat, sweater, and bra, then raised the knife high over his head and plunged it deep into her heart. And did it again. And again. And again until finally, her gurgling stopped.[3]

Tony looked down at Mary Anne's body and then, through the trees, at Pat's. He was trembling, and it felt as if the tremor started on the soles of his feet and coursed up through his entire body like an electric current—exhilarating and terrifying. His drug highs were great, but this was other-worldly. Along with power he felt rage: *Why did this bitch laugh at me? Stuck-up stupid bitch. I haven't even gone to college and I'm smarter than her. Is it any wonder I lost my temper? It's not my fault what happened. Not. My. Fault.* He felt with a thrill that an erection was pressing against his pants; he'd never felt bigger, and the urge to *show her who was boss* became unbearable. He looked down at Mary Anne's body; she'd be first.

When he was finished with Mary Anne and then Pat, he rolled away, zipped his pants, and vomited onto the frozen leaves. It was probably over. He'd gone too far this time. The two naked, twisted bodies were cold but all too real. It was getting late. He looked up through the canopy of pine trees and watched, mesmerized, as "the finger of light" from the Highland Lighthouse swung its arc through the darkening winter sky. He turned his tear-stained face "up to God" and prayed for Pat and for Mary Anne, "the poor little things." And for himself. And of course, for "Carl," who sat nearby watching him. Carl, poor, drug-addled Carl, for whom nothing ever seemed to go right. Carl—his accomplice, his friend, his confidant.

"The deed is done, and *we* are the victims, Carl," Tony said.

Carl didn't speak; the bastard didn't even say amen. But he was listening. Oh, he was listening, all right. Tony knew Carl heard every word he ever spoke.[4]

Tony was tired, now that it was all over. He'd never been so tired. Tired of everything—struggling to find work, scraping together the monthly payment to Avis, even taking the drugs—no, *especially* the drugs. He always seemed to be too high or too low—too many bennies or not enough. He couldn't imagine quitting, but it was all so exhausting. He watched the beam from the Highland Lighthouse course above him. He could never seem to get ahead; someone was always preventing him from the success he deserved, success he was *owed*. Avis, his nagging mother, his various bosses, his three pesky kids, who hung on his back begging for treats he didn't have. Christ! How tired he was of all of them!

Tony looked over at the gun, which had fallen on the ground earlier when he unzipped his pants. He picked up the gun; it was still warm. He ran his fingers down the barrel and over the handle. The urge became irresistible. He turned the gun, stared down the barrel, and pulled the trigger.

It clicked. He had run out of bullets.[5]

Tony, age nine

Tony and Avis at the Provincetown senior prom, 1962. She was thirteen years old.

Tony and Peter, 1964

THE *Royal Coachman*

RESTAURANT, LOUNGE, and MOTOR LODGE

Enjoy a
Royally
Relaxing
Vacation

where sea, sky,
sun, and sandy
beach join to
create the
most splendid
resort site on
the Cape.

Overlooking picturesque Provincetown Harbor / Route 6A / PROVINCETOWN, Massachusetts

Coachman Motor Lodge brochure, 1966, with Mom posing on the chaise longue

Left to right: Geoff, Gail, me, and Louisa on the Royal Coachman diving board, 1968

Mom and Auntie, Jekyll Island, Georgia, 1967

Clockwise from the top:
Geoff, Louisa, Gail, and me with Billy, 1966

My portrait done by a street artist
in Provincetown, 1966

5 Standish Street, 2020

MARY ANNE WYSOCKI
157 Superior St.　　　　　　R.I.C.
"Formed of joy and mirth"
— William Blake
Activities: Bowling 2, 4; Swimming 2; Skating 1, 2, 3, 4; Cageball 2, 3; Nine Court 2; Junior Alliance 3, 4; Junior Red Cross 2; Messenger 3, 4; Budget Collector
Remembered for: Her lavender cookies

PATRICIA HELENE WALSH
241 California Ave.　　　　　　R.I.C.
"Good humor is the help of the soul"
— Stanislaus
Activities: Bowling 2, 4; Swimming 2; Skating 1, 2, 3, 4; Cageball 2; French Club 3, 4; Junior Alliance 3, 4
Remembered for: "Me? Blush?"

Mary Anne Wysocki and Patricia Walsh's 1966 high school yearbook pictures

Pat Walsh, 1968, in one of the last-known photos taken of her

March 6, 1969, Tony after his arraignment (*center*) and Lieutenant E. Thomas Gunnery (*right*)

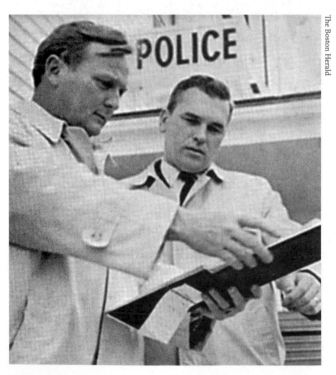

Detective Bernie Flynn and Lieutenant E. Thomas Gunnery, 1969

Tony running from court in the rain

Avis Costa, taken the day she testified

Bonnie Lee Williams, eighteen, taken shortly before her trip West with Tony

Barbara and Bobby Spalding, taken shortly after she met Tony

Susan Perry

Sydney Lee Monzon

Charles Zimmerman administering one of Tony's nine lie detector tests

Tony arriving at his trial

Tony's mother, Cecelia Bonaviri, at a conference with defense attorneys in 1969

Tony's mugshot taken upon incarceration at Walpole

Tony's mugshot, taken after eighteen months in prison

40

TONY

In the morning, Tony was awoken by a knock at his door. It was Mrs. Morton checking on rooms. She called through the door: *Do you need anything, Antone?*

Just some fresh towels, thanks.

Following her morning routine, Mrs. Morton continued down the hall, checking on the rooms, greeting guests, and collecting rents. When she climbed to the second floor, she found another note on a piece of the same brown paper grocery bag, this one tacked to the front door of number two. It read, "We are checking out early. We had a nice time. Thank you for your kindnesses." Mrs. Morton thought the plural use of "kindness" was odd. The note was signed "Mary Anne and Pat." Like she had with the first note, she grabbed this one and crumpled it in her hand and threw it in the trash, swiping her hands together, like a teacher at the chalkboard. *That's better!* She looked in the room and saw that it was empty. She'd come back later and change the beds after she continued her rounds.

Tony woke up feeling sick, again. He'd drunk the last of the women's Chianti, and his head pounded and his stomach was sour. Two mornings in a row. He got up and went to the bathroom. As much as he had always enjoyed bathing, he called that day's shower "a super pleasure." He looked at his reflection in the steamy mirror; his calm visage stared back. *Perhaps last night had all been a dream?* All night, snatches of memory, scenes really, had played through his head, horrific scenes of violence, blood, and death in the woods. *Maybe it was the LSD,* he thought. He'd often had terrifying, graphic dreams that were only made worse when he tripped on acid, and he definitely had had his share of the stuff the day before, punctuated by some serious hash oil. But still, something nagged at him, and it wouldn't let go. And then he opened his closet.

Fuck.

Piled on the floor of the closet in a great heap were all the clothes and shoes and shopping bags he had helped Pat and Mary Anne move into the house on Friday afternoon. And on top of the pile were his clothes from yesterday—striped pants and a jacket—with the unmistakable red stain of blood on them. In a sickening rush, he remembered coming home late, well, actually really early that morning; thank God the newspaper truck made its deliveries before dawn and had picked him up hitchhiking on Route 6. He had hopped in the back of the truck with the newspapers; he hoped the guy hadn't gotten a good look at him. After he got dropped off in town, he had tiptoed upstairs to the women's room, cringing every time a stair squeaked under his foot. He hadn't dared turn on the light, so he'd had to scramble around, gathering up all those damn dresses and sweaters and pants and underpants and coats and hats and *DAMN IT! Why had they brought so much shit for just two days?* He'd made two trips but finally had been able to gather it all up and bring it back to his room. And there it lay in his closet.

Fuck.

He pulled it all out and threw it into a great pile in the middle of the room and started pacing back and forth in front of it. *Shitfuckdamn. Now what?*

Suddenly he heard a knock and his friend Herbie Van Dam stuck his head in the room without waiting for Tony to open the door.

"Hey, dude! I've been knocking for ten minutes," Herbie said.

"I didn't hear you," Tony said, his eyes not leaving the pile of clothes.

"Yeah, duh," Herbie said. "I need my bike back. Where'd you stash it?" He finally looked down at the clothes. "What the fuck, dude? You into wearing women's clothing these days?" he laughed.[1]

Tony had known Herbie for years; just another one of his slightly loopy friends who could be trusted to forget what he was looking at as soon as he left the room. Tony wasn't worried. At least not about Herbie.

"These two chicks split and left their clothes here, and now I gotta get rid of them," Tony said.

Herbie didn't ask why the women left the clothes or why it was upon Tony to get rid of them. Tony was always up to some whack-job scheme; this seemed like another, and Herbie was already bored. He came to get his bike and hopefully to get high, not to fold clothes.

"Well, I came to get my bike. I came yesterday, but you weren't around," Herbie said.

"Yeah, I got wasted on some acid and walked the beach all night."

"Shit. Kind of a cold night for the beach, wasn't it?" Herbie asked.

"I walk fast," Tony said, reaching into a drawer. "Here, take some of these," he said, ending the conversation.

Tony gave Herbie a handful of Nembutals, took a handful himself, then lit a pipe of hash. *That should put Herbie off any possible scent.* It did. Herbie left soon after.

Tony resumed his pacing around the pile. As he stared at the clothes, fragmented memories of the previous day kept swinging wildly through his vision, like a bad dream. He knew one thing: his work wasn't done. Realizing he needed to focus, he took a hit of acid and decided *I'd better go check it out. Just to make sure.*

Still carless, he asked another boarder at 5 Standish Street to take him out to Truro; the man dropped him off at the end of Hatch Road, and Tony walked the rest of the way into the woods. He got in a few hundred yards and saw Pat's blue Volkswagen parked in a clearing in the woods. *Fuck. Her car.* Then, as he ran toward his old marijuana patch, he was struck dumb—a different human hand was sticking up from a pile of leaves. *It was no dream.*

He walked over to where the bodies were buried; *Well, not buried*, he could now see—*just covered*. He'd have to fix that. He went back to the VW and found it was out of gas. *Oh, right . . . last night was cold, and I ran the engine to stay warm. Shit. I'll have to carry the tools over a quarter mile from the crypt, where they've been since September—since Susan.*

Once back in the clearing with his tools, Tony put on a pair of gloves and laid out the ax, at least two more large hunting knives, and an industrial straight-edge razor tool and went to work. He'd learned from his previous "experiments" that there wouldn't be too much blood—it took less than an hour for the blood to solidify into something like red Jell-O, so things wouldn't be too messy. God how he hated a mess.

Tony was the only witness to the horrific scene that followed, but he admitted to being "fascinated" by dismembering bodies: "There is no comparison, you can't say it's like anything, because unless you actually experience it you don't know what it's like. It's something that you just can't experience normally. The LSD experience in looking at these things and going through this, it's like being in another world completely."[2]

After he had reduced both women to a pile of parts, he stood looking at the mess and was irritated; he realized all of it, all of them, wouldn't fit into one grave. Thinking, *Why the hell go to all the bother of digging another hole in this freezing-cold forest?*, he instead decided to use one of his earlier graves for the "extra" parts. As he dug down into the old hole—he couldn't remember which woman he'd put there—the smell of rotting flesh came out of the earth like a putrid gust of wind, hitting Tony with such force he vomited. He tried to breathe only through his mouth, but the cloying stench felt almost solid in his mouth; he could feel it on his teeth and knew it would linger on his skin and clothes for days, no matter how many showers he took. When he had dug down to where the shovel bit into the body, he jumped out and began haphazardly throwing Pat's and Mary Anne's various limbs into the two holes. Then he threw in Mary Anne's and Pat's clothing and boots, which he had reduced to shreds. Finally, he tossed in a purse. *One purse! Had Patricia had a purse? Shit. Fuck. Where is Pat's purse?* He looked around at the darkening woods and shrugged. *Ah, well, they'll never find them out here anyway.* The last thing he did before he covered the graves over was swallow the last of the drugs he'd stolen from Callis's office, and then he threw the empty pill bottles in on top and covered the whole grisly mess with dirt and leaves.

Late that afternoon, a friend of Susan Perry's and Avis's, Paula Hoernig, and her friend, Larry, were driving back to Provincetown when they saw Tony hitchhiking in North Truro, headed back to Provincetown with a duffel bag over his shoulder. They stopped to pick him up. He was wearing dark sunglasses; his clothes were filthy and looked as if he'd been in them for days. When they dropped him off in town, Larry turned to Paula.

"Christ, that guy smelled disgusting, like rotten fish."[3]

Paula had a head cold and couldn't smell anything. But she thought the comment odd, since it seemed as if Tony was always taking a shower, sometimes as many as three or four a day, whenever she had visited his and Avis's apartment. So why did he smell like rotten fish in the middle of winter?

When they dropped Tony off on the corner of Conant and Bradford Streets in Provincetown, he jogged up Conant to his mother's apartment for Sunday dinner—5:00 p.m., as usual. His mother put dinner on the table like clockwork; that night's was one of her staples—chicken in tomato sauce. After dinner, Tony and his son Peter, not yet six years old, went to the Laundromat to wash Tony's clothes.

41

LIZA

After Louisa's birthday was over and all our friends and their mothers had gone home, the house was quiet again. I followed Nana into the den, where she sat on the couch to knit and wait for Mom and Ron to get home from their dinner at the Red Coach Grill.

"It's bedtime for you, missy," she said, but she looked like the one who was about to fall asleep.

I kissed her cheek and headed upstairs.

I tiptoed into our room, where Louisa, Danny, and Jill were already fast asleep. I saw Louisa's haul of presents was neatly stacked on the dresser. Gingerly stepping over Danny in his sleeping bag, I crept across the room and stood by the dresser, examining each gift.

Her gifts were always better than mine. I'd get socks and old-lady white underwear and maybe a pair of school shoes, but Louisa got the good stuff, including little Holly Berry, even though Mom gave her away. This year's haul included a bendable Skipper with a full summer wardrobe for her days at the beach with Barbie; a matching hairbrush, comb, and mirror set, all in bright, shiny blue plastic; and, best of all, a bag of marbles. Careful not to upset the stack, I pulled the bag off the dresser and rolled each marble through my fingers. They looked to me like precious stones—mother of pearl, opal, even one that I was sure was a cloudy emerald.

I hated that Mom seemed to love Louisa so much more than me. Some days it felt so bad that I wished Louisa had been born to another family;

then maybe Mom would give me all the stuff she gave to Louisa. And the love.

I pocketed the emerald marble, put the bag back on the dresser, and went downstairs. Nana was asleep on the couch. I grabbed my coat and hat and went out the back door, quietly shutting it behind me. It was a cold night, and I hadn't thought to wear my boots or mittens. I walked around back and sat on the swing. As I swung back and forth, my hands getting numb holding the steel chain, I remembered that the first time Mom had really, really laid into me, it had to do with Louisa. It was early one Palm Sunday morning, and Louisa and I were kneeling in a "pew" that I had made out of the couch cushions, watching a church service on television. Suddenly Mom was standing in the door, her face creased with sleep and very angry that we'd woken her up. She looked over at a wastebasket that Louisa had put in the chair to make room for herself in the "pew."

"Who put that wastebasket in the chair?"

"Not me," I said, happy it was true.

"Not me," Louisa said.

Mom looked at me. "*You* must have done it, Liza. Your *sister* doesn't lie."

"She does too," I said, because she did.

I never saw it coming and heard rather than felt the *crack* of Mom's hand across my cheek.

"Your. Sister. Doesn't. Lie." Each word came with a slap. Finally, panting and standing over me with her hand still raised, poised to deliver another blow, Mom asked, "Have you had enough?"

I nodded, tears running down my cheeks.

"Good. Now put that goddamned wastebasket back where *you* found it and put these cushions back where they belong."

I wiped my eyes and nose on the sleeve of my nightgown and put the wastebasket and cushions back. As I edged by her through the doorway, she gave the back of my head one final smack. "And stop your crying, or I'll really give you something to cry about."

Sitting on the swing, I shivered with the misery of it all—winter, the pile of wonderful presents that weren't mine, and now a shameful guilt for wishing Louisa hadn't been born. I got off the swing and went back inside, longing for the summer.

It wasn't even February, and I was already dreaming of getting back to Provincetown.

42

MISSING

Robert Turbidy hung up the phone and smiled. In his conversation with Pat, his "unofficial fiancée," he told her of a "special surprise" but didn't tell her what it was. She asked if he'd made her another suede pocketbook. No, it wasn't another purse. She'd have to be patient. He was so brimming with love and desire after their weeks apart, he couldn't wait to show her the surprise. Two days later, on Saturday, January 25, he left the tattoo parlor and looked down at his shoulder: PAT in big, bold, capital letters. Straightforward and honest, just like her. He felt such a singular elation that he could have danced down the street.[1] On Monday, he finally left California and pointed the nose of his VW bus east, toward home and toward her, and smiled all over again.

Bob Turbidy had served three years in the US Navy as a legal officer, and when he retired from duty had returned to his native Providence and fallen in love with Patricia Walsh. Together, they had traveled the United States in his VW bus, camping their way across the country and back. They loved the freedom of the road and hoped to join President Kennedy's VISTA service program and teach school on the Navajo reservation in Northern Arizona.

But when he failed to reach Pat on the phone Sunday night, January 26, he started to get nervous. She had specifically told him in their last phone conversation on Thursday that she'd return Sunday from a girls' weekend in Provincetown because she had to be at work first thing Monday morning. By Monday night, he was frantic and called Pat's father, Leonard

Walsh, from a phone booth by the side of the road to see if he or his wife had heard from Pat. They hadn't. With three days of travel still ahead of him, Turbidy had trouble avoiding a speeding ticket as he raced home.

When Leonard Walsh hung up the phone from Bob Turbidy, he immediately called the Massachusetts State Police to see if any accidents had been reported involving a blue late-model VW Beetle with Rhode Island plates. No, the police told him, there was no report of any accident or breakdown of a car fitting that description. The next morning, Tuesday, January 28, before he left for work, Walsh called the Providence police saying their daughter had been scheduled to return from a weekend in Provincetown on Sunday but that she hadn't shown up for work Monday morning, which was out of character for the responsible, levelheaded young woman. Like many police departments across the country, Providence officials brushed off the parents' concern, citing the growing number of young women who went missing only later to be found after a drug- or alcohol-induced adventure. They assured Leonard and Catherine Walsh that they shouldn't worry. *This kind of thing happens all the time.* Their daughter would show up, eventually. Unwilling, perhaps unable to sit and wait, Leonard walked the few short blocks down to the police station on his lunch hour, where he made sure a missing person report was officially filed.

At the station, Sergeant Horace Craig reassured the anguished father that nearly every single missing person report ended up being something totally benign: flat tire, no pay phone, miscommunication. Something. He sent Leonard Walsh on his way with a pat on the back and a promise to call as soon as he heard anything about the women in the pale blue VW bug.

When Lt. Craig watched Leonard Walsh's sad, stooped shoulders head down the front stairs of the station, he said to his partner, Sergeant Edward Perry, "I don't like the look of this one." He didn't like the fact that two stable, mature women with jobs and no history of vagrancy or substance abuse vanished into thin air on a weekend girls' trip to Cape Cod. Perry agreed and picked up the phone to call the Provincetown police, giving them a description of Patricia, her friend Mary Anne Wysocki, and the VW Beetle with Rhode Island plates.

Provincetown patrolman James Cook took the call. He was fighting the flu, groggy with cold medicine, but nonetheless spent the afternoon driving the narrow streets from one end of Provincetown to the other looking for the car. He found no trace of it. He made a note of the missing women and their car in the police logbook in red ink to make sure "no one would miss it," and then went home to bed.

While they waited for word from Patricia, the Walshes paced their tidy living room. They didn't dare leave their house; they might miss a phone call or a knock at the door telling them their daughter was fine, the car had broken down on a remote road, the women had hunkered down in the cold, thankful that Pat kept a bedspread in the trunk. They had taught Pat to "prepare for anything on the road," especially during winter in New England. *They'll be home soon, chilled to the bone but fine! Just fine!* Perhaps Catherine Walsh made what felt like her millionth promise to God; *I won't even get mad that she caused her father and me such worry.* But in the endless nights after Pat's disappearance, it could only have been torture for the Walshes, not knowing where their little girl was, and that likely kept them staring at the ceiling, their hearts pounding in their ears; *Where are you, Pat?*

In the Wysocki apartment it probably was even worse. When the police failed to find a trace of their daughter, the couple had hired a private investigator. But the man was so incompetent or just plain lazy that after knocking on only a few motel doors on Commercial Street and not finding where Pat and Mary Anne had stayed, he reported to the Wysockis that "the girls never went to Provincetown."[2] Perhaps because the Wysockis and Walshes were not of the same social status and had never been to each other's houses for dinner, they didn't join forces to find their daughters. Instead, the Walshes waited in their home while the Wysockis waited alone in theirs, an attic apartment on Superior Street near Providence's old Highway 6. The waiting turned them from middle-aged to elderly practically overnight. Mary Anne was Walter and Martha

Wysocki's only child, their only hope for an old age surrounded by grandchildren at Thanksgiving dinners and noisy Christmas mornings. And with every passing day, they probably felt not age but death creep into their bones and backs and hearts. *She is gone*, the empty apartment around them whispered. *Gone.*

43

TONY

The Rhode Island women had been missing a week when, on February 2, Carl Benson, who lived just across Old Country Road from the Pine Grove Cemetery in Truro, piled his two children into the family car for a drive into town to get the Sunday newspaper. Rather than taking the long way around on the main road, he took a shortcut through the cemetery and the Truro woods on an old fire road.

"Daddy, what's that car doing there?" asked his son from the back seat.

Indeed, thought Benson, as he spied a blue Volkswagen Beetle parked just off the dirt road in a small clearing of trees. Pulling alongside the bug, he stopped and got out of his car for a closer look. As he walked slowly around the VW, noticing its Rhode Island license plates, he felt the hair on the back of his neck rise, and a prickle of nerves rush through his stomach. Suddenly, he thought he heard footsteps and then someone running through the woods. He spun around, his eyes searching through the thick trees; he felt like he was being watched. He looked over at his car and saw his two children, their faces large through the window, and quickly walked back to where it idled.

"What is it?" his daughter asked.

"Nothing," Benson said, his heart pounding. "Let's go get the paper." He tried not to push the gas pedal to the floor, because he wanted more than anything to get the hell out of those woods.

"Daddy! Don't go so fast," his children cried from the back seat.

Benson reluctantly eased his foot off the gas and slowed the car over the rutted road.

After getting the paper, he dropped the children at home and immediately drove to the Truro police station to report the abandoned car.

Chief Harold Berrio was on duty that Sunday. He was half of the two-man force that he had formed in Truro twenty years before, creating the town's first police department. Stocky and good-natured, Berrio was what might have been considered old-school; he called homosexuals "floozies" and women "broads" and thought every person under thirty was a dirty hippie and a wastrel. And even though Truro bordered Provincetown, Berrio disapproved of all the "funny business" that went on in the town just to the north because it was filled with so many of those very same dirty hippies and drugged-out wastrels. There was a reason, he thought, why Provincetown was sometimes called Helltown.

Berrio took Benson's report of the abandoned car and then asked if he would take him to the spot. Benson agreed and when the men drove into the woods where the car was parked, they found a note on the windshield. "Out of gas" was scribbled in red Magic Marker on a piece of torn, brown paper; it looked like a piece of a grocery bag.

"That wasn't there when I was here before," Benson told Berrio, the hair again prickling on the back of his neck. He knew with a cold certainty that he had been watched when he first sighted the car. The woods he had known and loved his entire life felt suddenly sinister. All he wanted to do was run.

The men walked around the VW, and Berrio took down the plate number, noting that it was from Rhode Island. The doors were locked, and nothing appeared amiss, but when they looked through the windows to the interior, Benson was again filled with dread. It wasn't that he saw anything obvious; it was just that he *knew* something had happened in that car.

The men parted and Berrio returned to the station, where he made a quick check to see if the car had been reported stolen; it hadn't. Satisfied that the car had in fact merely run out of gas and would be reclaimed by its owner soon, Berrio went home for the night and watched *The Smothers Brothers Comedy Hour* on television.

The alert about the blue VW with Rhode Island plates and the two missing women that Officer Cook had written five days earlier in red ink in the Provincetown police log hadn't been shared with the two policemen four miles down the road in Truro.

Meanwhile, Tony was itching to claim the VW in the woods. *Pat didn't need it anymore,* he joked to himself. *It's just sitting there. Why not take it? Why let a perfectly good car rot in the woods?* Besides, now that it had been spotted by that guy and his kids, Tony knew he had to move it or lose it.

Later that same night, Tony convinced two young kids whom he considered his loyal followers to help him get the car out of the woods and drive it to Boston. He'd figure out what to do with it from there.

Leonard Walsh called the Providence police every day, asking, no, *begging*, for information on Pat and Mary Anne, but still there was no word. Finally, on Monday, February 3, Providence police sergeant Edward Perry, frustrated with the lack of response from the Provincetown police, called the Massachusetts State Police barracks in West Yarmouth for assistance. Detective George Killen took the call.

Killen had earned the respect of his colleagues as well as his adversaries, many of whom called him "Old Stoneface." Responsible for criminal investigations and prosecutions, Killen, like Perry and Craig in Providence, immediately sensed something was wrong with the missing women's case; these women were no wayward hippies looking for an escape from their overbearing parents. These were two adult women with jobs, rents, and a practically new car. Killen called Chief Cheney Marshall in Provincetown, whom he'd known since they were teenagers, and hustled tips from tourists on the Provincetown pier. Marshall told him he'd follow up on the missing person report, but privately he was surprised that Killen was taking a personal interest; there were so many missing women, especially in vagrant-friendly Provincetown. *Why these two?* What he didn't know was that Killen's mother's maiden name was Walsh, the same as Patricia's.

The next day in Providence, Sergeant Perry issued a try-to-locate for the VW on the regional police teletype. Up in Boston, State Police detective lieutenant William Broderick was given the assignment to look around for the car. In his twenty years as a patrolman, Broderick had gained the reputation as a "knock 'em down, drag 'em out son of a bitch" cop, starting in 1952, when he was suspended for ninety days without pay for an unspecified infraction. But given that ninety days is far more than a slap on the wrist, then and now, it stands to reason whatever he did was high on the list of the state police's in-house sins. By 1969, Broderick had been stabbed three times in the chest, had had his first heart attack, and had no compunction about drinking on the job. When the try-to-locate came in, the police had a tip that the car might be in the city's Back Bay neighborhood.

"Jesus Christ," Broderick grumbled as he headed out, "there's gotta be ten thousand Volkswagens in that area."

The detective knew it could be a long night of surveillance so he called his wife to say he'd be home late then stopped by a local package store for a six-pack of beer. For two hours he drove slowly up one street and down another through a rainstorm heavy enough to be mistaken for a hurricane, holding his beer in one hand and driving with the other. He had just crossed Gloucester Street and was heading west on Beacon when there it was: a blue VW bug with Rhode Island plate KV-978 parked in front of 415 Beacon Street.

Broderick knocked on the first-floor apartment door and then watched about twenty young men and women, thinking it was a drug bust, jump out the front windows in a cloud of marijuana smoke and run down Beacon. He told the young woman who answered that it wasn't a bust; Broderick simply wanted to know who owned the car parked out front. She pointed him upstairs, where he found the apartment door ajar and, upon pushing it open, saw Vinnie Bonaviri and his girlfriend, Cathy Roche, having sex on the sofa.

Broderick cleared his throat. "I'll wait 'til you're finished."

Vinnie and Cathy jumped up and grabbed for their clothes. Once dressed, Vinnie told Broderick it was his brother's car but that he hadn't seen him in a few days. With orders to watch but not impound, Broderick left the brownstone and returned early the next morning to continue his surveillance. Around noon, he saw a tall, dark, neatly dressed man with wire-rimmed glasses emerge from the building. Again, with no evidence of a crime, Broderick didn't approach Tony, but he followed him as he got in the VW and drove to the Punch Bowl, a gay bar on Stuart Street near the old Hotel Statler (now the Boston Park Plaza), which Broderick had surveilled in the past.

Boston's gay scene was vibrant but still underground in the late 1960s. Adjacent to the city's infamous Combat Zone, there were entire blocks where bars and dance clubs catered exclusively to gay men and lesbians, and Tony knew where to find them. The Punch Bowl was one of them and was famous for its annual Beaux Arts Ball, where men sported chiffon gowns and the women wore tuxedos. But unlike in Provincetown, where everyone knew everyone else's business, in Boston Tony was able to frequent the gay bars in anonymity. An hour later, Tony left the bar alone and returned to Beacon Street. Broderick stayed on his post, and later that same evening, he again spotted Tony leaving the apartment. Once again, Broderick followed him to the Punch Bowl and sat at the bar three stools down and watched Tony "play the guys, lead them on. But he always left alone."[1]

The next morning, the car and its driver were gone. According to Broderick's account of the incident, the initial try-to-locate bulletin inexplicably did not include that the VW belonged to two missing women from Rhode Island, or instructions to question the driver. Even more curiously, the report that the car had been located in Boston did not appear to reach either Providence or Provincetown, where police continued to search for the VW on the Outer Cape.

That same afternoon, Russell Norton was sitting in the Rhode Island College Student Union. Norton, Mary Anne's friend, had hitched up from

Provincetown to meet the women two weekends before, but he'd been unable to find them. They never showed at the Fo'clse as planned. Sitting at the Student Union on February 6, he overheard a man say that he'd met two Providence women at a rooming house in Provincetown. Norton ran to a pay phone and called Bob Turbidy with the information.

Immediately after Turbidy had returned from California on Thursday, January 30, he'd driven straight to Provincetown and asked at every inn and motel if anyone had seen the women. Not realizing the Standish Street Guest House was open, he drove right by it. Turbidy also spoke to Police Chief Marshall, who all but rolled his eyes at the distraught boyfriend's concern, telling him she'd *show up soon; they all do.*

But when Turbidy called the station again on February 6 with Norton's information that the two women had rented a room at 5 Standish Street, Marshall and sergeant Jimmy Meads sat up a little straighter in their chairs.

Meads called Patricia Morton, and she confirmed that the women had arrived on Friday the twenty-fourth for the weekend, but she hadn't seen them leave; they'd left a note, which Mrs. Morton told Meads she'd found on Sunday morning. She also volunteered that she had found another note on the women's closet door asking them for a ride to Truro. That note was signed "Tony Costa."

Tony Fucking Costa, Meads thought. *That guy is trouble.* His name just kept coming up; Callis had fingered him for the May 17 break-in and robbery at his medical offices; the owner of a lumberyard in Maine suspected him of stealing a list of expensive power tools; Bob Murray's Drugstore and Adams Pharmacy burglaries had Costa written all over them; and Arnold Appliances reported a television and stereo missing after their padlock had been cleanly picked. *Damn.* Meads had known Tony and his family forever, and after Tony had been their snitch in the Von Utter bust, Meads had even vouched for the guy to get him out of jail early on his nonsupport rap. Reluctantly, Meads called Cecelia, telling her he needed to talk to Tony about two missing women who had stayed in the same rooming house.

"Is my Tony in trouble?" Cecelia asked.

He told her no, simply that he hoped Tony might have information about two missing women's whereabouts.

With nowhere else to look, and unaware that the car had been spotted in Truro *and* Boston, Meads instructed patrolman James Cook to once again head out to look for the VW. Maybe it had broken down somewhere and the women had abandoned it. As he drove out of Provincetown and south on Route 6, Cook saw Chief Berrio's cruiser idling on the side of the road, pulled up alongside, and rolled down the window.

44

LIZA

Winter always felt lonely in West Bridgewater. It was just Mom, Louisa, and me in our little house, and I missed the freedom and fun of Provincetown. I also missed Tex; after Mom made me return his ruby ring, he kind of disappeared from my life. I occasionally saw him getting into or out of his family's car, but he never looked toward our house, and eventually I stopped looking toward his.

Ever since we left the Cape in the fall, I'd been nervous, even more nervous than usual, and the eczema flared up from my fingers to my elbows. I didn't know what it was about, but I thought it probably had to do with our having left Provincetown so suddenly; I hadn't had a chance to say goodbye to the few friends I made in school, and I didn't want them to forget about me, the way townies always forgot the summer kids. But worst of all, I hadn't had a chance to say goodbye to Cecelia and Tony. I missed them both, and even though I didn't do it as much once Mom bought the Bayberry Bend, I missed following Cecelia around while she worked. I loved helping keep her supply of toiletries and towels well stocked on the maid's cart as she cleaned room to room and helping her fold the laundry warm and fresh from the dryer. As she worked, she told me stories about Tony and Vinnie and about how she grew up in Provincetown when Commercial Street was a dirt buggy path and the harbor was full of fishing trawlers and nets laid out on the wharves to dry in the sun. She talked so quietly I often had to bend toward her to hear her over the drone of the laundry machines. Sometimes I just let her talk, even if I couldn't hear what she said, because her soft voice could lull me to sleep on top of the warm towels in the bin. I loved the clean tidiness of it all; shelves of perfectly folded towels and sheets, baskets of little square soaps and towers of neatly stacked toilet paper. There was peace in its order. The room was always toasty warm, and while on some days it must have been downright stifling, it never felt so; to me it was a cozy and safe place to hide.

As I looked out the window at cold, bleak West Bridgewater, I tried to imagine what Tony and Cecelia were looking at out their window.

45

THE FIRST BODY

"Christ! I can take you right to the car!" Chief Berrio told Officer Cook.

It was February 7, a full week since the car had been spotted in the woods by Carl Benson and two weeks since the Rhode Island women were last seen. Berrio was miffed to learn that Provincetown police had kept the information about the missing women and their car "all to themselves." It only confirmed his worst opinions about the goings on "up there" in Helltown.

When Cook pulled up alongside Berrio's cruiser, the chief was pleased to be the one to take the Provincetown cop right to the missing car in the woods. But it was gone.

"It was right there," Berrio said to Cook, pointing to a small clearing.

They parked, got out of their cruisers, and walked west into the woods on the dirt road. Within a hundred yards, they found torn and scattered papers, including an insurance policy and registration with Patricia Walsh's name on it. They looked at each other, each with a growing sense of dread; car owners are not in the habit of tearing up the registration and throwing it out the window. They also found an empty gas can.

"The note on the car said 'Out of gas,'" Berrio told Cook as the two men stared down at the can on the ground.

When Cook returned to Provincetown with the report that Berrio had seen the car in the woods and that its registration and insurance papers had been found nearby, the police finally began to realize that Pat and Mary Anne hadn't just wandered off on a girls' weekend gone a little wild, that they hadn't just walked away from the car and gotten lost in the woods, and that they hadn't decided to just blow off work and school to party. They were missing and it was now apparent that their last known whereabouts was somewhere between Provincetown and the desolate Truro woods.

Down in Yarmouth at the State Police barracks, George Killen had still not been informed that the car had been spotted in Truro or Boston. When Provincetown police called with the news that Truro Police Chief Berrio had actually seen the car one week earlier, Killen too got a sick feeling in his gut and brought in Detective Bernie Flynn, one of his best detectives, to spearhead what was finally an investigation.

Detective Flynn was a good-looking man, blond and blue-eyed, with the cocky swagger of someone totally at ease in his own skin. He had served as a seaman second class in the Coast Guard during World War II, after which he attended the State Police Academy, where he graduated at the top of his 1946 class. After graduation, he'd joined the New Bedford Police and was respected by just about every man he worked with as a "hellava cop" and a tenacious investigator who didn't mind kicking down the occasional door.

"If you want to be a nice guy, maybe you should get into another line of work" was Flynn's motto.

In 1966, when he was offered the chance to work with George Killen at the State Police barracks in Yarmouth, he jumped at it, and he became the stereotypical "bad cop" to Killen's "good cop." They were a tough pair to outfox.

When the call came that the missing VW had been spotted (but astoundingly, *still* not any information about the car itself having been located in Boston), Killen organized a small army to finally search the Truro woods.

The Outer Cape is famous for a dazzling quality of light that is like no other place on Earth. Some of the magic has to do with the land being surrounded by water, but it's also because that far north of the equator, the sunlight enters the atmosphere at a low angle. Both factors combine to leave everything it bathes both softer and more defined. For centuries writers, poets, and fine artists have been trying to capture its essence. Some have succeeded, but most have only sketched its truth. That's no reflection of their talent, because no matter how beautiful the words or stunning the painting, Provincetown's light has to be experienced.

The light is one thing, but there is also the way everything smells. Those people lucky enough to have experienced the Cape at its best—and most would agree it's sometime in the late days of summer when everything has finally been toasted by the sun—know that simply walking on the beach through the tall seagrass and rose hip bushes to the ocean, the air redolent with life, is almost as good as it gets. If in that moment someone was asked to choose between being able to see or smell, they would linger over their decision, realizing the temptation to forsake sight for even one breath of Cape Cod in August. Those aromas are as lush as any rain forest, as sweet as any rose garden, as distinct as any memory the body holds. Anyone who spent a week in summer camp on the Cape can be transported back to that spare cabin in the woods with a single waft of a pine forest on a rainy day.

Winter alters the Cape, but it doesn't entirely rob it of magic. Gone are the soft, warm scents of suntan oil and sand, replaced by a crisp, almost cruel cold. And while the seagrass and rose hips bend toward the ground and seagulls turn their backs to a bitter wind, the pine trees thrive through the long, dark months of winter, remaining tall over the hibernation at their feet. While their sap may drain into the roots and soil until the first warmth of spring, their needles remain fragrant through the coldest month, the harshest storm. And on any particular winter day on the Outer Cape, if one is blessed enough to take a walk in the woods on a clear, cold, windless day, they will realize the air and ocean and trees all talk the same language and declare *We are alive.* Even in the depths of winter: *we are alive.*

It was on such a cold February morning with bright, piercing sun that a small army of men found themselves in a thick forest of pine and scrub oak, searching for what they feared they might find. Most of the men knew these woods; they had grown up there, boys exploring its dark recesses, playing tag through the trees, daring one another to go a little bit farther into the dark shadows, and then, stealing their first kiss in its lovers' lane. And now here they were, grown men—park rangers, firemen, members of the Truro Rescue Squad, and state and local police—all called to the woods to search for two missing Rhode Island women.

With Killen calling the shots from State Police headquarters, Chief Berrio was the de facto leader of the search, and he strutted through the woods, eager to assume the role; it was his town, after all, and he'd actually seen the car. And while no one relished finding any bodies, his little hamlet of Truro rarely garnered such attention, aside from tourists who got lost looking for the National Seashore. Watching him lean on a shovel and pose for the police photographer, Provincetown Police Chief Marshall remarked, "That guy's as useless as a tit on a bull."

The search party slowly walked past where the VW had last been seen and deeper into the woods on a narrow dirt road, so overgrown with saplings that any vehicle attempting to drive in would lose a fair amount of paint on both sides. About twenty minutes down the road, members of the Truro Rescue Squad spotted a patch of ground about ten feet off the road that was slightly sunken, about four feet long and two feet wide, that looked like it had been recently disturbed. They called the detectives over to take a look. Among them was trooper Tom Gunnery, the same officer who had pulled Tony over for a noisy muffler in September. As he approached the area, Gunnery saw the edge of a piece of green cloth sticking up out of the soil at the bottom end of the depression. He pulled on the cloth; it was the strap of a US Army duffel bag with what looked like blood on a small hook at the end of the strap. When he pulled the bag loose from the ground, a foul stink escaped with it, like something had rotted beneath. Gunnery felt the ground under his feet; it was slightly spongy. He got down on both knees and began digging with his hands; the sandy soil came away easily. With other officers now gathering to watch, Gunnery dug down about twelve inches when he felt something hard beneath his fingers.

"I've got something!" he shouted, as he pulled an object from of the hole.

"Jesusmaryandjoseph!" he exclaimed, falling back onto the pine needles and leaves as the men stared.

It was a human hand.

The search was immediately suspended while Lieutenant Killen was called to the scene. Killen then called Flynn and Dr. Daniel Hiebert, who would act in his other capacity as Barnstable County's medical examiner, and instructed them to meet him in Truro. The old doctor put on his heavy winter coat and headed out the door, telling his patients in the waiting room that he'd return as quickly as possible.

When the call came into the Yarmouth barracks looking for Killen and Flynn, Bob Turbidy and Gerry Magnan, Mary Anne's on-again, off-again boyfriend, were standing at the front desk talking to the duty sergeant. The two men had driven up from Providence and were at the station delivering photos of Pat and Mary Anne, at the request of Bernie Flynn, whom Turbidy had spoken to the day before. When Turbidy overheard that a body had been found in the Truro woods, his blood went cold.

"You better get down there," the desk clerk said.

Turbidy got directions to the scene, and he and Magnan jumped back into his VW bus and sped to Truro.

When they reached the entrance at the end of Hatch Road, a police officer was walking out of the woods. His face was ashen, and his eyes looked a bit too large for his head.

"We found a body," the cop said, stating the obvious.

When Turbidy explained that he and Magnan were looking for Bernie Flynn, they were then allowed to ride in the back of the medical examiner's truck taking Hiebert to the scene. As the truck bumped along the rutted road, Hiebert complained to the driver, "Why do they always have to find bodies on Saturday?"[2]

They came to a stop, but only Hiebert was allowed out of the truck;

Turbidy and Magnan were told to stay put and away from the dig site—police protocol when human remains were being exhumed. Turbidy for one didn't want to dig up any bodies, especially if it was Pat's.

In the woods, the digging resumed with Killen, Flynn, and Hiebert now part of the crowd gathered around the hole. First, Gunnery unearthed the remaining arm, then part of a leg and then the other separated arm—all of which looked as if they'd been chopped off by an ax. In particular, the left thigh had almost no soft tissue on it, indicating repeated and irregular cuts that sliced away much of the meat before the limb was successfully severed. At the end of the arms, both hands were clenched into fists, and on the left ring finger there was a gold ring with five small diamonds in it. Below that they found the pelvis and hip joints, separated from the torso at about the belly button. The skin from both the anterior and the buttocks had been entirely removed; it was never found. Then below that mess was a human head in a plastic bag with the words *Horizon Electric Blanket* on it. Untying the knot in the bag, Gunnery removed the head and saw that it was a woman whose face was frozen in a grimace of terror and pain. Whoever she was, she had taken a ferocious beating; the nose and left cheekbones were broken, nearly flattened, the face was bruised, and four upper teeth were missing, Digging deeper, he finally revealed the torso, around which was wrapped an industrial-size white cotton laundry bag (forty-five inches by sixty-six inches), the sort that motels use. Gunnery removed the bag; like the pelvis, the torso had large sections of skin that had been peeled back, cut away in a sweater-like pattern. The breasts, which were still attached to the loose flap of skin, were missing their nipples. Finally, at the bottom of the grave they found a pair of blood-soaked pink bikini panties with *Thursday* embroidered near the waistband.

The officers stood over the obscene pile of body parts. Whoever this poor girl was, they knew that the face was neither that of Patricia Walsh nor Mary Anne Wysocki.

Suddenly a routine search for two missing Rhode Island women had become a grisly murder investigation of now a third, unknown woman.

That afternoon, George Killen and Chief Berrio held a news conference announcing that a grotesquely dismembered body had been found in the Truro woods but that it was neither of the missing Rhode Island women. And, Berrio added, the shallow grave had recently been disturbed by an animal. Little did they know the animal had a name.

When word of the discovery hit the Sunday papers, Susan Perry's mother finally filed a missing person report, six months after anyone had last seen her daughter. When asked what took her so long to contact the authorities, she answered, "You never know with kids these days."

46

TONY

Bob Turbidy watched the police, rangers, and plainclothes detectives walk down the path in a somber line. They looked like a squadron of defeated soldiers after a nasty battle in the trenches. He asked which man was Bernie Flynn and was pointed to the detective. Flynn looked as if he might have aged a decade while he was in the woods. His face was etched with exhaustion and sadness, and his trench coat and pants were covered in filth—both dirt and something else that Turbidy couldn't distinguish but could smell. Flynn positively reeked of rot. Both he and Gunnery would later burn every article of clothing they wore that day; no matter how many times their wives put them through the wash, they could never entirely get rid of the stench.

"Officer?" Turbidy said, silently praying. "I'm Bob Turbidy. Pat Walsh's boyfriend. Is it . . . ?" he nodded his head toward the woods.

Flynn slowly shook his head.

"It's not Patricia," he said, and then looked at Magnan. "Or Mary Anne. We don't know who it is, but it's not either of them. You should go."

Turbidy nodded, his knees weak with relief. He nodded at Magnan, and the two men walked the half mile out of the woods and back to their VW bus. As the car bumped back onto Hatch Road, they decided to head into Provincetown and check out the women's rooming house at 5 Standish Street.

They introduced themselves to Mrs. Morton as friends of Pat and Mary Anne, there to find out anything they could about the missing women. The men found Mrs. Morton "scatterbrained" and a real "cuckoo clock" as she showed them through the guesthouse. As she walked, she rambled on about her various renters and about how one tenant, Antone, had been moving stuff out of his room all week and just yesterday his mother had called demanding Mrs. Morton return his hair dryer; something she refused to do until *Antone* returned his room key.

"She says to me: 'I don't want my Tony to get into no trouble.' Real townie, you know what I mean?" Mrs. Morton said.

Mrs. Morton said she hadn't seen Antone in over a week, so she supposed he had moved out, but did he tell her he was leaving and return the key? *No siree, he did not.* Did the men have any idea how much money she'd spent on lost keys and replacement locks? *It was a small fortune, but you know tourists and renters—totally oblivious as to what it takes to run a guesthouse!*

But Turbidy and Magnan were no longer listening to her chatter; they were looking at each other, each silently wondering: *Why does a man need a hair dryer?*

"Could we see Antone's room?" Turbidy asked.

She walked them into what she called her best room—the Bay Room, number four.

"The police were here last night, so I don't know what it is you'll find," she told them as she pushed the door open and stood aside.

Turbidy and Magnan walked by her and slowly circled through the room, looking under the bed and mattress, into drawers and behind the desk. When Turbidy opened the closet door, he saw three sweaters folded on the shelf.

Turbidy reached up and pulled one down that looked familiar to him; it had a distinctly female scent. "This looks like Pat's," he said to Magnan.

Then on the closet floor they saw the electric hair dryer in a faux alligator case. Magnan turned to Turbidy. "I'm pretty sure it's Mary Anne's."

They asked Mrs. Morton if they could use her phone. First, Magnan called Martha Wysocki in Providence and had her describe Mary Anne's hair dryer; he'd been right—the one in Costa's closet was hers.

Turbidy couldn't believe it. "Hell, the cops were right here and they overlooked everything."

The men called the Provincetown police. Turbidy told Sergeant Meads that Mary Anne Wysocki's hair dryer and a sweater he believed was Pat's were found in Tony Costa's room and that they should pick him up immediately for questioning. Again, Meads dismissed his concerns. He also wasn't thrilled about being told how to do his job by two hippies from Providence in a VW bus.

"I'll talk to Tony," Meads said to Turbidy. "He owes me a few favors. I'll find out where the girls are."

Not for the first time, Turbidy and Magnan wondered whose side the cops were on—theirs or this Costa fellow's.

On their way off the Cape, Turbidy and Magnan stopped at the Yarmouth barracks, where the duty officer paid little attention to their concern, insisting that there was no evidence of a crime in relation to the two Rhode Island women.

"This guy Tony Costa is the missing link," Turbidy insisted.

As they all stood in the barracks talking, the phone rang; this time it was Meads in Provincetown, saying that Tony had called to say he knew where the girls were: "They went to Montreal to pick the lock." The duty officer relayed the conversation, explaining to a perplexed Turbidy that "picking the lock" was slang for having an abortion.

Turbidy was outraged. Not only was Pat on the pill, but she would have been overjoyed to find herself pregnant because they both wanted to have children; they had recently talked about marriage and starting a family. Nonetheless, the officer began grilling Turbidy as if he were a suspect in his girlfriend's disappearance. Magnan had heard enough.

"This is total bullshit," he said and turned to Turbidy. "Let's get the hell out of here."[1]

On the drive back to Providence, Turbidy remembered his last conversation with Pat; it had been the Thursday before she and Mary Anne left for Provincetown. He remembered them laughing because he refused to tell her his surprise. He remembered his elation after leaving the tattoo parlor, the ink still wet on his shoulder. He remembered standing on that sunny California street corner and feeling as if she were right by his side. Then, with a sudden chilling shock he realized it had been Saturday, January 25, around 2:00 p.m., Eastern time.

Bob Turbidy's blood went cold and he wondered if that was the moment when something terrible had happened to Pat.[2]

47

LIZA

The Provincetown friend who visited us the most in West Bridgewater was Billy, who worked at the Royal Coachman and whose father had also tried to date my mother. At first, I had really liked Billy. Tony considered him a "cool cat," and so did I. He looked like one of the Beach Boys, and he taught me, Louisa, and Geoff how to jackknife dive in the RC pool, while Gail had to watch from the sidelines because she was still too little. And he always had a smile for me, like Cecelia and Tony. But somewhere along the line Billy's smile seemed to change and he would look at me in a way that made me nervous. After that, I just tried to avoid him. But inevitably Mom would send me to the supply room for more toilet paper or towels or to the cigarette machine.

"Hey there, Liza," came his high, squeaky voice from the front desk as I scurried through the lobby. "Why you in such a hurry? You got ants in your pants on the other side of France, or something?"

I was only a little girl, but I knew Billy shouldn't be thinking about my underpants.

Then one day in late February, Billy showed up at our house out of the blue. I heard the car before I saw it—the souped-up engine sounded like a race car coming into the pit at the Indy 500. I was out playing in the snow and looked up as the car drove into the driveway. I saw Billy and waved and watched him climb out of the car, a newish Pontiac. I knew my Pontiacs; Dad drove one so I was always on the lookout for them. Mom opened the door just as he was about to knock. I ran over and followed him into the house.

"Hey there, Liza! What's shakin'?" Billy asked as Mom pointed at my feet.

"Take those boots off and put them in the kitchen," she said.

Billy smiled at me, and even though it was his best smile, he looked awful. His summer tan had faded, leaving his skin kind of a sickly yellow. I'd never seen him with acne before, but he was sprouting a chinful of zits, some of which looked newly picked. His eyes were rimmed in red, and topping it all off, his blond hair was long and greasy and hung limp, almost to his collar. I took a step back at the sight of him.

"Hi, Billy," Mom said, as I went to the kitchen. "What are you doing here?"

He laughed. "That's some welcome! Aren't you glad to see me?"

I didn't hear her answer, and it didn't matter anyway; he wasn't looking for one.

When I came back into the living room, I could smell something weird and rank about him. I couldn't quite name it, but it made my stomach do a little flip-flop. Maybe it was the heavy winter clothes; I had only seen him in his shorts and polo shirts. But my winter clothes didn't smell, so I doubted it was the clothes.

"What brings you up to West Bridgewater?" Mom asked again, leaning toward him and giving his zitty cheek a kiss.

"I'm meeting some buddies on the Common. Thought I'd swing by and say howdy."

"How's my favorite place in the world?" Mom said.

"Things are pretty crazy down there right now," he said, looking over at me. "There's some wild shi— I mean wild stuff going on."

Mom got the hint.

"Liza, go finish washing the dishes and make sure you dry them carefully and completely before you put them in the cupboard. Last night's dinner dishes were still wet when you put them away."

I didn't argue, even though *she* had done the dishes the night before.

"Hey, when you're done with the dishes," Billy said, "maybe I'll take you and Louisa to Pomeroy's for a doughnut before I head into the Common." Again, he smiled that best smile, but it was still ruined by the rest of his.face.

"Sure," I said, heading back to the kitchen. A Pomeroy doughnut was usually a big treat, but I realized I didn't want to drive anywhere with Billy, to sit next to him on the Pontiac's bucket seat, to be that close to his pimply face and greasy hair and dank smell.

I went to the sink and pulled the step stool over so I could better reach the dishes. I tried to not make a sound; I wanted to hear every word about the "wild shit" going on in Provincetown. But I would have had to be sitting in their laps to hear what they were saying; their voices were that low. I just heard a word here and there.

"Body . . . Truro . . . cemetery . . ." Then Billy forgot to keep his voice down.

"The place is crawling with cops!" he almost shouted. "I had to get away from the whole scene."

But his voice went low again, and I gave up and started rinsing and stacking the dishes in the rack. Then, as I reached for a plate to begin drying, I heard a name clear as a bell.

"Tony Costa."

48

TONY

At the same time the police were digging up the body in the Truro woods, Tony called his mother from Burlington, Vermont, eager to report that he'd been hired by the Vermont Furniture Company; he was to start work first thing Monday morning. He'd arrived there only a couple of days before from Boston and he already had a job. Cecelia's news was less cheerful: police had called her asking where Tony was; they had some questions about two missing women from Providence.

"Tony, I'm scared," Cecelia said.

Tony told her not to worry. He hung up and immediately called his "buddy" Jimmy Meads and began to weave what would end up being the first of his convoluted tapestries of lies. He told Meads he'd met the women, not at Standish Street but at the Fo'csle, where he'd had a few drinks with them. Unaware that the hair dryer and sweater had already been found in his room, he didn't tell Meads the truth of where he had met the women because he wanted to keep police from searching Standish Street. He also told Meads that the women were headed to Montreal so Patricia could get an abortion. Regardless of how outlandish it would be for a woman to tell a virtual stranger about her need to obtain a still-illegal abortion, Meads seemed to buy it. As they hung up, Tony assured Meads he would be in touch if he heard from Pat and Mary Anne.

The next day, Tony called Meads again, telling the sergeant he decided to come back to Provincetown and all but demanded an appointment with Chief Marshall Monday morning to "clear things up on my behalf" regarding the missing Rhode Island women.

Meads asked him why the urgent return to Provincetown.

"Jim," he said. "I have their car."

One of the ironies of the entire Costa case was that if he hadn't been greedy in wanting to keep Patricia Walsh's car, he in all likelihood would have walked away from the murders—all of them. Yes, he had met the women at Standish Street, but so had several others. Yes, he had a few of their belongings in his room, but he could have said the women left those items in his room when they used the adjoining bathroom. Yes, they gave him a ride to Truro, but he could have said they dropped him off where he wanted and he never saw them again. But Tony wanted that spiffy car, and it became his Waterloo.

Tony left the car parked at a gas station in Burlington and took the bus back to Provincetown, arriving sometime Sunday evening. Monday morning, February 10, in preparation for the interview with state and local police, Tony shot himself up with four heads of speed. Tony was sure that his "super intellect" would convince even the most seasoned detective of his innocence. It didn't work, and after his rambling, often contradictory, and somewhat incoherent answers, police never seriously entertained any other suspects in the women's disappearance. Still, Tony impressed Bernie Flynn with this clean-cut good looks and polite manners; he was not the sleazy Provincetown hippie Flynn had been expecting to see walk in the door.

The six-hour interrogation began smoothly enough, but when Flynn started asking about how Tony had come to be in possession of the women's car, Tony's slick cool evaporated and his story began to unravel, starting with his claim that although he had bought the car from Patricia Walsh for $900, he hadn't actually given her the money. Flynn pounced.

"You want me to believe that the Walsh girl, a girl you just met that day, signed her 1968 Volkswagen car over to you without receiving any payment for it?" Flynn asked.

"I told her I would pay her in the morning," Tony said.

Then, when Flynn questioned why Tony had asked Pat for a ride to Truro if he now owned her car, Tony replied, "I didn't need it right away and wanted to be a good fellow to the girls."

"Didn't you find it strange that these girls would put their car in the middle of the woods in Truro?" Flynn asked.

"No, I just went along with them."

"How did the girls get out of the woods after leaving the car there?"

"I don't know."

"Why didn't they park it in front of the rooming house where it would be convenient to you?"

"I don't know."

It only got worse from there.

What is this bullshit? Flynn thought.[1]

He then read Tony the names of eighty girls and women one-by-one who were reported missing in New England. Already suspecting that Tony was directly involved in Pat's and Mary Anne's disappearance and possibly in more missing women's cases, Flynn wanted to gauge Tony's reaction to the list. Other than fidgeting, running his hands through his hair, and looking around the room like a squirrel on a high wire, Tony remained unfazed.

Sergeant Jimmy Meads was also in on the interview and tried to appeal to Tony's paternal instincts, telling him that the parents of the missing women were concerned for their daughters' safety and if Tony knew anything, he could help relieve their anxieties. Tony paused and placed his head in his hands. Meads and Flynn waited, expecting a confession of sorts. Instead, Tony took a deep breath and raised his head.

"Jim, if I could help you, I would. But those girls are a long way off, and I doubt it you will ever find them."

The moment had passed, and from that point on, Tony doubled down on an ever-changing story about the fate of the two Rhode Island women.

On February 14, with still no sign of Patricia Walsh or Mary Anne Wysocki, Bernie Flynn drove to Providence to interview the women's parents. He found Leonard Walsh a passive, slight man and his wife, Catherine, a strong, outspoken, and very angry woman. Catherine Walsh had good reason for her rage; it had been nearly three weeks since her daughter was last seen in Provincetown, and yet that town's inept police seemed to be sitting on their hands. She let Flynn have it between the eyes for the police's failure to connect the dots, for their dismissal of Turbidy's concerns and information, and for their letting *seventeen damn days* go by without so much as a phone call to them before this. Flynn could only let the woman vent her anger and fear, while he stood in the living room, hat in hand.

Flynn then drove across town to the Wysockis' and walked up the two flights of stairs to their three-room attic apartment above a bakery. The couple seemed more like the grandparents of a twenty-three-year-old woman rather than the parents, and Flynn felt a deep sense of regret having to invade their privacy with such painful questions about their daughter, brutal questions really, in light of what everyone now feared had happened to Mary Anne.

By the time he returned to the barracks, Flynn knew in his gut that the women had been murdered and that Tony Costa was somehow involved.

Police in Burlington, Vermont, located the VW where Tony told them he had left it in the gas station parking lot, and Gunnery and Flynn drove up to bring it back to Massachusetts for forensic tests. While the autopsy was being done on the body found in the woods and investigators searched the VW for any evidence of a crime, Tony made a pest of himself at the Provincetown police station, dropping in unannounced and demanding to see certain officers and detectives. Every time he talked, he told a different story about how he had met the women, why Pat "sold" him the car, where they had gone, and when he last saw them. He had read somewhere that liars cannot meet the gaze of those questioning them, so Tony trained himself to stare unblinkingly into the eyes of anyone who challenged him. It was more than unnerving to the cops. When he wasn't trying to win staring-down contests, Tony delivered frenetic monologues in a "high, soft baritone articulated with a precise, almost effete accent," one that was out of character with Provincetown locals' *you knows*. Flynn thought it was obvious that Tony had a high opinion of himself; Antone Costa did not want to be mistaken for a tough townie.

What Flynn didn't know was that when Tony was twelve, he had gotten his hands on a tape recorder and heard his voice played back for the first time. Always having disdained as low class the Portuguese accent of nearly everybody around him, including his mother, Tony spoke into the recorder and listened to his voice, practicing various intonations, emphases, and pronunciations until he came up with a style of speaking that was a strange mix of effete Boston Brahmin and a local trying a bit too hard to sound worldly. It was that odd and variable speaking voice that Flynn, and later a long list of interviewers, would notice, wondering why Tony tried on his various accents like a selection of hats.

Finally, Flynn had had enough of Tony's circle-talking around questions.

"The next time I talk to you, you'll be under arrest," Flynn told him.

Tony jumped out of his chair, upsetting it onto the floor. "Are you accusing me of killing these girls?"

Flynn was surprised; Tony had made the leap from the women being missing to their being murdered.

"I never said anything about those girls being dead," Flynn said, his voice cool and smooth as ice.

"I want out of here!" Tony shouted.

Flynn pointed toward the door. "You're free to go."

A few days later, George Killen also had had enough.

"Tony," Killen said, "before you say anything else, you should know you're a suspect in the disappearance of these girls and the theft of their Volkswagen." He proceeded to read Tony his Miranda rights.

Tony listened patiently, then started right back in, avowing his innocence and spinning yet another contradictory version of where the girls had gone and why he had their car.

Killen held up his hand in Tony's face.

"Just stop. You're getting in deeper and deeper, and I suggest you stop talking right now and get yourself a lawyer. It's time for you to leave my office."

Ever the gentleman, Tony shook Killen's hand and left the police station.

Even though police knew that Tony was deeply involved in the disappearance of the women, they couldn't make an arrest without at least having evidence that Pat and Mary Anne had met with foul play. So they kept him in their sights and on Monday, February 24, when Tony took the bus out of Provincetown, Bernie Flynn followed it to Hyannis. As Tony got off the bus, Flynn put a restraining hand on his arm; he felt Tony flinch.

"Listen, Tony, all of this will be cleared up once we hear from the girls. That's all we need, and we'll stop bugging you."

Flynn thought he saw a light bulb go off behind Tony's eyes. He pressed his point. "Let us know when you hear from those girls."

"Oh, I'm sure I'll hear from them soon," Tony said.

Flynn all but gave himself a high five; Tony had taken the bait.

Tony got on the bus to Boston and from there traveled on to Buffalo, New York. The next day a telegram to Tony from "Pat and Mary Anne" was delivered to Cecelia's apartment; Tony told her to take it right down to the police station.

She did, and as she handed it across the counter to Bernie Flynn, she said, "Now, maybe you'll believe my Tony."[2]

With the bogus telegram in hand, Bernie Flynn knew they finally had their man.

49

TONY

Tony was now squarely in Bernie Flynn's crosshairs; the fact that they hadn't been able to nail him yet was just Tony's dumb luck. *Emphasis on the* dumb, Flynn thought.[1] Flynn began interviewing all of Tony's friends and family, beginning with Avis. When Flynn went to her apartment to conduct his first interview, it didn't go well. Not only did Avis squirm her way through the meeting, but Flynn was also shocked and disgusted by the state and stench of her apartment. Three small children played on a floor littered with dog feces, a few teenage kids with filthy clothes and greasy hair flopped on cushions, beer bottles covered the coffee table, ashtrays brimmed with cigarette butts, and dirty dishes and rotten food filled the kitchen sink and counters. The grimy teens never budged from the couch, not that he would have taken a seat if offered; Flynn remained standing. He made a mental note to shift from foot to foot to prevent cockroaches from crawling up his pant leg. He left soon after he arrived, having learned almost nothing new. Avis avoided answering any question with a straightforward answer and was a staunch defender of her ex-husband. Flynn suspected that she'd lied to him when answering even the most basic questions about Tony's whereabouts and actions, but then again, so did most of the locals when questioned by police, starting with Tony himself. His friends were circling their wagons.

In the Truro woods, the searches continued for the bodies of Mary Anne Wysocki and Patricia Walsh. Even the most seasoned police officers and detectives hated venturing into the thick forest, and Chief Marshall admitted that he was afraid he'd get lost and never find his way out, even with a compass. Officers tied yellow ribbons on the trees as guideposts and told Marshall, "If ever in doubt, keep the sun over your left shoulder and walk due west and out."[2] It didn't really help. It was a land without landmarks. Standing in the middle of the thicket of brambles, bushes, and trees, it was almost impossible to determine which way was west, sun or no sun, and more often than not there was no sun in the winter sky. Police often had to honk a cruiser's horn to help guide an officer out of the woods.

As police continued their research into their only suspect, in early March they learned that two years before, Tony had been cited in an "accidental assault," hitting one of his "kid chicks," Marsha Mowery, with an arrow in those very woods. They called her in for questioning. She initially refused, but after Killen called her parents, she was brought into the station by her father the next day. She told Killen, Flynn, and Marshall that she believed Tony had purposefully aimed the arrow at her, but that "it had been a joke" to scare her. Nothing more. The police then marched her through a freezing rain into the woods to show them exactly where it happened.

"There," she said pointing. "That's where he hit me with the arrow."

Flynn felt an excited flicker go through him; this was a half mile from where the car had been parked and one hundred yards farther into the woods from where the body had been found and earlier searches had been conducted.

Police quickly organized another search party, and on March 5, Chief Marshall, George Killen, Bernie Flynn, Jimmy Meads, and Tom Gunnery were headed back to Truro, accompanied by two national park rangers. Not knowing if they'd find anything in yet another search of the woods, they held off summoning old Dr. Hiebert. If they actually found a body, protocol would demand that a medical examiner immediately be called and then be present for the removal of the corpse. So Flynn, Killen, Marshall, and the rest of the men went in, shovels and probes in hand, trudging through a new dusting of snow.

This time, one of the state troopers had brought his hunting dog and boasted, "Cookie here'll find something if there's anything to find."

Flynn wasn't so sure. The dog seemed much more interested in running through the woods like a crazed bird dog on uppers, lifting his leg on every branch, tree, and brush. Flynn called out to Gunnery, "Don't stand still too long or that damned mutt will piss on your leg!" As the dog ran through the woods in its manic frenzy, Flynn suddenly saw it stumble and roll through the underbrush; his hind leg had caught on something that tripped him.

"What the hell?" Flynn said as he moved toward the spot. There he saw a leather strap sticking out of the dirt. He pulled it, and a suede pocketbook emerged. It looked handmade; somebody had put a lot of work into its crafting. After weeks of frustrated searching and a growing sense of dismay that nothing else would be found in the grim woods, Flynn's relief was palpable. He could have kissed the purse strap. They were on their way.

"I got something here," he called to Killen.

Even though the women's bodies hadn't been found, police knew they were close. Chief Marshall said to Killen, "Both women were probably killed one after the other, so one of them would have had the chance to run." The men surveyed the woods around them. "And she would have gone up that hill," Marshall said, pointing. "People always feel safer on heights."[3]

The men looked up the hill and saw a large, oddly shaped pine tree with a branch that had broken off, about six feet up. Walking to the tree, they saw strands of rope clinging to the branch and bark, and at its base they found empty vials of pills and strewn bottle caps, some bearing the pharmaceutical brand *Wallace*. Nearby, Gunnery found some solidified, pinkish matter that crumbled in his fingers. Then something glittering in the dirt caught his eye; fishing it out he saw that it was a gold earring.

Gunnery's stomach clenched, and the muscles of his neck and back became taut with tension. He'd been here before. He called Flynn, Killen, and Marshall over.

Gunnery cleared away surface leaves and twigs and the outline of a recently dug hole emerged. He picked up a shovel and started digging, but the roots of the tree hampered his progress, so he knelt down, as he had a month before, and started clawing the loose sandy soil with his bare hands. Kneeling beside him, Flynn watched his progress and felt the cold through the knees of his trousers.

About eighteen inches into the hole, Gunnery's fingers hit something solid.

"There's something down there," he said, leaning back from the hole, almost unwilling to repeat his own history in the ghoulish woods.

Marshall bent to have a closer look and saw something white under a thin layer of dirt. Killen knelt and brushed the dirt away. Both men jumped back.

"Jesus Christ!" Marshall said.

All four men looked down at a human hand, almost reaching toward them.

Once again all digging stopped while Dr. Hiebert was called to the scene. When he arrived, they resumed what was now an exhumation. Flynn bent down and began clearing handfuls of dirt from the grave, revealing a clump of matted brown hair. He pulled the hair and realized it was not attached to a scalp. He then climbed into the hole and carefully brushed dirt away and saw the back of a head. He gently pulled the head; it had been severed and came easily out of the ground. He cradled it in his arm, brushing the dirt from its open eyes and mouth. With a heavy sadness, he recognized the face from the photos Bob Turbidy and Gerry Magnan had brought to the barracks; it was Mary Anne Wysocki.

The men took turns digging and hauling out the corpse; it had been cut into five pieces, and with each new discovery, their horror grew. None had ever seen anything like this, and each man silently envisioned the brutality it took to wreak this much damage. Then, as they placed the body parts on the ground near the grave, they realized there must be yet another grave; the corpse's left leg was missing.

Nearby, a park ranger was staring at an odd scattering of soil on a pile of leaves, something that wouldn't occur naturally. He felt the ground beneath the dirt was soft under his feet. He called Flynn and Gunnery over.

Again, they began digging into the loose soil with their hands, and within less than eighteen inches they uncovered another tangle of body parts. Flynn once more climbed down and tried to pull out what appeared to be the lower half of a female, severed just above the hips, but it was too heavy, and Gunnery had to help him get it out of the grave. Under it, they found a torso, arms, and head; somberly, Flynn recognized the face as Patricia Walsh. Under her body they found various articles of clothing, including a man's jacket with *Turbidy* written on the inside collar.

Along with the body parts came a powerful stench so putrid the men began breathing through their mouths. It was the stink of decomposition, and the men knew it wasn't either body they were smelling; these women had been in the ground only a month, and because of the winter cold, their bodies hadn't yet begun breaking down. Again, the men took turns digging, and their noses ran in the cold March air. Reflexively, they wiped at the drips with the backs of their gloves and instantly recoiled at the horrific stench already soaked into the leather.

Finally, under the body of Patricia Walsh they found the blackened remains of yet another dismembered woman. But unlike Pat, Mary Anne, and the body found the month before, these body parts had been carefully reassembled and laid out, almost reverently, as if in an Egyptian tomb. The face was ruined by decomposition, making an immediate identification impossible. Underneath the body they found a pair of sandals, a bloodstained shirt, and a pair of bell-bottom jeans with a $10 bill carefully folded in the back pocket.

At the base of a tree they found a knife, a gun, and a Warner #108 single-edged razor-blade tool, used in cutting heavy fabric and wallpaper.

"Go grab the son of a bitch,"[4] Killen told Flynn.

No one had to ask which son of a bitch he meant.

Lieutenant William Broderick, the same Massachusetts State Police detective who had tailed Tony in Boston the month before, was sent to arrest him. When he and two of his colleagues got to the Beacon Street apartment where Broderick had first spotted Tony, they were told Vinnie had moved, so they went to Macy's Liquor Store in the North End where he worked.

Broderick recognized Vinnie from their ignominious meeting at the Beacon Street apartment and dismissed him as not the brightest bulb on the Christmas tree. Small, dark, and looking somewhat slow-witted, the kid had evasive eyes that the seasoned cop had seen countless times.

"I haven't seen Tony in ten days," Vinnie said, his eyes shifting.

Wise to obfuscation, Broderick and the two other detectives went to Vinnie's new apartment on Marlborough Street.

When the knock came at the door at 4:20 p.m., less than an hour after the three bodies had been found, Tony calmly greeted the detectives in their khaki trench coats.

"Hi, Officers. What can I do for you?" Tony said.

"You are . . . ?"

"Vincent Bonaviri."

"Good try, pal," Broderick said, recognizing him from his surveillance of the VW. "We just spoke with Bonaviri at Macy's Liquors. Wanna try again?"

"All right, I'm Tony Costa," he said, a guileless smile spreading across his face.

"You're under arrest."

Because he was a flight risk and they didn't have a warrant yet for the murders, Tony was initially arrested for grand larceny of an auto and was again read his Miranda rights. The Massachusetts State Police then called Provincetown, and Officers Flynn and Gunnery immediately got in a squad car and drove to Boston to take Tony to the Barnstable County House of Correction.

During the two-hour drive from Boston to Hyannis, Tony never said a word.

It was his son Michael's fourth birthday.

50

LIZA

It seemed as if I was hearing "Cape Cod" and "Provincetown" and "Truro" all over the news. Mom snapped off the radio or television as soon as the story said anything about those places, but I heard enough to know something had happened, something bad. I asked her what, but she shot me a look and muttered, "Nothing," and I knew not to push it. Besides, I was busy planning my upcoming birthday. My tenth. A big one, and I wanted it to be perfect.

Now that the snow had stopped falling for the winter, the early spring rains began and the days were cold and wet and miserable. I couldn't wait for summer to arrive so we could get back down to Provincetown and I could work on my tan. I thought about Bob Stranger and little noisy Duke. I thought about Cecelia and Tony and driving to the dump with him. I thought about biking to the Penney Patch for waxed lips and candy dots and swimming in the RC pool with Gail and Geoff. And I thought about what sort of bathing suit I'd get this year. I had grown so much since last summer, even Mom agreed I'd need a new one. In the past she had sometimes made our suits out of scraps of fabric she brought home from her home ec classroom, and all I could do was pray that she'd be too busy or distracted to force me into one of those. They were always baggy in the wrong places and tight where it was most uncomfortable. This year, now that I was going to be ten, I wanted something pretty and that fit me. *Please.*

One day after school we all went shopping, but not for bathing suits.

Mom needed something at the drugstore, and I wandered down the hair products aisle; along with a new suit I wanted blond hair. One of the girls in my class had put Sun In in her hair and *presto chango* she was a blonde! I was reading the directions on the bottle when Louisa walked up.

"Mom says let's go," she said, and I kicked her in the shin as she passed.

"Ouch. What did you do that for?" she said, her hand reaching down to rub her leg.

"*Ouch. What did you do that for?*" I said, mimicking her in a high, whiny voice.

Just then, my head was swatted from behind.

"I heard that," my mother said. "Why *in hell* are you so miserable all the time?"

I looked at the Sun In bottle in my hand.

"Can we buy this?" I blurted out without thinking.

Mom looked at me, her eyes wide with disbelief that I would ask for the Sun In right after being smacked in the head for being a brat. Then her eyes narrowed dangerously, and she gritted her teeth and grabbed my upper arm, digging in her nails. The bottle of Sun In fell to the linoleum floor and rolled away under the shelf.

"*Buy me, buy me, buy me,*" she hissed. "That's all I ever hear from you. Now get your ass to the car."

I pulled free from her grasp and ran out of the store, through the parking lot and kept going, all the way into the woods behind the shopping mall. Humiliated and furious, I vowed that someday I'd get her back. Hit her back. Threaten to spank her in public. Make her cringe with shame. It was getting dark but *no way in hell* was I getting back in her car. So I ran through the woods toward home, pretending I was running away. I wasn't scared of the woods. I knew them the way I knew the dunes in Provincetown, and I felt safe in them because I knew my mother would never set foot in them. *She'd never find me in here.*

I followed the abandoned train tracks out of the woods and back up to Crescent Street about a mile from our house. Once on the road, anybody could pick me up and maybe I'd never be seen again. I sort of wished any-body would. That would show Mom.

If Tony lived nearby, he would have picked me up if he'd seen me walking alone through the woods. Tony would have, but he was far away in Provincetown.

51

TONY

The day after his arrest, Tony was transported from Barnstable to the Provincetown district court and arraigned on two counts of murder in the first degree. Avis and Cecelia sat among the spectators, most of them women, crammed into the courtroom on the town hall's second floor. All rose as Judge Gershom Hall entered. He looked at the rare spectacle of a crowded court and then took his time seeing to the other business of the day—speeding tickets, fishing violations, eviction disputes. Finally, he turned to Tony and asked him to rise. As the judge began, Tony's eyes looked around the room vaguely, not focusing on anyone or anything besides a painting he loved, *The Fish Cleaners* by Charles Hawthorne, which hung on the wall. Then when the second charge, "murder in the first degree of Mary Anne Wysocki," was read, Tony bowed his head and stared at the floor.

With the arraignment over, Tony was led down the town hall's impressive stairs that bracketed both sides of the two-story lobby and ushered out the double front doors. As the doors opened, a crowd of nearly 150, including his old buddy Woody Candish, greeted him with cheers and shouts of support: "We're with you Tony!"

Bernie Flynn descended the stairs behind Tony, frowning in disdain. *Who are these freaks? Celebrating a guy who butchered four girls?*[1] It confirmed for Flynn the worst of the hippie culture, American youth, and, most of all dirty, desolate Provincetown. It didn't help his opinion of the place that nearly every local had stonewalled him, refusing to answer even the most basic question. He looked forward to seeing it in his rearview mirror when the case was over and he could leave, *permanently*.

Tony smiled, raised his shackled hands, and waved. The crowd cheered. He walked down the stairs like a movie star on the red carpet, enjoying the spectacle of it all, particularly the attention and praise bestowed on him. As he drove away in the back of a police cruiser, he flashed a peace sign for the photographers; the picture appeared on the front page of the *Cape Cod Times* the next day.

"They seemed like a nice couple with young kids," David Raboy, the man who had rented Tony and Avis the Shank Painter Road cottage, said. "You don't expect he's Jack the Ripper."[2]

"Everyone feels bad it had to be a Provincetown boy," admitted the mother of one of Tony's friends.[3]

Many in Provincetown agreed, believing that Tony Costa never could have murdered the four young women. Not "our" Tony, they said, the handsome husband and father of three, the part-time babysitter, carpenter, and plumber who just about everybody considered the friendly, even charming guy next door. In fact, many people thought he'd been railroaded. Dr. Hiebert was upset that Tony had been arrested and felt that the police were "persecuting the boy."

And those who didn't think he was innocent kept their opinions to themselves. One of them was Woody Candish's wife, Donna.

"I wasn't shocked," she later admitted. "He sat on my counter and told me there were three things he could never be forgiven for. The worst sin is killing, right?"

Jim Zacharias agreed. "I learned that Tony treated Avis like an animal." Capable of anything. "There was just something about him that creeped me out."[4]

While his defense team began to search for other potential suspects, Tony wrote Avis from jail, demanding that she falsely accuse other possible suspects in the murders as well as claim to know Chuck Hansen, a character Tony had concocted to foil police. She refused to do both.

It wouldn't be until forty years later that Avis would admit, "No one wanted to believe when the last two girls went missing that Tony could have been responsible, but we all suspected it was true. I, more than anyone, knew it was." She went on to write, "There was a month between the discovery of the first body and the last two [*sic*˙] . . . a month in which we all came apart and started whistling in the dark . . . sleeping with one eye open, if at all. A month where not one of us would tell the others what we suspected. To say it outloud [*sic*] was to die. That's what I thought, anyway."[5]

Because Tony was known around town as some sort of stoned Santa Claus who would pass out drugs like gifts to his minions, some locals suspected that sooner or later "he'd be picked up for the slayings."[6] But publicly they defended Tony, talking out of both sides of their mouths to reporters and investigators, as if it were a game of cat and mouse—as if it were the locals versus the outside world. In short, the locals had created an almost Mafia-like code of silence to insulate themselves, Tony, and those in his crew who broke the law. When brought before the police and questioned about Tony's drug possession, theft, even assault and domestic violence, many openly, even brazenly, lied.

Back in Hyannis, Bristol County district attorney Edmund Dinis called a press conference for the following day at 8:00 a.m. Dinis, a lifelong politician, had doggedly worked his way up from New Bedford city councilman to the Massachusetts House of Representatives and then the State Senate. In 1956, he became the first DA of Portuguese descent to serve Bristol County, which then included the Cape and Islands. When the press conference was called, it rankled the Provincetown police, who felt Dinis was overstepping his bounds, but Dinis was a showboater who couldn't resist the cameras.

It was like nothing sleepy Cape Cod had ever seen. Dinis stood in front of the packed room and detailed the most atrocious aspects of the police

---

˙ The correct number was three.

findings, including the erroneous detail that the bodies had been "cut into as many parts as there are joints," and that the hearts had been removed from the bodies and had not been recovered. He also claimed that one body had teeth marks on it. But what Dinis didn't understand, and no one in the room clarified, was that an "incised wound" was not a result of incisor teeth but rather one caused by an incision, the type a knife or other sharp instrument would make. When asked by a reporter if the killer was a "Cape Cod Vampire," he agreed that perhaps that's exactly what they had on their hands. The moniker "Cape Cod Cannibal" was born.

The locals were outraged by the horrific murders, garishly portrayed in the carnival-like press coverage. Truro residents bemoaned that children used to wander through the woods hunting for blueberries without fear but that now those woods were a place of horror.

Perhaps the only people enjoying themselves, besides Tony, were the press. For them, the entire spectacle was catnip. No matter how mawkish the headline, they couldn't sell their papers fast enough. Desperate for any new detail to splash on the next edition, they camped out in front of Avis's and Cecelia's apartments, 5 Standish Street, and both the Provincetown and Truro police stations.

"You gotta give me something," they begged Truro Police Chief Berrio as he got out of his cruiser and headed into the station.

"I gotta give you nuthin'!" Berrio bellowed as he pushed past the throng into the building. "Now get the hell outta here!"

Berrio told Killen that as bad as the press was, "the tourists are even worse." The woods became prime real estate for souvenir hunters, many of whom brought their children along for the search, as if it were a holiday or a day at the beach.

In Provincetown, a reporter with the *Cape Cod Times* quoted an unidentified long-haired kid who watched from the Benches, muttering as the newsmen milled around Town Hall.

"It makes me so mad; they're making a circus out of this," he said.

And it was a circus that sold out the big tent, every day.

52

TONY

A month before, when police had warned Tony that he needed an attorney, his uncle Frank Bent had called his friend and one-time fellow town councilor, Maurice Goldman, asking him to represent his nephew. Now that Tony had been arrested and charged, Goldman took the case, perhaps as a favor to his old friend Frank, perhaps because it sounded more interesting than his usual docket of probating wills and litigating property liens in sleepy Brewster.

Born in Canada on July 4, 1900, Goldman immigrated to America with his family when he was a toddler. He had a scar over his right eye from a fight when he was six years old over territory for his paper route. He'd been a Boston city councilor, a state senator, and a Suffolk County assistant district attorney before he went into private practice. At almost sixty-nine years old, Goldman was portly with pale, hooded eyes and a strong, thrusting profile. Proud that he often took on pro bono cases, he called himself "the poor man's lawyer." And with his last $3 in his pocket at the time of his arrest, Tony was nothing if not poor.

On March 8, two days after Tony's arraignment, Goldman and his co-counsel, Justin Cavanaugh, drove to Bridgewater State Hospital, where Tony had been taken for thirty-five days of court-mandated psychological examinations to determine whether he was legally sane and therefore eligible to stand trial. Until the bodies had been found, Goldman thought Tony's involvement with the women could have been purely coincidental but not necessarily criminal. Now, with the bodies at the morgue and

Tony having told a string of lies about how he came to possess the women's car, Goldman got right to the point.

"I'll ask it bluntly, Tony. Did you kill those girls?" he said.

"I had nothing to do with it. I have killed no one," Tony replied in his best *I'm offended you'd even ask* voice.

For the next two hours, Goldman and Cavanaugh had Tony detail everything he knew about Patricia Walsh and Mary Anne Wysocki, starting with where they met and how they looked. As Tony wove his tale of professed innocence, part fact, part fiction, the narrative included a list of those he said were most likely responsible, starting with a man named Chuck Hansen.

"Find Chuck Hansen," he told Goldman and Cavanaugh, "and ask him where he was that weekend."

Cavanaugh promised they'd put finding Hansen high on their agenda. As he and Goldman watched Tony get escorted back to his cell, Cavanaugh thought their client was innocent. He found Tony too soft-spoken, too mild, too polite to have killed and killed in such a heinous manner. *Impossible.* He turned to Goldman and remarked that Tony seemed scared. Goldman didn't seem to share Cavanaugh's opinion of Tony's innocence.

"Of *course* he's scared. You'd be scared too if you'd killed four people," Goldman said.

After Tony's admission to Bridgewater and for the next thirty-five days, he was interviewed by a caravan of doctors, psychologists, psychiatrists, and social workers. One session included thirteen professionals, all holding clipboards. Everyone in those diagnostic sessions was impressed by Tony's utter calm, poise, eloquence, and intelligence. He did not have the usual profile of an inmate accused of such barbaric crimes, although few of the professionals in the room had ever seen this degree of brutality. While various doctors cited "sexual identity confusion," "possible schizoid personality disorder," "lack of personal insight," and "a narcissistic, inadequate man who needs to manipulate people, especially women," none found him psychotic or criminally insane. At the end of his examination period, the determination of the entire Bridgewater staff was that "Mr. Costa showed no psychological illness"[1] and was therefore deemed competent to stand trial.

On April 10, with all of his psychological examinations complete, Tony was transferred from Bridgewater back to the Barnstable County Jail, where he would remain throughout the investigation and trial.

A dreary two-story brick edifice built in the 1800s on the hill behind the courthouse overlooking Cape Cod Bay in the distance, the Barnstable County Jail was something out of a Dickens novel—dark, dank, and claustrophobic, with imposing steel bars every twenty feet through its halls. Each six-by-nine cell had cinder-block walls, a metal cot, a stainless steel sink and toilet built into the corner, and a four-by-twelve-inch opening in the solid steel door through which a plate of food or a letter could be passed. Though Tony was not the only prisoner in the jail's history to be held for more than fifteen months, he was certainly one of its most infamous.

While Tony had been undergoing his examinations in Bridgewater, the two partially decomposed bodies found with Pat's and Mary Anne's bodies in the woods were finally identified as those of two other missing Provincetown women, Susan Perry and Sydney Monzon.

The search for Sydney Monzon, the pretty girl people called Cricket who wanted to be a stewardess and travel the world, was over.

In remembering Susan Perry, Alice Joseph, the librarian, thought of the William Wordsworth line: "A Maid whom there were none to praise / And very few to love." Someone would later post a variation of the epitaph on Susan's online memorial page.

53

LIZA

Spring finally arrived in West Bridgewater, and Mom was starting to make summer plans again. Things were looking up.

Dad had briefly resurfaced in our lives, promising to take us to have Easter dinner with his new family. But we waited in our Easter bonnets and shiny patent leather shoes on the front lawn all day, and he never showed; judging by Mom's fury, he didn't call to say why. All she knew was that he had ruined her plans to have a fancy Easter dinner with Ron at the Ritz-Carlton in Boston, where she'd heard there was a huge buffet with a bottle of champagne on every table. All of that and no kids. But then Dad ruined it. "Mr. No Show" had struck again.

At the start of the summer, Mom sent me to a two-week YMCA camp in Plymouth. I had tried to fight it because I wanted to be in Provincetown, swimming, biking, and riding to the dump with Tony. But she couldn't be budged; she was sick of my questions and my rolling my eyes at everything she or Ron said; she wanted a two-week "Liza-Free Zone," and she would have it. Camp actually wasn't bad at first, but after a couple of days I broke my big toe. Still, she refused to come pick me up; she had paid for two weeks, and two weeks is what I would stay, broken toe or no broken toe. Geoff had gone to camp with me, but he hated it and wrote a note home that only had one word—*HELP!*—and before I knew it, Uncle Hank arrived, scooped him up, and took him home, leaving me and my broken toe behind. So instead of playing hide the flag and diving off the dock into the lake, I sat in my bunk and wrote my first full-length story. It was about

Tex, the boy who had moved into Nana and Grampa Georgie's house next door to us. My goal was to write one hundred pages about him and how he had made me feel. I finished, writing *the end* in big cursive letters with my purple pen, just one day before everyone was due to come get me so we could all head to the Cape. I didn't often feel pride, but staring at *the end*, I wanted to hug myself. I had done it, without any help, and no one could take it away.

I waited all day for them to pick me up, and it was almost dark when the car finally pulled into camp. Most of the other families had already come and collected their kids, but I was still there, waiting on my crutches. Mom was behind the wheel of her convertible with a scarf around her head, smoking one of her little cigars. Ron sat in the passenger seat, smoking his bigger and smellier cigar. Louisa, Jill, and Danny sat in the back seat. When no one got out to help me, I struggled to open the door, clumsily laying my crutches on the floor, and then crawled into the back seat for the hour-and-a-half drive from Plymouth to Provincetown.

I scrunched in next to Louisa and pulled the story out of my bag. My stomach felt like ants were crawling through it and my heart was pounding, but I was eager and proud to share it. One hundred pages! And I'd written every word.

"I wrote a story at camp. Wanna hear it?"

I looked up at Mom and Ron in the front seat. They exchanged a look that didn't make my stomach feel any better.

"Sure," Mom said, with a chuckle. "Why not?"

My hands shook, so I pressed the pages into my lap and began.

"It's called 'The Boy Next Door.'"

Before I could finish reading the first paragraph Mom snorted, and then Ron snorted. I looked up, and Mom was looking over at Ron; they were both snickering and looked like they were going to burst out laughing at any minute. I felt a hot surge of embarrassment, but I really, really wanted them to hear my story. I knew if they heard it, they'd stop laughing and tell me it was quite good and that they were proud that I'd written a whole hundred pages all by myself. I looked over at Louisa, Jill, and Danny, and they all looked at me, but they weren't laughing. I continued reading, but I only got through another sentence or two.

"Okay, okay," Mom said, glancing in the rearview at me. "I think that's enough. We get the picture." She and Ron both laughed again.

I quickly shoved the pages back into my bag and scrunched as low in the seat as I could, out of Mom's line of sight.

When Mom's and Ron's laughter finally trailed off, she wiped at her eyes under her sunglasses. "'The Boy Next Door.' Now I have heard everything!" she said, and that sent them into another round of laughter. No one else said a word.

As we drove, the sun set and I sat against the car door, twirling my hair with both index fingers—a double twirl. I watched the oncoming headlights on the other side of the road, wondering how I could run away from home, and from Mom. I doubted Mom would come after me, so maybe I didn't even need to run. I could just stroll away from home and then find another mother, maybe even one who wanted to have me around and hear my stories.

Like always, as we drove up and over the Sagamore Bridge, officially leaving the mainland and landing on Cape Cod's sandy shores, my mood got a little better and Mom's positively soared; I would be back in Provincetown soon, and she was headed to her Eden. Even though she spent a lot of her time cleaning toilets and making beds, she loved owning the motel: "It doesn't even feel like a job, that's how much I love P'town!" she said. With Mom happier, I was happier.

54

TONY

While Tony sat in his jail cell and counted the days until he was sure they'd find him innocent and set him free to get high and walk the dunes again, Goldman was busy building a defense that might save his client from the electric chair. The lawyer's first stop was Cecelia Bonaviri's gloomy, second-story apartment, where Goldman had asked that the family gather for a group interview. The weather was even more bleak than usual for March on Cape Cod and when Goldman and Justin Cavanaugh got out of their car at 9 Conant Street, they had to bend their heads against the gale-force winds. They entered the tiny apartment and found it uncomfortably stuffy and crowded with consoling relatives. Goldman handed a pack of cigarettes to Avis as introductions were made. He took note of Cecelia's sad, stooped posture, her threadbare yellow sweater, and her mournful eyes. He began by asking her about Tony's childhood; as she spoke, wind rattled the windows and silent tears streamed down her cheeks. She gazed out into the storm, her words drifting into a mumbling dream world.

"California," she said, her voice barely audible. "I loved it so much. That's where my Tony was made when his father and me were there during the war. It was like all my prayers were answered."

No one in the room knew what to say. Her California dream was now an unspeakable nightmare.

In order to have some privacy, Goldman asked Avis to come out to his car for her interview. She agreed, and in her typical forthrightness, she spared no detail of the troubled past between her and Tony.

"He changed when he started on drugs," she told Goldman. "I think he's schizophrenic, because when he got mad, really, really mad, and showed any kind of violence, he was a different person. He would flip out if he was nagged. But he got over it fast. Then he wouldn't admit he was ever sore."

She told Goldman that Tony was never particularly fond of his children, except for the baby, Nichole, whom he named.

"You see, he always wanted a girl."

When Goldman and Cavanaugh finally stepped out of Cecelia's building, both felt relieved to be out of the depressing apartment. Both men took in huge lungfuls of the fresh air blowing in off the ocean.

Goldman knew Tony didn't have a dime to his name, so he petitioned the county to pay for his and his defense team's work, agreeing to repay the money, if necessary. But the county refused, so Goldman came up with another strategy to eventually get paid: a book and possibly even a movie deal.

"Murray always had an angle,"[1] Tom Gunnery observed of Maurice Goldman.

Goldman relished the prospect of not only defending Tony Costa, the already infamous Cape Cod Cannibal, but of selling a book with all the lurid details of his crimes. Gerold Frank's book on the Boston Strangler was on the *New York Times* bestseller list and rumor had it a film was in the works. It didn't hurt that Tony's crimes were even more grotesque than Albert DeSalvo's. And it would only add fodder to the public's appetite for horror stories to have the villain a soft-spoken family man, polite to a fault, "adored" by his ex-wife and children, looked up to by the young and old alike, a man who worked hard to pay his bills, as a carpenter no less, very Christlike, Goldman thought. Goldman had even hired Tony to do work on a few of his properties around Provincetown, so Goldman himself would be able to add a personal anecdote or two about what a good guy he was. It was the perfect scenario for a bestseller. Goldman could wait the year or two for his payoff; it would be all the sweeter when it became a blockbuster film as well.

The first order of business was to have Tony and Avis sign over the rights to their life story, which they did; after all, what choice did they have? Tony needed an attorney, a good one, and they could barely afford to put food on the table. Then Goldman called his friend Kurt Vonnegut and told him about his new client and how he needed a kick-ass writer to write the book. Vonnegut was intrigued, but when he demanded a larger percentage of the advance and royalties than any of the legal team would receive, including Goldman, Goldman went looking elsewhere. One of the writers he found was Victor Wolfson, an Emmy Award–winning writer for his work on a Winston Churchill biopic. At first, Wolfson was optimistic about the book, but after learning the hideous details of the murders and their unrepentant perpetrator, Wolfson told Goldman there was no way he could "clean up" Tony enough for a book that would have mass-market appeal. Finally, a local writer, Lester Allen, took on the task. Allen was a little-known and semi-retired contributor to the *Cape Cod Times* who had never written anything longer than a two-column piece for the paper. While certainly not the big name he had hoped to get in Vonnegut or Wolfson, Allen, Goldman assumed, would at least be able to capture the essence of Tony, his rather salacious sex life, and his grisly crimes.

As Goldman began planning what would be the defense strategy, Allen went to work interviewing Tony and every available person in his life, particularly Avis, whom he spent more time with than anyone else, save Tony. Through the interviews, she suffered under his invasive and often lewd questioning. His interviews with her read more like interrogations, and sleazy interrogations at that. Allen seemed fixated on the more erotic if not lurid details of Avis and Tony's sex life, repeatedly bringing the beleaguered Avis "back to the subject"—Allen's subjects of cunnilingus, fellatio, sodomy, masturbation. He wanted to hear, almost eagerly, every intimate detail.

"Did he want you to take his member into your mouth?" "How many times did he masturbate onto your naked body?"[2]

Today, Allen and Goldman might well be sanctioned and Allen sued for sexual harassment.

As abusive and inept an interviewer as Allen was, he was the only member of the defense team who was paid, receiving more than $650 in fees and expenses, nearly $4,500 in today's money, all of it out of Goldman's pocket. (It's also worth noting that this bare-bones defense team rewarded itself mightily, spending more than $3,000 on just four meals at the Dolphin Restaurant in Barnstable, across from the district courthouse and jail, receipts of which were submitted to the county for reimbursement but were rejected. Along with his expensive fish, Goldman ate what he claimed were nearly $8,000 worth of defense team costs, more than $48,000 in today's money.)

55

LIZA

After running the Bayberry Bend pretty much single-handedly the first year, Mom decided she needed a manager and once again hung a HELP WANTED sign in the front window. Ron spent the workweek in Boston and only occasional weekends with us on the Cape, leaving Mom to happily run *her* motel. I'm not sure if she interviewed anybody else, but within a couple of days of opening the place for the second season, Frank appeared on the doorstep. He was an odd man who always seemed to have eyeliner and a dab of lipstick on his otherwise pasty, puffy face. He tapped on the front door and stuck his head inside the office.

"Hellooooooo! Are you still looking for help?"

Mom hired him on the spot and put him to work that day. Frank's résumé, credentials, and references to manage a motel? Not so much.

"I couldn't run the place alone, could I?" Mom said.

Even though Frank often looked like an unmade bed, he was a hard worker. He was average height and pudgy, especially around his belly, with brown hair that was long, but not hippie long, just long enough to curl uncombed over his collar. He was jolly, silly even, and laughed a lot, strutting around Bayberry Bend as if it were his personal vaudeville stage. Behind his back, Mom called him a "flaming fag," but I think she was actually really fond of him. We all were. And he seemed to like me and Louisa. He took us to the dump to collect scrap sheets of plywood so he could make us a fort in back of the motel. And whenever Mom disappeared down the road, he stepped in to look after us. It must have been more than he signed up for, but he didn't complain.

"Frank just loves being a fag," Mom said under her breath probably once too often, but I don't know if he did love it. Sure, he loved wearing lipstick and mascara, he loved tight, colorful clothes, and he loved mooning after other guys, but sometimes it seemed like all of his dancing around, happily fluttering his hands, was somehow an act. At times he looked so sad it made me wonder about his "loving being a fag." It was illegal to be gay in those days, even in Provincetown, and Frank talked about being homosexual in a whisper. How much could anyone love *that*?

And gay or not, happy or actually sad, he was nice to me. Everyone liked Louisa, but I was the difficult daughter, the "one that's gonna put me in an early grave," my mother often said, and most people seemed to agree. But not Frank. I guess Frank appreciated that I was different, like him maybe.

One June evening, as Mom was getting ready to go downtown to see Bobby Short and his orchestra at the Crown & Anchor and Louisa and I sat on the bed reading, Frank appeared at the screen door, drink in one hand, cigarette in the other.

"Yoo-hoo! Come on, girls, open the door for Frank!"

I looked at Louisa, but she kept her eyes on her book, *Charlotte's Web*, so I got up and went to the door.

He waited on the other side of the screen with a toothy grin.

"Evening, sunshine!" he said, laughing.

I smiled; he always made me feel better. I unlatched the hook and held the door open for him.

He was dressed in a skintight stretchy paisley shirt and white hip-hugger bell-bottoms with what looked like Mom's wide white leather belt that made his stomach hang over the buckle. He jumped through the open doorway into the room, causing the entire place to shake under his weight, then did a wide-armed pirouette, not spilling a drop of his drink, and announced, "I am what they call downtown a whole mouthful." Louisa and I looked at each other and laughed; we didn't understand exactly why what he said was funny, but we knew just looking at him was.

"Big night for old Frank, ladies! I shaved my legs," he said with a wink. "Wanna see?"

We giggled, and he put his drink on the side table and made quite a show of pointing his toe like a ballerina and pulling up one of his pantlegs about six inches to reveal a fleshy, pasty calf with now-smooth skin.

That summer, the Provincetown Players were staging a play called *Camino Real*, and while Mom couldn't afford to go to the theater, she heard it starred some handsome new actor. His name was Richard Gere, and he was evidently a "real swoon." Bob and Frank talked about him so much I half expected to one day find the "dreamboat" actor smoking cigarettes with them on the lawn chairs in the back of the motel, all wearing Ray-Ban sunglasses and holding up reflectors to work on their tans.

After a few weeks back in Provincetown, I realized something big had happened there that winter and wondered if it had anything to do with Billy's visit to West Bridgewater. But no matter how much I listened to the adults around me, I couldn't get the details of exactly who was involved or what had happened. They always stopped their whispering as soon as I came into the room. I wondered if they were deliberately keeping something or *someone* from me, but I'd felt that way my whole life. Everything seemed to be a secret. I had always been so good at eavesdropping on people, but all of a sudden it felt like the volume had been turned way down. All I knew was that my mother started locking our doors and windows at night, something she'd never done before.

By midsummer, the whispering stopped and everyone was talking out loud about murdered girls buried in the woods. As the rumors and fears circulated around Provincetown, I tried to make ten-year-old sense of it. The woods of the Outer Cape and behind our house in West Bridgewater had always been peaceful for me. Places where I played with friends and alone for hours. Places where I felt happy and safe. And in Truro, a place where I had been with Tony many times.

I thought back to those drives to the dump and to the Truro woods with Tony and remembered how grateful I was for the fresh air coming in the windows as we drove back down Route 6 toward home. Inside the truck often smelled bad, sort of like lobster and clamshells when they've been in a hot dumpster too long. *Maybe that's why those seagulls always followed the truck*, I thought, remembering our usual trail of birds.

Then suddenly I thought of something from one of those drives, but it was dreamlike and fragmented, and I wondered how much of it was true or if the scary rumors around town were making me remember things that weren't real at all. In that foggy memory, we were driving down Route 6 and Tony started in on a long list of complaints about his life: Avis, the kids, his brother, his boss—they were all *stupid jerks and ding-a-lings and lowlifes*, and he needed to get the hell out of Provincetown for good. When we got to the woods, he parked the truck and told me to stay put; he had to check on things, and he'd be right back. But he wasn't right back, and I nearly fell asleep waiting in the front seat, lulled by the summer heat. He finally came back, and as we drove out of the woods, he stared straight ahead out the windshield, his eyes unblinking. I felt bad for whatever was making him so sad. Neither of us spoke as we drove back to Provincetown.

Dream or not, I missed those days. I wondered if I was ever going to see Tony or Cecelia again.

56

TONY

As the man charged with designing and executing a successful defense for a man now accused of not one but four infamous and monstrous murders, Maurice Goldman had few options. He also had a client with a history of prolific lying, most of it to the Provincetown police and all of it admissible in court. Goldman knew the prosecution's first line of attack would be the simplest: the innocent don't lie.

He began by looking for Chuck Hansen, the man Tony first implicated in the murders, in the slim hope that the case against Tony was one of mistaken identity. But all too soon, Goldman realized it was a fool's errand.

"Listen, fella," he told Tony, "this Chuck Hansen doesn't exist. If he existed, we would have found him by now. Trust me."[1]

After Hansen failed to materialize, Tony then named an ever-lengthening list of "friends" who probably killed the women, first among them Cory Devereaux, his young acolyte who had sold him the .22 revolver. Tony not only tried to frame Cory for the murders, he also told investigators that he had a strong love-hate relationship with Cory that had been "homosexual but not homogenital . . . whatever that distinction means," his defense team noted.[2]

When Goldman informed the prosecution that Tony had named Cory Devereaux as the guilty party, Bernie Flynn was sent to check him out. Flynn found the teenager squirrely but credible; Flynn even admitted to a grudging admiration for the street-tough kid, seeing a bit of himself in the troubled teen. But Cory had a solid alibi, and he passed three polygraphs.

When Goldman informed Tony that Cory was innocent, he became incredulous, insisting that the evidence was there and then that the cops were "hiding something" in order to nail him.

Goldman's best chance at a defense, and one that if successful would have changed criminal defense law, was to petition the court for a plea of "guilty but insane" as opposed to "innocent by reason of insanity." Goldman knew that once the jury heard the details of the murders, as well as viewed autopsy photos of the brutalized bodies, those twelve men and women would never be able to look at Costa and deem him "innocent."

Because the Bridgewater team had declared Tony competent to stand trial, Goldman enlisted the services of his own team of psychologists and psychiatrists who would, he hoped, be able to reveal the truly crazy, if articulate and poised, man who had eluded detection at Bridgewater.

In the thirteen months between his return from Bridgewater and the start of his trial on May 11, 1970, Tony continued to undergo what became an unprecedented number of examinations, including ten by doctors brought in to evaluate his mental state and four full physical examinations. Tony wrote in his prison diary, marveling at all of the attention he was getting. His genetic and chromosomal makeup was also tested to determine whether Tony had a so-called double Y chromosome. If he did, Goldman could use that disorder's traits—among them impulsivity, explosive temper, hyperactivity, and antisocial behavior—in his defense. But those tests showed no abnormalities; Tony was an otherwise healthy specimen.

Through the barrage of examinations and interviews, Tony proved to be a prolific and "extraordinary liar, deluded by his own skill in weaving tales . . . either to fill in events which he cannot remember or to conceal from himself what he does not want to remember."[3] To test that memory, the defense team gave Tony copies of the gruesome autopsy reports; he only pretended to read Susan Perry's and refused to even look at Patricia Walsh's. When challenged in one of his lies, he erupted in rage, yelling that he was being framed, and then later was "all smiles" and said he made a mistake in what he had earlier told investigators. His facile manipulation of truth and his endless lies frustrated Goldman and made it impossible for him to know exactly what he would be facing from the prosecution when the case went to trial. It also made it very hard to nail down a clear story for the book in progress.

Nearly every examination and interview with Tony was tape-recorded, and on those recordings he assumed various personae, his voice veering from that of a New England fisherman to Ivy League highbrow to whispering child. His examiners were curious about Tony's odd elocution—prissy, almost effeminate in its precise, fussy pronunciation, and how it was totally out of character with his masculine good looks.

In one of Tony's meetings with his attorneys, Goldman began the session asking Tony to recall the exact timeline of January 25, the last day Pat and Mary Anne had been seen alive.

"Well, I can tell you it was a *brilliant* day," Tony said.

The attorneys all looked at one another, eyebrows raised. Tony sounded like Prince Philip, or rather, Queen Elizabeth. For whatever reason he had assumed a fey British accent for the meeting.

"Tony, why are you talking that way?"

"I am sure I don't know what you mean, Maurice."

He also spent more than forty-five hours being interviewed by Lester Allen, more time than he spent with any other member of his defense team, his family, or his psychiatric examiners combined. In those sessions Tony frequently answered Allen's questions in an arched, affected manner—"This I do not know," "Yes, I too am strong on that idea." "I don't rightly recall," and "I am as perplexed as you by this."

When asked about his philosophy of life, Tony said his "figure for identity" was Jesus Christ and that "if someone is hurting or slandering or destroying someone else, they in turn must be destroyed."[4]

Between Tony's British lord, pious martyr, and stuffy professor, the defense team had enough Tony Costas to fill an entire cell block.

The most thorough psychiatric evaluation of the prisoner was done by Dr. Harold Williams from McLean Hospital outside of Boston, the oldest mental hospital in New England, ranked as the best free-standing psychiatric facility in the country. Tony boasted to his attorneys that because of his drug dealing, organized crime might be involved in his case, so Williams, who bore an uncanny resemblance to the actor Larry Hagman, took a loaded .357 magnum with him to the jail. After one of his visits, he ran into Avis as he waited for his gun to be returned to him from the safety lockup. He noted that she stood transfixed, watching him reload the gun and snap its barrel back into position.

Williams walked away from each session with Tony emotionally and physically exhausted after spending so much time with the "evil" that surrounded Tony and permeated the room.

"I felt the devil was watching . . . from Costa's side of the table," he told Goldman. Coming from a man who dedicated his professional life to working with the criminally insane, that said something. Yet despite his personal revulsion, he was able to provide what was the most detailed explanation of Tony's history, psychosis, and murders.

Williams postulated that Tony's obsession as a young boy with his dead father and then his feeling of abandonment sparked by Cecelia's marriage to Bonaviri and birth of Vinnie were at the root of Tony's pent-up fury against all women. The murders, and specifically raping and dismembering the corpses, allowed him a "glorious" release as he acted out a horrific drama of incest and matricide during which he returned to the blissful state of infancy when he had Cecelia all to himself.[5] And finally, because Tony told Williams that "the real Tony" was "buried deep," the act of burying his victims ensured they would be "with him" forever.[6]

Maurice Goldman heard of all this in a stunned silence. While he knew Tony was guilty of the murders, having Williams lay out the measure of his ruined and dangerous psyche was shocking. But at the end of Williams's evaluation, even with his damning indictment of Tony's moral and ethical code, the doctor was unable to render Tony legally insane. Unlike a true psychotic, Tony knew right from wrong, and further, he had consistently tried to cover up the murders—another indication that he knew the degree of his crimes. Finally, Williams told Goldman that he deemed Costa a sexually dangerous person who should be sent to prison, not a psychiatric hospital. Rather than accept the lurid diagnosis, Goldman fired Dr. Williams and began looking for yet *another* psychiatrist to tell the defense team what it needed for an insanity defense.

57

LIZA

One day while I was hiding in the Bayberry Bend laundry room reading a Nancy Drew mystery, I heard Frank and Bob chatting as they sunned themselves on the lawn behind the office. They were talking about how the "murdered girls" had been "all cut up and shit" and how the hearts had been removed and had teeth marks on them. "Someone really did a fucking number on those girls," but Frank and Bob didn't believe *he* could have done it. I didn't know who *he* was, and I didn't want to come out of my hiding place to ask.

The one person not talking about the murders was Tony, but that was because he'd disappeared. At camp I'd finally smoked my first whole cigarette, and I wanted to show him how I had learned how to blow smoke rings, just like he did. I asked Auntie if she'd seen him, but she just gave me a weird look and said no. Then, I went looking for Cecelia and found her in the laundry room at the Royal Coachman. She looked awful and more tired than usual, with the circles under her eyes nearly black. She hugged me as always, but as I lingered in her arms I smelled liquor on her breath, and it made me sad. It had never smelled so strong, and I didn't like it. I pulled away gently and asked her about Tony, but she just shook her head and looked away. When she turned back, I could see she'd been crying. She reached out and patted my shoulder.

"I'll tell him you were asking for him. He loved you girls," she said, pausing to adjust her sweater, then continued folding a pile of towels.

Loved, I thought. *She said* loved *not* love. *He can't be dead. I would have heard if he was dead, wouldn't I? He must have left town.* Tony had always talked about going to California. I figured he had gone there for the winter and just hadn't come home. And just like that, he became another man who disappeared from my life without saying goodbye.

As I walked back across Route 6A to the Bayberry Bend, I imagined him driving west into the setting sun with the top down, singing "I Heard It Through the Grapevine" at the top of his lungs.

Tony must be gone for good, I thought. No wonder Cecelia looked so sad.

A few days later, as I took clean sheets out of the washer, a station wagon pulled into the parking lot, even though we had the NO VACANCY sign hanging out front. Mom was working at the front desk, and she grumbled *What the hell do these people want?* The screen door squeaked open, and a man in Bermuda shorts and a pink golf shirt walked into the office.

"Which way to the woods where that man killed all those girls?" he asked.

Mom barely looked up from the column of figures she was adding and gave a wave of her hand with her index finger pointing south.

58

TONY

In addition to the slew of psychiatric evaluations, Goldman had Tony undergo a series of polygraphs with the aim of getting something from him that he refused to give: the truth of what happened to the women in the woods, as well as the three women who had vanished after their encounters with Tony—Bonnie Williams, Diane Federoff, and Barbara Spalding. There were also as many as five more young women whose disappearances in the same time frame were eerily similar, and Tony's own defense team suspected he may have killed and buried those missing women in remote graves as well.[1]

With the truth, Goldman would be better armed in facing the prosecution and for building his "guilty but insane" defense. And a confession wouldn't hurt book sales either.

Maurice Goldman asked Bridgewater State Hospital's lead polygraph examiner, Charles H. Zimmerman, to conduct the tests. Zimmerman knew a thing or two about dealing with pathological liars and violent criminals. Born in Germany in 1920, he had had an illustrious career at the German crime laboratory in Frankfurt before immigrating to the United States and becoming a citizen in 1964, where he worked on high-profile intelligence matters, some with the CIA. In his career, he conducted more than ten thousand tests, including those on Patty Hearst and each of the suspects in the Boston Strangler case. Charlie, as he was called by friends and colleagues, spoke in a soft voice with a slight German accent, and his modest humility hid a ferocious tenacity that could disarm even experienced criminals. Through his career, in addition to bolstering the state's evidence, Zimmerman often worked with defense teams, believing that "informed counsel is brilliant counsel."

Zimmerman not only respected Maurice Goldman; he embraced challenging cases, and Tony's proved too irresistible to pass up. He and his wife had a summer home in Sandwich on the Upper Cape and Zimmerman agreed to work on weekends with Tony at the nearby Barnstable County Jail. It didn't hurt that Goldman talked big about the huge payoff the book and movie deals would bring, a piece of which would presumably go to Zimmerman because while he submitted bills for his time to Goldman, none of them was ever paid.[2]

After Zimmerman finished a session with Tony, he turned to a colleague who had observed the proceedings and asked his opinion.

"Charlie, he's got problems," the man said.

Indeed.

While Tony had denied any direct involvement in the murders, he had had "reactions" to nearly every direct question about the crimes, indicating considerable knowledge. And, Zimmerman knew, innocence did not leave traces on a lie detector test.

In the polygraphs, Tony proved himself a master at manipulating the dialogue away from the question at hand and diverting it to subjects that Tony then rambled on about, often incoherently. Fellow inmates had assured him that it was a breeze to beat a lie detector; you had to breathe slowly and methodically and just keep talking. *That* Tony could do.

As early as June 1969, Zimmerman got Tony to admit to "being the cause of" Christine Gallant's death and to helping dismember Patricia Walsh and Mary Anne Wysocki, but, as had been his pattern, he maintained that Cory had done the actual killing. Susan Perry's and Sydney Monzon's murders, he continued to insist, were a "mystery" to him. It would take nine polygraphs in all and countless re-creations and variations of his story before Zimmerman finally seemed to break through

Tony's wall and get him to admit to not only knowing about their murders but to knowing details that only someone who at least smelled the smoke of the gun would know.

In one of the tests, Zimmerman did all the talking for the first twenty-six minutes. When Tony finally spoke, he asked Zimmerman to turn his eyes away; he didn't want Zimmerman to look at him while he told him something. Zimmerman complied and turned toward the window away from Tony, but it wasn't enough.

"You can see me in the reflection. Could you please put your coat over the window?" Tony said.

By hooking his jacket over the window lock, Zimmerman was able to cover enough of the glass to satisfy Tony. He sat back down, made sure all the connections were solid, and waited.

When Tony began speaking, he sounded wounded, upset, scared, as if the reality of his prison cage was finally hitting him. Then, he described in terrible and precise detail how Pat and Mary Anne were murdered, again insisting it was Cory who did the killing. But in this test, he finally revealed that it was he who stabbed Mary Anne in order to silence her "gurgling." It was, he insisted, the "humane" thing to do. Then, he described cutting off her head. In a voice flat and without affect, Tony said he'd grabbed her head by the hair, wedged the knife against her throat, and cut back and forth, as if slicing salami, until he'd severed the head completely. He then carried the head by the hair to where he threw it into the hole, on top of Sydney. In the process he had hacked off a handful of hair and threw that in the hole as well. Zimmerman was shocked by the admission; never before had he had a patient feign innocence of murder but admit to dismemberment. When he asked Tony why he went to the incredible labor of cutting the women into so many pieces, he responded easily, even pleasantly, "so they would fit in the hole," as if pointing out the pure logic of it.

In the last test, on October 26, Tony finally came clean.

"The fact is, I do remember committing these murders. Why, I don't know. I'd like to have someone study it. They were committed by me though, for reasons I don't really know. There's a lot that I don't remember."[3]

Zimmerman asked him, "Now, as you look back on these acts and the realization that you're the person who did it, do you feel that you are mentally sick?"

"Oh, yes," Tony said eagerly. "I believe so. This is a problem that needs to be ironed out. There has got to be something there, otherwise they wouldn't have been committed. There has to be something from that."*[4]

Zimmerman concluded his sessions and felt as though he'd never witnessed such cold-blooded displays. Like Harold Williams, Zimmerman found that his time with Tony left him exhausted and depleted.

Tony's case personified an issue that had nagged Zimmerman. He felt that the United States should have one federally funded institution where mass killers, like Tony Costa, could be studied in order to better understand what caused their violent rage. The killers' psychological profiles could eventually establish a set of guidelines for psychiatry at large and for the courtroom. Zimmerman's hope was to develop a psychological test for mass killers that could reveal the early signs of psychopathy, prevent a possible recurrence, and create a central data bank to provide psychiatric guidelines for judges, probation officers, and criminal justice professionals.

Although the FBI created a Behavioral Science Unit in 1972 to research a rise in sexual assault and murder,[†] Charlie Zimmerman would likely be disappointed that progress on a data bank to identify and prevent those offenders from committing violent crimes before they occur has not yet been reached more than fifty years later.

---

* Within weeks, Tony had recanted his confessions, again insisting that various friends, real and imagined, had committed the crimes. He would maintain his innocence for the rest of his life.

† It was Robert Ressler, an investigator on this FBI team, who coined the term "serial killer" and would later be profiled in the Netflix series *Mindhunter*.

=====

Because of the laws surrounding attorney-client privilege, Tony would have had to agree to share his confession with the prosecution. He didn't, so the state's case against him was purely circumstantial; although he was the last person to be seen with each of the dead women, there was no evidence, no eyewitnesses, and because he had been very careful to wear gloves, no fingerprints that linked him directly with the murders. (Although Tony had raped the corpses, it wasn't until 1984 that DNA was discovered as a unique marker.) Nonetheless, Goldman struggled to build a credible defense because of Tony's profligate lying. Finally, he was left with no other option than to claim that Tony's drug use made him do it. During several jail cell consultations, Goldman, Cavanaugh, and Allen tried their damnedest to explain their strategy to an uncomprehending Tony.

"Mr. Commonwealth of Massachusetts, you have no evidence against Tony Costa," Goldman began, illustrating how he might address the court. "But if you did, the man did it completely under the influence of drugs, barbiturates, and he was in a state under which he didn't know what he was legally doing."[5]

That too was going to be a hard sell, because since the day of his arrest Tony hadn't shown any sign of addiction or withdrawal. Still, the drug-addiction claim was all Goldman had left.

The last psychiatrist Goldman hired was Dr. Jack Ewalt, who held the Bullard Chair of Psychiatry at Harvard and was the architect of President John F. Kennedy's task force on mental health. Now that Tony had finally put the knife in his own hand at the scene of Pat's and Mary Anne's murders, Goldman hoped that Ewalt would be able to break through Tony's defenses and get the entire story. Ewalt interviewed Tony eight times, during which Tony warmed to the idea that even if he did kill the women, it wasn't his fault, *the drugs made me do it*. He told Ewalt about the girls' murders as a series of flashbacks, as if they were drug-infused dreams rather than a clear road map of his crimes. Even as Tony got closer to telling the truth, he again dodged an actual confession by claiming a sort of selective amnesia. In his "memory" of killing Sydney, Tony once again blamed the drugs, and, speaking in the third person, feigned shock and horror at "his" having killed Sydney, then stripping and raping her body. He described the scene to Lester Allen:

> First there was a memory of Sydney holding his hand as he guided her through the woods from the road where the car was parked to his cache of stolen drugs. Then there was a glimpse of her kneeling and watching him dig up the ammo can. She said something and he strained to hear her soft voice. And then the memory of a flash of a knife and her small sigh as she tumbled backward, her lovely hair covering half her face as she laid on the dirt. How small and childlike her body was when he stripped off her clothes. How vulnerable she seemed under the frenzied stabbing. And finally, the memory of a voice, his voice, screaming "Why?! Why?!" [6]

In his report to Goldman, Ewalt apologized for not being able to deliver what the attorney most wanted—a clear diagnosis of Tony's psychosis. Just as Williams had, Ewalt told Goldman that Tony clearly knew the difference between right and wrong, and therefore he would face the full extent of punishment for his crimes.

59

LIZA

Mom loved her life on Cape Cod. She loved being her own boss and sweeping the warm sand from *her* motel's walkways. She loved the energy of all the weird and wonderful folks who crowded Commercial Street in their flamboyant outfits. And she loved dancing the nights away. Most nights, Louisa and I were still left with Sally, the chambermaid, in number nine. Mom figured between Frank and Sally we no longer needed a traditional babysitter (as if we'd ever had one of those).

Frank had been a wonderful find for her; he felt more like a girlfriend than an employee. On nights when she was headed to the clubs, she would pour them both a "dressing" drink while she put on what Grampa Georgie called her war paint. As she teased her hair into the perfect beehive, the two of them would laugh, and Frank would try on her different lipsticks and teeter around our tiny room in a pair of her high-heeled mules, with a cheap feather boa that she'd found at a flea market flung around his neck. (Why Frank was allowed to play with her lipsticks and makeup and high heels and boa but Louisa and I were absolutely forbidden to touch anything of hers, *period*, I didn't dare ask.)

Some nights she went to the Pilgrim Club on Shank Painter Road, which was rapidly evolving into what would become Piggy's, a wildly popular dance bar that welcomed both gay and straight patrons. Other nights, and with Ron at home in Newton, she'd head out with Auntie to what was known as the "dyke bar," the Pied Piper. At the Pied Piper, they became fascinated with a lady singer who frequently entertained there. The woman had been married with twin daughters, but she left her husband and children to move in with her *girl*friend. It was the first Mom and Auntie had ever heard of a woman leaving her husband to live with a *girl*friend, and they were obsessed, and even a little envious at the thought of it.

But as the summer rolled on, Mom and Ron suddenly broke up and her already sporadic good mood vanished altogether. She was *pissed*. She had tried to plan a "family" trip to Disneyland, and I guess the problem was that we weren't, in fact, a family. Louisa and I had barely figured out where Disneyland was on the map when Mom started in on Ron, asking when they'd be married; maybe they should do it in Disneyland? He didn't lie.

"I don't want to get married again. And," he added, "I don't want any more kids."

It didn't take a genius to figure out that he meant Louisa and me. I wasn't surprised; nobody seemed to want us around, besides maybe Cecelia and Tony and sometimes Grampa Georgie. But I know she hated seeing what she had hoped would be her ticket to an easier life disappear. I took extra care to avoid her because it didn't take much for her to backhand me for telling a lie I hadn't told or to chase me down and drag me to the sink and wash my mouth out with soap if she so much as imagined I'd used the *s*-word, which by now I was doing a lot. I usually said it under my breath—"What a little shit," or "What a shithead," but not as under-my-breath as I hoped, so she would bend me over the hard edge of the sink and run the bar of soap across my clenched teeth. She asked me where I learned to talk like that, and it took every ounce of my self-control not to answer, "Duh, I wonder."

Her drinking started earlier and earlier in the day. One day she had a meeting in town and no one around to look after Louisa and me, so she took us along. Afterward, we all went out for a rare treat: chowder and a foot-long hot dog on MacMillan Wharf. We sat at a picnic table outside the hot dog place and ordered our food, but Mom just asked for an ice water. When it came, she drank the water and poured gin in the cup from a bottle hidden in her purse. After our meals were brought to us and before

I thought to keep my mouth shut, I complained that my clam chowder was too hot to eat. Without taking her eyes off mine, she reached into her drink, took out a few ice cubes, and threw them into my soup, splashing the hot chowder in my face.

"There. That should cool it off, *princess*," she said, taking a swallow of her drink and eyeing me over the rim of the cup.

I wiped bits of clam from my cheek and nodded, picked up my spoon, and hoped she couldn't see the tears gathering in my eyes.

Mercifully, her mood was somewhat softened when two new guys came on the scene. One was a married lawyer with an office on Commercial Street who took her out for drinks, and the other, Steve, was a frequent guest at Bayberry Bend who came to Provincetown, he said, for the fishing. His arms and legs were deeply tanned but so hairy you could barely make out the skin beneath. He took us for rides in his Jeep and for cookouts out on Long Point. He was nice, like Tony, so I forgave him for all that hair and gave him about a seven on the boyfriend scale. But then one weekend he brought his girlfriend to Provincetown with him, so that was that. When we were cleaning their room, I watched Mom dip her fingers into the woman's face cream and spread it slowly up her neck and all over her face.

"Someday," she said, leaning into the mirror and watching her hand smooth the cream, "I'm going to have expensive cream like this."

I looked away, a little sad for her.

In mid-July, Ron suddenly reappeared. He flew into Provincetown Municipal Airport on a private plane and took Mom to a champagne lunch at the Provincetown Inn overlooking Long Point and the harbor. Over dessert, he presented her with a two-carat diamond. She came home holding up her left hand, turning the ring this way and that, marveling. Two days later, she left Frank in charge and she and Ron flew to South Carolina to elope. Again, I don't remember any goodbyes. What I do remember is Frank announcing that Mom had "run off" with Ron to get married and that she'd be home in a couple of days. I couldn't help but wonder why in the world she'd run off and marry Ron, a mere five and a half on my boyfriend scale. And why Ron's sudden change of heart about marriage and more kids? I worried about that, but Mom didn't question her good fortune.

I'd have a stepfather. I remembered that Tony had talked a lot about this *stupid stepfather*, and I hoped Ron wouldn't turn out to be stupid too.

When they returned, and even though she was now married, our summer in Provincetown didn't change much. She moved us into one of Bayberry's two-bedroom cottages, because we couldn't very well sleep in the same room with her and Ron, and now we had Jill to help with cleaning toilets and hairy drains. Danny, because he was a boy and the youngest of us, was off the hook.

That summer, along with a stepfather, another sister, and a little brother, I also got my period. Not that anyone noticed.

60

TONY

Late in 1969, both the defense and the prosecution were wrapping up their investigations and compiling their list of witnesses. But then on December 21, one witness was taken off the list, permanently. Cecelia Costa Bonaviri suffered a brain aneurysm and died in an aisle of King's Department Store in Hyannis while shopping for Christmas gifts.

Tony, still being held at the Barnstable jail, blamed himself for her death.

"I feel as if I've lost my last friend," Tony told Justin Cavanaugh. "I might as well've killed her myself."

It may have been the truest thing Tony Costa ever said.

Her body was taken back to Provincetown, where viewing hours were held at Nickerson Funeral Home, the same mortuary where the autopsies of Patricia Walsh, Mary Anne Wysocki, and Sydney Monzon had been conducted nine months before. Tony was then taken to the mass at St. Peter the Apostle. He was allowed to be unshackled; Chief Marshall had received a tip that there could be an assassination attempt on Tony's life, so security was already at a maximum, and the shackles would be overkill. After the service, Tony watched Father Leo Duarte give the last rites over his mother's grave. He stood shoulder to shoulder with Avis and remained dry-eyed throughout the ordeal, but as he was led back to the police cruiser, Tony's shoulders sagged, and once seated between the two officers in the back seat, he put his head in his hands and wept.

In the year since the murders, Provincetown locals had become desensitized to the horror. "Tony Costa digs girls!" and "Chop Chop Costa" were among the one-liners that went around town like the bad jokes they were—cocktail-party banter, otherwise funny if one discounted the brutal murders and mutilations of four women.

Tony loved all the attention he was getting. A popular joke circulating around the Cape made macabre fun of the particular way in which the women had been killed: "Tony Costa walked into a Cadillac dealer and asked the price of an Eldorado. 'Oh, it'll cost you an arm and a leg,' the salesman said. 'It's a deal!' Costa replied." Tony even embellished the joke: "I said, 'This is the car I want.' And the salesman said, 'Son, you can't afford it; it'll cost you an arm and a leg.' And I said, 'If you have a shovel handy, I'll be back in ten minutes.'"

In April 1970, with the trial only weeks away, Goldman staged his last-ditch effort to get information out of Tony that might help bolster the defense: hypnosis. With a proper confession and detailed information about the murders, Goldman could plead either diminished capacity due to his heavy drug use or use his "guilty but insane" defense. He felt that Tony, while undoubtedly a killer, belonged in a state hospital for the criminally insane, not a federal prison.[1]

But after three tries, the most the hypnotist, Dr. Judianne Densen-Gerber, got out of Tony was an admission that "I just got to" commit murder, but no explanation of why. However, the tapes and transcripts of her three sessions with Tony curiously never ended up in the case files and archives. What remained was the repulsion Stephen Lipman, one of Tony's defense attorneys, felt after having sat in on two of the sessions. "Quite frankly," he later said, "it was disgusting. I couldn't attend the third [session]."[2]

Inside the Barnstable County Jail walls, Tony's days were grim. He had a lot of time to consider his crimes and perhaps feel real remorse for having taken the lives of at least five women. But true to his pattern, his abiding sorrow was only for himself. In one letter to Lester Allen he wrote, "The hostile sensations have gone, but the sad, lonely memory remains forever. To live with such inner sorrow and regret with no contrition available ever, is punishment beyond which any man's sadistic qualities could possibly contrive."[3] Once again, it was all about Tony.

He spent his days pacing his cell, writing furiously in his journals, and urinating in paper cups because he couldn't bring himself to use the stainless steel toilet in the corner.

"He's a very sick guy," Armand Fernandes, the assistant district attorney for Barnstable County, observed.[4]

61

TONY

After fifteen months and all of Goldman's machinations, countless psychiatric evaluations, polygraphs, and hypnosis sessions, it was over with barely any fuss.

On May 11, 1970, the bailiff escorted the jury into the famed Barnstable County courtroom in single file. He wore the traditional eighteenth-century garb of the court—a long blue coat and tails—and carried a tall staff. Tony wore a suit Goldman's wife had picked out of Maurice's closet; she had let out the cuffs of the jacket and pants, but they were still inches too short.

Instead of trying him on four counts of murder, the prosecution opted for the two in which they had him dead to rights because of the stolen car: those of Mary Anne Wysocki and Patricia Walsh. They concluded that since it's not possible to serve more than one life sentence, they didn't need to try him for the murders of Sydney Monzon and Susan Perry. Although Massachusetts had enacted a "mercy bill" in 1951 that removed the mandatory death sentence for murder in most cases, given the heinousness of the crimes, the prosecution left open the possibility of sending Tony to the electric chair.

Before testimony began, the jury was taken out to the Truro woods to view the burial sites. A caravan of National Guard jeeps drove nearly thirty-five people, including the defense and prosecution teams, Judge Robert H. Beaudreau, state and local police, the press, and of course, Tony Costa, into the woods, the heavy brush scraping both sides of the vehicles.

They parked in the clearing and the group was walked down a narrow path to a small hole dug into the side of a hill.

After the "tour" ended, the caravan drove back into Provincetown, where Tony's friends who were walking on the sidewalks paused to watch the cars pass. They cheered and yelled, "Yay, Tony!" and a teenager spotted Tony's car and trailed it on his bike through the streets. Tony sat smiling, accepting the adulation like an astronaut returning from the moon. He waved with shackled hands through the window.

With the trial having formally begun, the prosecution opened its case. The Wysockis were too ill and perhaps too broken to attend the trial, so Patricia Walsh's father was the first witness called to the stand. When asked to identify his daughter's cable-knit sweater found in Tony's closet, Leonard Walsh fought back tears as his fingers hovered over the sweater; he couldn't seem to bring himself to touch something that intimate to his daughter's skin. But when handed a picture of her blue VW bug, he clutched it to him like a talisman, and identified the car as belonging to Patricia. Catherine Walsh followed her husband to the stand, and as she answered questions, at one point she paused and leaned forward, almost out of her chair, fixing her eyes on Tony until finally Armand Fernandes, the assistant district attorney, noticed what was happening and distracted her with another question. When Bob Turbidy took the stand, he identified the suede handbag found in the woods as belonging to Patricia Walsh.

"How do you know it was Patricia Walsh's?" Fernandes asked.

Turbidy put his head down briefly and took a long breath. Then, he looked up at Fernandes.

"Because I made it for her."[1]

Goldman didn't cross-examine, and in fact would only cross a handful of times as the state's parade of witnesses gave their testimony.

When the prosecution rested, the defense began, and over the next two days called ten witnesses, but the only one who got a reaction out of Tony was one of the last—Avis. He cried as he watched her take the stand, steam gathering behind his glasses. He removed his glasses and Goldman handed him a handkerchief to wipe his eyes and clean the lenses.

In the months before the trial started, Avis had told Tony's defense team that she felt as if she was "going to lose my mind" and "totally freak out on the stand." When asked if she'd seen a doctor about it, she said she hadn't because she feared something might be wrong. "I think I have leukemia or cancer and they're going to tell me I'm going to die pretty soon."[2] Lester Allen promised they would give her something to calm her nerves when she testified; "After all," he told her, "we have an obligation to help you out . . . a contract with you . . . and it's in our interest to keep you healthy and to keep you functioning."[3]

When the day of her testimony finally came, Avis was indeed functional, but visibly nervous and giggling and waving at Tony as she passed the defense table. She wore a plaid miniskirt with a crocheted vest over a turtleneck jersey and a peace-sign medallion around her neck. Long bangs covered her eyebrows, and tinted aviator glasses obscured her eyes. Once on the stand, she held one hand in front of her mouth, possibly to hide her crooked teeth, and in the other she held a sprig of white lilacs. She was repeatedly admonished to "Speak up so the jury can hear you."

"I'm talking as loud as I can, okay?" she retorted, again covering her mouth and giggling. Goldman chided her, telling her to "Pay attention! It's not fair" to Tony. Meanwhile, Tony sat at the defense table, tears streaming down his cheeks.

Avis finally stopped her odd antics when district attorney Edmund Dinis approached the witness stand to cross-examine her. In all the prior interviews she had given the defense team, the police, and the prosecution, she was asked again and again to discuss her and Tony's sex life. She had spoken about her promiscuity, her drug use, and their sexual history casually, almost as if she'd been reciting a recipe. But when Dinis began his questioning by asking her about her overdose of chloral hydrate, she refused to discuss it, as if she had suddenly become very aware of just how much she was revealing.

Dinis: Would you tell us about the incident with Dr. Hiebert that happened early in your marriage?

Avis: No. I really would rather not.

Dinis: You would rather not?

Avis: Yeah.[4]

Avis admitted to Tony's defense team that she and most of Tony's friends weren't "afraid to lie to police or in court. They don't think anybody's going to find out. If I was caught up in something this big, and asked to put my hand on the Bible, it wouldn't matter to me. You can find justification for lying."[5]

As Avis left the stand, she blew Tony a kiss and then formed her fingers into a peace sign.

Goldman called a long list of Tony's friends, colleagues, and followers, several of them still in their early teens, to the stand. Each told a variation of the same story: Tony was high, Tony was depressed, Tony was out of work, Tony was a mess, Tony liked to talk, but Tony was never angry: "I never saw Tony yell"; "Tony was super mellow"; "Tony wouldn't hurt a fly." And on and on as the team tried to build a case that, if not for the profligate drug use thanks to Dr. Callis, Tony would have been a model father and husband, a talented carpenter with plenty of work to support his family.

In a case wrought with damning details, Goldman was gratified that none of the grisly facts about Susan's and Sydney's deaths was permissible in the trial because Tony was only charged with the murders of Pat and Mary Anne. In particular, Goldman was relieved that the jury never learned that Susan's body had basically been "dumped by the side of the road."[6] Unlike the other three women who walked unaware into their burial sites, Susan was transported in pieces to hers and hastily buried only feet from where Tony parked the car on the dirt road. Goldman justifiably feared that if the jury knew and envisioned that chilling scene, it would have assured that Tony went to the electric chair.

One of the last witnesses to take the stand for the defense was Tony's brother, Vinnie. While police suspected he had been less than truthful in his numerous pretrial interviews, he admitted that when Tony was arrested, his father, Joseph, instructed him to cooperate fully.

"It's over and done with," Joseph told Vinnie. "There's no protection now."[7]

And Vinnie did cooperate, telling police that Tony had been in possession of a pistol, a large hunting knife, and Patricia Walsh's blue VW bug with Rhode Island plates. Even with his having implicated Tony in possessing two of the murder weapons and a victim's car, when the time came Vinnie testified for the defense, not the prosecution. Presumably well-coached by Goldman, Vinnie reaffirmed Tony's heavy drug use and how it changed his very character, echoing the defense's strategy that, in essence, the drugs made him do it.[8]

When the defense wrapped up its case and both sides were set to rest, Tony insisted on taking the stand in his own defense. Goldman flatly refused to let him, saying he would absolutely, positively not stand up under Edmund Dinis's cross-examination. Tony, eager to parade his super intellect in front of the court, asked that he be allowed to at least read a statement to the judge and jury. Goldman wasn't happy about it, but he agreed, knowing that in death-penalty cases the defendant is allowed to address the jury without that testimony being under oath or subject to cross-examination.

For a rambling ten minutes, Tony expounded on his theories of life, love, drug abuse, and the future of America's youth to a rapt audience. He was calm, reasoned, articulate, and passionate—not exactly a case for the insanity defense, and both his team and the prosecution knew it. But he thought he'd "done it."

"Christ!" he exulted to Goldman. "I think I just won the case!"

At the prosecution table, Dinis sat back stunned. He agreed the case had just been won, but not by the defense. He turned to Armand Fernandes.

"There goes their insanity plea."

After Judge Beaudreau gave the jury its instructions, it took only six hours for them to find Tony guilty of two counts of first-degree murder. They also suggested clemency, saving Tony from what would have been an almost guaranteed death sentence. Beaudreau complied and immediately sentenced Tony to life in state prison in Walpole without the possibility of parole.

When the verdict was read, an incredulous Tony murmured, "It can't be," and told Goldman on the spot to appeal. "We'll win," he said.[9]

As everyone left the courtroom, many jurors shook hands with Dinis and Fernandes, congratulating them on a job well done. Others approached the defense table and told Goldman and his team, "It was a really difficult decision." As Goldman had feared, it was hard for them to say the words *innocent* given the ghastly evidence presented and Tony's unchallenged role in the murders.

One reporter later wrote, "Tony Costa made the Boston Strangler look like a choir boy."[10]

As Tony was driven away, this time to Walpole State Prison for the rest of his breathing days, Bernie Flynn turned to George Killen.

"He won't last very long in there," he predicted.

62

LIZA

I never learned what happened to Tony, and by the time the summer of 1970 rolled around, I stopped asking. The murders were no longer the talk of the town, but every now and then I'd hear Frank and Bob talking about how they just couldn't believe it, but that *he* must have done it since they were sending him to Walpole for life. From what I heard, Walpole wasn't anywhere I'd want to spend much time, and it sounded like this *he* was going to be there a long time.

Besides, I was eleven now and had other things to be concerned about. For one thing, now that Ron and Mom were married, Ron wanted to buy a boat, sell the Bayberry Bend, and get the hell out of Provincetown. I didn't want to leave the one place where I felt at home. The thought that we might leave kept me awake at night, my stomach a jangle of nerves and my eczema leaving raw patches all over my body. Most days I had to wear a shirt over my bathing suit because the rash was so ugly. Then one night, my normal level of anxiety became white terror.

It was a Saturday night, and Frank was on duty in the office, keeping an eye on us while Mom and Ron went out to dinner. That night the motel was full and the NO VACANCY sign was hanging out front, squeaking as it swayed in the breeze. Our cottage felt safe and warm, glowing with a rare sense of safety and family. Louisa and I and Jill, Danny, and Gail were all eating hot dogs and beans. I don't know where Geoff was that night. After dinner, Jill and I were doing the dinner dishes and listening to the radio, dancing to the Jackson 5's hit "ABC," when the phone rang in Mom and Ron's bedroom; I answered it. It was Frank.

"Listen to me," he said, his voice low, almost a whisper. "Lock all the windows and all the doors. There's been another murder, right behind you in the cottages. I'll get there as soon as I can."

My throat tightened, and my heart pounded in my chest. *Another murder. Right behind you.* I ran back to the kitchen, yelling for Jill to grab the kids and get under Mom's bed while I locked all the windows and doors. Then I grabbed a carving knife out of the drawer and ran to Mom's room. I dialed the operator and told her to connect me to the restaurant where Mom and Ron were eating.

But before the call could be put through, there was a loud banging on the side of the cottage, and quickly after that, another outside the bedroom window.

"LET ME IN!" a man demanded.

I dropped the phone on the floor without knowing I had.

Peering through the partially closed blind I saw a man with a nylon stocking over his head.

"I said let me IN!" His teeth were bared against the stocking.

He banged on the windows of the cottage as he made his way around to the front door. The kitchen knife shook as I held it straight in front of me and walked back into the living room. I couldn't have screamed if I had tried. I was frozen with fear. Jill had come out of the bedroom, and we stood with our backs against the wall and watched the doorknob jiggle, back and forth, back and forth.

Suddenly, the door was flung open, and the man in the nylon stocking stood in the doorway. My legs gave way and I slid down the wall like molasses. As I hit the floor, the man peeled off the stocking and laughed. It was Frank.

"Scared ya, didn't I?" he shrieked, then started laughing again.

After that, I was okay with Ron's plan to get the hell out of Provincetown.

A year later, the Bayberry Bend Motel and Cottages were made into individual residences and sold off, one by one. They were some of the first condos ever sold in Massachusetts.

The captain of industry had struck gold once again in the burgeoning condo market. He made a killing.

63

TONY

For the first year of his incarceration, Tony received a lot of fan mail from strangers, most of it from women. He also did his fair share of writing, mostly to his legal team lambasting them for the job they'd done that put an "innocent man" behind bars: "I am not a murderer," he wrote Goldman on December 28, 1970, "I am instead a victim. I am a victim of a drug-pushing doctor and ultimately of drugs."[1] It was always somebody else's fault. When he wasn't haranguing Goldman, he was begging the man for money to fund whatever scheme he was cooking up that month—a leather business, a jewelry business, a typewriter with which to write his memoir, pocket change for toiletries and cigarettes; it was always something. Goldman usually responded with $20 or $30, sometimes $50, but not the hundreds that Tony insisted he needed.

In addition to letters, Tony wrote a memoir of sorts, calling it a "factual novel," perhaps stealing the idea from Truman Capote, who called *In Cold Blood* a "nonfiction novel." Tony titled his book "Resurrection," a suggestion of his Christlike fantasies. He was sure it was going to be a huge bestseller and provide for his children while he was in prison (he continued to believe he'd eventually be free on appeal, even though his appeal had been denied without challenge). The four-hundred-page manuscript never sold.

"Resurrection" makes for disturbing, often loathsome reading. In it, Tony again demonstrated his intelligence, writing long and convoluted treatises, one explaining his sympathy for and kinship with other fatherless children, and what a strong need they had for solace, protection, and love.

A coward to the end, he blamed two of his alter egos, fictitious drug buddies whom he called Eddie and Carl. In a rambling, violent, and lurid reconstruction of Susan Perry's murder, Tony recounts how "Carl" described what happened. It is most likely as clear a blueprint of the crime as we'll ever get.

> Susan died in my room. Then Eddie and I were trying to decide how to get the body out of the house . . . she was too big to fit in the duffle . . . he came up with the idea of cutting her up into chunks . . . he ran some cold water in the tub . . . put her body in a kneeling position . . . a huge hunting knife . . . gripped her by the hair and tilted her head back . . . put parts of her body in the duffle bag . . . my mom came home . . . what a hassle she gave me when she saw the blood and guts laying in the tub . . . she cursed me then cursed Susan. She told me to get rid of the mess fast and to clean up the place and hope for the best.[2]

Among the repellent details in this quasi confession is the astonishing claim that Cecelia walked in on Susan's dismemberment, cursing Tony, then cursing the victim herself who lay in ruined pieces in the bathtub. If even marginally true, it reveals just how far she was willing to go to protect "her Tony." If, on the other hand, Tony made up the story, why would he insert his mother, over whose grave he had grieved just months before, into such a ghastly scene? Leo Damore, who would go on to write an exhaustive account of the case and its investigation, acknowledged, "The terrible part is, I think his mother knew."[3]

Donna Candish agreed. "He was her pride and joy. He could do no wrong. If she walked in on Tony doing something [like that], she would never have said a word."

Further, Tony cut Susan up into more pieces (eight) than any of the other three women, because unlike Sydney, Pat, and Mary Anne, Susan wasn't killed in the woods. And as a result, he himself later explained, he had to cut her into parts small enough to carry and to transport without detection. Whatever the truth of Cecelia's involvement, in one of her last comments on the charges against her son, charges that included killing four women and then raping, dismembering, decapitating, and burying their bodies in shallow graves only a few miles from her doorstep, Cecelia was quoted as saying, "If our Tony cut up those girls, he must have had a good reason."[4] It will never be known if Cecelia was mentally ill, but the possibility that she was aware of his crimes and said nothing adds an entirely new layer of outrage. Had she spoken up, it very likely would have saved the lives of Christine Gallant, Patricia Walsh, and Mary Anne Wysocki.

With Cory exonerated and none of Tony's companions ever linked to Susan's or any of the other murders, the reality of his crimes was finally revealed by his own pen: Tony brutally beat Susan, cut her body into eight pieces, very possibly in his own mother's bathtub, put those pieces in five separate bags, including one for her head, and dumped them in a shallow grave next to the dirt road in the woods. Afterward, he rode his bike into Provincetown, had a cup of tea with his Lorna Doone cookies at Adams Pharmacy, and gossiped with the women behind the counter.

When Goldman read "Resurrection," he finally learned the revolting totality of the murders and warned Tony, "Don't let this fall into any-one else's hands!" But Tony had already shared it with most of his cell block mates and submitted it to Houghton Mifflin, where it was quickly rejected.

His prison file notes that he was "polite, cooperative and friendly—no trouble," but prone to depression and anxiety that he "salts away with in-tellectualizing and manipulation. He definitely must keep his time occu-pied."[5] And he did, working in the warehouse, with his leather business, and with a list of prison help groups—Christian Action, the Lifers' Group, and one combatting drug abuse—as well as participating in ongoing coun-seling with prison doctors.

While he was a model prisoner he was also a pontificating one, coun-seling younger inmates on the perils of drug addiction. One can only imagine how being lectured to by a pious Tony Costa, who was fond of saying "I live for God,"[6] went over with the hardened Walpole population.

Perhaps not well, because he was subjected to "pranks." What kind of pranks or how humiliating they may have been was not divulged by Tony or prison officials, but according to Goldman, Tony was continually sexually molested, and fellow prisoners called him "Choice Cuts." His request to be relocated to the Norfolk prison due to Walpole being too "stressful" was denied.

In the end, he found love, or at least a warm body to help him feel safe. He told Maurice Goldman of a prison romance with Peter Olsen, a man serving a three-year sentence for petty crimes; Olsen had a rap sheet pages long with crimes ranging from breaking and entering to drunk and disorderly conduct and illegal possession of a narcotic, but nothing close to horrific quadruple murder. Still, the heavily tattooed Olsen and the clean-cut Costa found each other.

On May 12, 1973, Olsen was found dead in his cell by suicide. At least that's how it was recorded. Why a man with less than a year left on his sentence for petty crimes would kill himself was apparently not asked at the time. Tony never mentioned or wrote about it, so it is difficult to judge how the death of his friend and sexual companion affected him. However, only days after Olsen's death, Walpole's acting superintendent petitioned for Tony's recommitment to Bridgewater for sixty days psychiatric observation. When Tony returned to Walpole in July 1973, the Bridgewater doctors reaffirmed Dr. Ewalt's 1970 determination that he was a sexually dangerous man. In their notes they also cited his "hopelessness" at failing to gain a new trial on appeal. Again, Olsen's name was never mentioned.

Exactly one year later on the anniversary of Olsen's death—May 12, 1974, and also Mother's Day—Tony was found dead in his cell, hanging from the bars by a belt he had made in leather shop. His tongue was bitten nearly in half, and he'd urinated down the front of his prison uniform. It's not known whether a note was found. And while his death was also ruled a suicide, it was believed by several who knew him that he had been murdered by other prisoners. Maurice Goldman was one of them. He believed that Tony had received intense sexual harassment from other prisoners and that after Olsen's death, Tony, "still a young man—attractive, muscular, good-looking . . ." may have rebuffed other prisoners' advances, and paid the price of that rejection.

Attorney Stephen Lipman agreed: "The prison population is a conservative one. They don't usually go for Tony's type of crimes."[7]

Donna Candish also believed Tony had been murdered, years later saying, "I was surprised to hear he'd committed suicide, because the person I knew Tony to be would never take his own life. Even after what he said to me. I think he was just planning on living out his life. He was very righteous."[8]

Dr. Nicholas Groth, who evaluated Tony in prison and hoped to get him transferred out of Walpole and into a Connecticut prison where Groth ran a clinic for the sexually dangerous, commented, "His death has always puzzled me. I guess psychologically he was capable of suicide, but there were underground rumors about his being murdered and it being made to look like a suicide."[9]

One of Tony's fellow prisoners at the time was another serial killer, Albert DeSalvo, the notorious Boston Strangler. Like Tony, DeSalvo enjoyed a piece of gallows humor and would sign Gerold Frank's biography of him "Sorry to have missed *you*." It's probable that DeSalvo and Tony knew each other, given that DeSalvo, like Tony, crafted a plethora of leather goods while in Walpole. Regardless of whether they shared a love of leather, neither was a particularly popular prisoner. On November 25, 1973, DeSalvo was found stabbed to death in his cell; fellow prisoners said it was retribution for his having run his own amphetamine business, undercutting the prison syndicate's drug pipeline. Six months later, Tony would also be found dead.

"This case has haunted me for fifty years," Lipman said in 2018. That's in part because what the defense team feared the most happened: they saved Tony from the electric chair, but they couldn't save him from death at his own hand or at those of other Walpole inmates.

On Tuesday, May 14, 1974, an invitation-only funeral service was held for Tony at St. Peter the Apostle Catholic Church in Provincetown.* Immediately following the service, he was buried next to Cecelia in an unmarked grave. After a lifetime of trying, Tony finally had his mother all to himself.

---

* With Cecelia gone, her sister wouldn't collect Tony's personal effects at Walpole for another year, and only then at the insistence of prison officials.

64

LIZA

2020

On August 1, 1988, I went into labor and headed to Falmouth Hospital, about twenty miles down the road from where I was living in Sandwich. An hour later, my mother showed up and tried to bully her way onto the maternity ward, but the nurses wouldn't let her into my room. Then, just as my labor was kicking in hard, I heard a loud knock on the room's first-floor window. I looked up and there was my mother, waving wildly, giving me a thumbs-up. When a nurse saw what was going on, she pulled the shade and I heard Mom run off laughing. *Thumbs-up.*

The next morning, August 2, my son, Will, was born; my mother rejoiced that "she" finally had her boy. Had Tony Costa lived, that same day would have been his forty-fourth birthday.

Six months after Will's birth, I went back to work. Within the first week my mother appeared at my office and plunked herself in the chair on the other side of my desk with a great *harumph*.

"You don't return my calls," she said, reaching for a cigarette. I pushed the ashtray toward her but didn't respond. Her eyes narrowed, and through a puff of smoke she said, "I *will* have a relationship with my grandson, you know."

I felt the rage bubble up in my throat and had to swallow hard before I could speak.

"Not if you lay one hand on him, you won't."

She looked me square in the eye. I stared back. It was almost as if she'd been waiting my whole life for me to stand up, to call her bullshit, to stop her from ever harming me again. We sat in silence, staring each other down, neither knowing what to say. She at least knew not to protest, not to call it a lie—that she'd never laid a hand on me or that she'd had to discipline me because by the time I turned four I was "a nightmare." She knew she had to keep her mouth shut if she wanted to see Will, let alone have him in her life. And to her credit, she did. She wanted it that badly. Even so, I blinked first and looked away. She had won the staring battle, but I had won the war. I hoped.

After she left, I called my therapist. She encouraged me to compile my questions about my childhood and then ask Mom to lunch. A few weeks later, Mom and I were settled in a pine-paneled booth at the Bee-Hive Tavern in Sandwich. Once Mom's glass of white wine and my iced coffee were in front of us, I took a deep breath and began.

"Why did you have such a hard time with me when I was a kid?" I could feel my heartbeat throbbing in my throat. Why in hell was I still scared? I was a grown woman, a wife, and now a mother and a stepmother myself. But still, my fear of her raced through my body like an electric current.

She picked up her wineglass and turned up the corners of her mouth, revealing her canines, which even though she'd long since had them filed down were still fangs. It was somewhere between a smile and a sneer. I held my breath.

"I don't know what it was about you," she began, the smile-sneer holding her mouth. "But from the day you were born, I always felt you were out to get me."

I raised my eyebrows, trying not to gasp. "Why?" I managed to ask.

"Well," she said, taking a deep breath. "You were conceived on our first time on our wedding night. And I didn't want to be pregnant yet. And then"—she continued as if she had been waiting a long time to get this off her chest—"you were a girl. *Everyone* wanted a boy first." She spilled some of her wine as she waved the glass in emphasis.

Two strikes, I thought. I didn't have to wait long for the third.

"And *then*"—she paused, readying her final blow—"you were just so damn stubborn. Impossible really. Just like your father." She sat back and took a healthy swallow of her wine.

There it was.

The air around me felt heavy and time slowed. I think she kept talking, but I couldn't hear the words. It felt like I'd passed out and just regained consciousness. She was telling the truth, but I was hearing it for the first time. She hadn't wanted to get pregnant on her wedding night. She hadn't wanted a girl. And then that unwanted girl had a mind of her own. My mother's worst "nightmare." Had I even stood a chance? She had always considered me a threat, a living, breathing mistake, and as with all her other mistakes, instead of examining herself as the possible cause, she turned her frustration and anger outward. And I was her favorite target.

I don't remember much more of that lunch, except that I felt an odd lightness, as if I'd been unburdened. That, and trying not to cry into my French onion soup. But over the following weeks and months I realized she'd done me a great favor. For the first time in my life I understood that my mother's resentment toward me was formed before she even gave birth. Who I was had never been the problem. The fact that I existed at all was the issue. Before I had ever opened my infant mouth and let out my first cry, my mother looked at me as her adversary. And somehow, it was my fault. My entire life I had felt as if I was fundamentally bad. That something was wrong with me at my core, something that could never be cleansed or confessed away and that everyone could see from the outside, like a scarlet letter or a third eye. But that moment in the Bee-Hive Tavern felt like the beginning of a new life. Unwanted was different than bad. It was somehow workable. I could climb out of unwanted, but bad was a death sentence. Unwanted at least had a chance at life.

It was ten years after that painful lunch that my recurrent nightmares began and eventually brought me back to my childhood, my summers in Provincetown, and my friend named Tony. Only then did I realize the true depths of my wound: in addition to her abuse and neglect, my mother had been so self-absorbed that she unwittingly left her children in the care of a psychopath.

Since beginning this project, I have been asked one question above all others: *Why didn't he kill you?* Why wasn't a little girl for whom he bought Popsicles and drove countless times to the clearing in the Truro woods among those he killed, violated, dismembered, and buried? The only answer that makes sense is my age. I now suspect that Tony was grooming me to be one of his adoring "kid chicks," his harem of young, troubled girls; I certainly fit the description. Mercifully, by the time he was arrested, I was just turning ten—too young to sexually arouse him.

Then again, maybe it was just luck. When I told Judge Armand Fernandes, the last surviving member of the prosecution team, of my history with Tony, the first words out of his mouth were "You're lucky to be alive."

After Mom blithely told me, "Well, I remember he turned out to be a serial killer," those summers with Tony came rushing back, and I decided I needed to learn everything there was about him and his crimes. As my research began, I thought about my recurrent nightmares and their violence. Had I witnessed something in those Truro woods as a child? Did I, like perhaps Patricia Walsh and Mary Anne Wysocki, stumble upon one of Tony's haphazard graves, seeing something that my brain couldn't comprehend at eight or nine years old but that continued to roil through my subconscious as I matured?

Over lunch one day with my childhood friend, Gail Becker, we reminisced about the Royal Coachman, those summers in Provincetown, and our mothers. She suddenly fell silent, her head bowed over her plate. When she looked up, tears were running down her cheeks.

"What is it?" I asked.

"I don't know," she said, her voice quavering. "I just never felt that anybody had your back."

"That's because they didn't." As I said the words, their full weight hit me. Gail hadn't been much older than a toddler in those days, but even she knew.

I'll always struggle with my mother and the flashpoint anger I inherited from her. But this process has laid bare my life and opened every wound I have. And here is the deepest of those wounds: I have always felt as though there was something wrong with me, inherently deep and dirty and dark. Something unlikable and unfixable and worst of all, unlovable. And I believed it. As a result, I spent my childhood more afraid of my mother than I was a psychopathic serial killer. Finally, when I became a mother and in spite of my fear, I was able to stop what had been generations of physical abuse. It ended with me.

During the laborious process of writing this book, I visited my mother often to tap into her memories of people and events. She's in her eighties now, and as with so many wounds, time has healed some of ours. In one conversation we talked about the late 1960s and how it was a hell of a time to grow up; the Catholic Church was still unchecked in its abuses, the country was embittered by an ongoing guerilla war in Southeast Asia, and indiscriminate sex had become common, fueled by ready access to birth control and street drugs of all kinds. Finally, at the time of Tony's arrest in 1969, there were thousands of missing girls and young women across the nation, and overwhelmed police departments could do little to find them. In that perfect storm of chaos and neglect, children often survived by taking care of themselves. Louisa and I certainly did.

Mom has no regrets, at least none she'd ever admit to me.

"That's just the way it was back then," she said recently, and chuckled softly, remembering her golden days on Cape Cod. "Boy, oh boy, I sure had a good time. But then I remember I had two little kids and I wonder who the hell was looking after you girls."

Who indeed.

EPILOGUE

One of the most fascinating aspects of this story has been trying to solve the puzzle of Tony Costa: What happened to the bright young boy who turned into a heinous serial killer? What makes a monster? While those around him never imagined the evil lurking beneath his handsome facade, Tony knew something was wrong. He had terrifying, graphic nightmares and violent thoughts he couldn't control. He read a library shelf of books on mental illness. He pored through his stolen copies of the *Physician's Desk Reference* and the *Diagnostic and Statistical Manual of Mental Disorders* (or *DSM*, the bible of psychiatry) cover to cover, over and over. But there was nothing written at the time that would have prepared him, his family, local police, psychiatrists, the district attorney, or his defense team for the horror of who he was and the hideous brutality of his murders.

"That's not just a serial killer," Dr. James Fallon, author of *The Psychopath Inside*, said of Tony Costa and his butchery. "That's a whole different animal."[1]

In 1969, there wasn't even a term for serial killers, let alone treatment or a cure. It wasn't until early in the twenty-first century that scientists and psychologists linked a trifecta of potential causes to the development of psychosis: (1) chromosomal, genetic, and hormonal abnormalities; (2) low-functioning prefrontal cortex; and (3) childhood neglect, trauma, and/or abuse.

According to Bessel van der Kolk, who wrote a seminal book on childhood trauma called *The Body Keeps the Score*, "Fifty percent of the people who seek psychiatric care have been assaulted, abandoned, neglected, or even raped as children, or have witnessed violence in their families."[2] He goes on to say that trauma experienced in childhood changes the brain's actual viscera by releasing certain hormones and chemicals; it literally rewires the circuitry and reorganizes the way the mind and brain work. Trauma recovery coach Michelle Rosenthal agrees: "Every cell records memories and every embedded, trauma-related neuropathway has the opportunity to repeatedly reactivate."[3] In other words, once rewired by trauma, the brain can experience an explosive misfiring whenever and however triggered.

One indication of Tony's possible childhood trauma is van der Kolk's belief that "If you've been traumatized, being in silence is often terrifying. Memory is stored, so when you are stilled, demons come out." Time and time again, Tony professed to being terrified of both noise and silence; change in his pocket was maddening, as was the quiet of the St. Peter sanctuary, where instead of peace Tony heard accusatory voices.

From what we know, Tony didn't fit the classic profile of a serial killer: he wasn't orphaned at an early age or sent to a string of gruesome foster homes. His mother, Cecelia, while a drinker, wasn't a staggering alcoholic, and there are no reports that she or his stepfather, Joseph Bonaviri, beat him. However, Tony *was* reportedly tied up and raped in his early adolescence, and while Tony himself dismissed it as "nothing of great consequence . . . it wasn't even really an attack,"[4] the assault apparently left its mark. A reporter who followed the case closely and interviewed many of Tony's closest friends noted in her file that Cecelia had caught Tony masturbating on a young girl whom he had tied up and hung by her ankles in his bedroom closet. After rescuing the girl and sending her home, Cecelia then tied Tony to a chair as punishment. The story is inflammatory and unverified, and yet, Tony *did* tie up his young neighbor in Somerville, his wife, and possibly his four victims who were found in the woods along with strands of bloody rope. If even marginally true, the story's odious details offer another hint into what might have set in motion Tony's savage, sometimes uncontrollable rage.

Something happened to Tony, but whether it was his brain chemistry, genetic makeup, or the events of his childhood, we can't definitively know. However, current research suggests it was a combination of all three. While the truth died with him, to the end Tony tried to frame Cory Devereaux for the murders, attributing to Cory a confession that likely reveals his own dark despair.

"It was a compulsion, I had to do it. . . . But I don't know why."[5]

And finally, there were the women who disappeared and were presumed to be among those he killed—Diane Federoff, Bonnie Williams, and Barbara Spalding. In writing about these three women, we were unwilling to cut and paste from previous chroniclers' accounts the sentence, "She was never seen alive again," since we didn't know for a fact that it was true.

We asked ourselves, what might have happened in 1969 when police, investigating other suspected victims of Tony Costa, knocked at the door of Spalding's commune in Haight-Ashbury, looking for a woman and a drug addict who was already known to the welfare department and the city's emergency rooms? Our guess was that the men in blue uniforms carrying guns on their hips were stonewalled by Barbara's commune mates, if in fact the door was even opened.

So, fifty years later, we did our own investigation. With a combination of databases, we cross-referenced every possible Barbara, Diane, and Bonnie until we had a short list of women and their relatives, and then we began writing and calling. After nearly a year, we found out what happened to each of them and have been able to correct decades of erroneous chronicling of their murders. Here are their stories.

The evening of Bonnie Williams's 1966 graduation from Manatee High School in Bradenton, Florida, she left a suitcase in the bushes underneath her bedroom window, and when the family had gone to bed she jumped out of the house, grabbed the bag, and hit the road with her friend Diane Federoff, their thumbs pointing north. Diane was just sixteen and Bonnie only weeks from her eighteenth birthday. By the time they got to Provincetown, they'd been on the road for a couple of weeks and were tired, hungry, and reeking of dank seaweed from sleeping in a barn near Mac-Millan Wharf. When Tony took them home to Avis and their cramped apartment, the girls must have felt like they were being taken to the Four Seasons Hotel.

Tony and the two young Florida women left Provincetown in early June and headed to California. After several days and as many as three thousand miles, Tony left them somewhere between Arizona and the Bay Area—exactly where will never be known. But at some point the women did make it to California and after nearly a year of panhandling around San Francisco and dropping acid in Haight-Ashbury with the members of a new rock band named Jefferson Airplane,[6] Diane decided to stay, leaving Bonnie to hitchhike home to Florida alone. Among Bonnie's wild adventures was meeting Clint Eastwood at a party, who was "a real asshole," she later told her sister. When she finally got home to Bradenton, she fell in love twice, losing both men tragically—the first stepped on a landmine in Vietnam in 1968 and the second wrapped his sportscar around a tree. Somewhat on the rebound, she married in 1969, had three children, and died in 2010 of brittle diabetes, a rare and severe form of the disease, after a lifetime of heavy drinking and smoking.[7]

Diane Federoff fared much worse. According to her sister and eldest daughter, Diane was a "tortured soul,"[8] most likely because she was sexually abused by her stepfather and then abandoned by her mother, who chose the abusive husband over Diane.[9] Beautiful, almost ethereal, she married three times and gave birth to three daughters, naming her eldest Raven in honor of Edgar Allan Poe. She died in 1995 when her husband drove their car into a retaining wall after a bitter argument.[10] The man was tried and convicted of drunk and reckless driving and vehicular homicide, but inexplicably served just three years in prison.[11] As horrific as Diane Federoff's death was, Tony Costa had nothing to do with it.

Likewise with Barbara Spalding, the troubled young mother in Haight-Ashbury. When investigators tried to find her in 1969, Barbara indeed couldn't be found, but it wasn't because she was in a shallow grave somewhere along the Pacific Coast Highway as many, including Tony's own defense team, believed. Her daughter speculates that when the police came looking for her after Tony's arrest, she may have been in prison or deep in the recesses of Haight-Ashbury's drug dens.[12]

After her brief relationship with Tony, Barbara, who had married and divorced before she met him, went on to marry twice more, each marriage miserable and short, and in 1975 she had a daughter, Athena. Athena survived heartbreaking abuse at the hands of Barbara, who was drunk or high the entire twenty-one years Athena knew her.[13] Grace, Barbara's sister, last saw Barbara in the mid-1980s, when she arrived drunk and volatile to pick up Athena and was thrown off the naval base where Grace's husband was stationed. That was it for Grace. She never saw her sister again.[14]

Athena hadn't seen her mother in three years when, in September of 1999, the Social Security Administration sent her Barbara's death certificate; her body had been found in a flophouse hotel in San Francisco, hanging over the edge of a trash bin.

"I've never even seen a picture of my mother," Athena told us over the phone when we finally found her in 2019. "We were always moving, always on the run. We'd have to leave in the middle of the night, because the rent was due or the place had been trashed. Sometimes our boxes followed us, but most times they didn't. I don't even have a baby picture of myself."

But we had pictures of both. So with Athena on the phone, we sent her images she had never seen—of herself at ages five and six and of her still-beautiful mother before the drugs had wreaked their havoc.

"Oh my God. She was so pretty." In Athena's voice we could hear poignant tears of all that was lost and of what might have been, if only her mother had been able to escape her demons before those demons killed her.

And so, while we know Tony Costa killed five and, according to police as well as his own defense team, was suspected in the disappearances of several more,[15] fifty years after the fact we now know that Diane, Bonnie, and Barbara weren't among them.

Some mysteries do get solved.

When the siblings and children of these three women discovered that their loved ones had been reported as "missing" fifty years ago and were assumed murdered by Tony Costa, a serial killer, they all were understandably shocked. While the women died too young—Diane at age forty-five in 1995, Barbara at fifty in 1999, and Bonnie at sixty-two in 2010—they didn't mysteriously vanish; they went on to marry, have children who love and miss them, and live their lives for years after their encounter with Tony Costa.

Bonnie Williams's sister shared a wonderful musing of what Bonnie's reaction might have been upon hearing the news of her presumed murder fifty years before:

> I can picture Bonnie sitting there with a scotch, a cigarette in her hand, slapping her leg and laughing hysterically saying, "You mean that wuss from Provincetown was a serial killer? No way. I could have taken him down with one arm behind my back."[16]

Oh, that Bonnie had had the chance to stop a serial killer.

AUTHORS' ACKNOWLEDGMENTS

This book percolated, on and off the front burner, for fifteen years, so there are a lot of people to thank. We urge you to read every name because, like the names of soldiers on a polished granite wall, absolutely none of this could have been accomplished without their love, expertise, tenacity, help, and sacrifice. So many kind, generous people gave the gift of their time and knowledge to us so that we could make this story come to life. We are in their debt.

First and in many ways foremost, an enormous thank-you and debt to Amanda Faehnel at Kent State University's Special Collections Library Archive in Kent, Ohio, for her kindness, patience, and willingness to always help. Her expert curation of the voluminous Tony Costa files is every biographer's dream.

We thank the families of Barbara Spalding, Bonnie Williams, and Diane Federoff for helping us unravel the more-than-fifty-year-old mystery of what happened to their loved ones: Grace Dickey, Athena Martinez, Robert Spalding Sr., Denise Williams Carson, Rex Williams, Kris Blaylock, Claudia Federoff Musgrove, Bruce Dean Cornwell, and Celeste Cornwell Dawson. For them, sharing the stories of what actually became of these "wild child" girls of the sixties was an often-painful reopening of old wounds, and we are eternally in their debt for their candor and bravery.

For sharing their stories, old files, newspaper clippings, faded photos, and fabled memories of the 1960s in Provincetown, we'd like to thank Dan Jarvis, Herbie van Dam, David Raboy, Charlie Souza, Bob Anthony, Jack Englert, Gretchen Neal, Channing Wilroy, Johann Englert, Frank X. Gasper, David Tankle, Fred Zimmerman, Ruth Ann Turbidy, Magnolia Turbidy, Nick Damore, Massachusetts State Police sergeant E. Thomas Gunnery (retired), Carolyn Enos De Leon, Christine Groom, John Wilson, Edith Vonnegut, James Zacharias, Donna Candish, and especially

Cory Devereaux, whose brave honesty in sharing his story and some of its dark chapters was nothing short of heroic. In addition to these generous individuals, there are several more who shared their stories but preferred to remain anonymous, and we have respected that request.

Although we reached out to Avis Costa Johnson many times, we understand why she preferred not to speak to us directly about her complicated history with Tony Costa. Nevertheless, we thank her for sharing so much of her life on Facebook, where she reveals not only astonishing candor but often brilliant writing. After nearly twenty years of addiction, she stopped using and drinking in 1983 and recently celebrated thirty-seven years of sobriety.[1] She reports that she hopes to one day write her story. We fervently hope that she will.

For providing their professional experience and opinions, thanks to Dr. Michael Baden; Aja Worthy-Davis, the executive director of public affairs for the New York City Chief Medical Examiner's Office; Sergeant William Doogan of the Boston Police Department; Judge Armand Fernandes; Attorney Stephen Lipman; Dr. David Bernstein from Forensic Consultants, LLC; Dr. James Fallon; Jamie Lewis at the Massachusetts Department of Correction; Diana Gaumond and MaryPat Kane-Oropallo of the Cape Cod Medical Reserve Corps; Joseph Gordon of the Barnstable County Sheriff's Office; Dr. Kent Difiore; physician assistant Stephen Webber; Lisa Huntska with the Upsala College Archives; Dr. Noemi Mattis; Betsy Sativa with the Arizona State Library Archives; Dean DiMartino with the Massachusetts State Archives; Lieutenant Craig Danziger with the Truro Police Department; Maria with the Providence Rhode Island Records Department; Margaret Sullivan, the Boston Police Department's Records Manager & Archivist; Dr. Mike Aamodt of Radford University's Department of Psychology; Felicia Sanchez; Dr. Anne Dowton; Elizabeth Bouvier, Head of Archives, Massachusetts Supreme Judicial Court; Kate Silvia, Director of Communications at the Massachusetts Department of Corrections; Hillsborough County (Florida) deputy sheriff Grita Perry (retired); Jason Dobson, Deputy Director of Communications at the Massachusetts Department of Corrections; Chloe Grinberg, Boston Globe

Photo Archivist; Cara Gilgenbach, head of Special Collections and Archives, Kent State University; Lester Allen III; photographer Merrily Cassidy at the *Cape Cod Times*; Kim Reis at USA Network; graphic designer Kelly Nolan; and Jennifer Smith at Eco-Gals.

For availing their quiet rooms, expert staff, and carefully cataloged archives, we'd like to thank the librarians and staff at Sturgis Library in West Barnstable, Massachusetts; Cape Cod Community College; Provincetown Public Library; Boston Public Library; and the Family History Library in Salt Lake City.

Jonathan D. Finn has been our friend and photographer of choice since our days at UMass Amherst together, and we thank him for hosting us during one of our research trips to Cape Cod and for the rocking photo of 5 Standish Street in Provincetown herein.

As well to Anne Bernays and Polly Kaplan, who provided what has to be the most luscious house in the most gorgeous location any writers could hope to find themselves for a chunk of the research we conducted in Truro. And to Kay and Charlie Walker who shared their casita overlooking the red rocks of southern Utah. We have been remarkably blessed by generous people sharing their spectacular homes for our research and work. Thank you all.

To Professor Christopher O'Brien of New Haven University's Forensic Science Department, for braving the Truro woods with us and for sharing his invaluable expertise in cold-case forensics. (We hope you were able to buff the scratches out of your Pathfinder's doors.)

Chelsea June Adams did what perhaps no one else has done in listening to and transcribing nearly fifty hours of interviews between Tony Costa, his defense counsel, lead investigators, and polygraph experts. In some ways, she now knows Tony better than anyone. God help her.

Thanks to the entire team at Simon & Schuster/Atria Books, and in particular our editor Trish Todd; every sentence you touched made this a better book. And thank you to attorney Elisa Rivlin and copyeditor Erica Ferguson for your painstaking work at getting it right.

And finally, our agents at Kneerim and Williams, Jill Kneerim and

Lucy Cleland, who both adored this book from the first pitch. Thank you for making it real. And a special shout-out to Jill, for somehow always having the perfect words of encouragement, comfort, advice, and humor for two very different clients. We don't know how you do it, but we are so very grateful you do.

In addition to our professional thanks, we both have a list of those close to our hearts without whom none of this would have been possible:

A FINAL NOTE FROM JENNIFER JORDAN

None of my books would have made it off my computer without my "perfect reader's" careful eye and spot-on suggestions. Every writer has to have one, and I am so blessed that mine is also my oldest friend and sister—Alice Webber. Our mother, Nan Inskeep, and brother, Jeff Gear, are also endless sources of love and support, as well as being voracious readers and careful editors, even though the vagaries of this thing called the "interweb" often confound her. Hang in there, Mother. You're doing great.

When I left Boston and moved west twenty years ago, I left a city (and region) I love, but not those whom I love in it, including the dear Marcie Saganov and Susan Maclure, who always provide a safe haven on my various trips "home," including those to research this book. I can't wait to walk the dogs in the arboretum and laugh like nobody else makes me laugh.

Writing is often a lonely enterprise, a lot like quarantine during a pandemic—oh wait, *exactly* like a quarantine during a pandemic. It requires near-total solitude, silence, endless rewriting and rereading, fact-checking and rechecking, and sometimes an entire *delete* and starting over. And those are the good days. When the bad days hit, and they always do, I am one of the lucky ones in having a partner and husband who knows when to keep his distance and when to bring me an egg-and-bacon burrito or a vodka soda, depending on whether five o'clock had arrived.

He has been that sounding board, shoulder on which I've cried, chef, bartender, and always, unconditional support. I love you, Jeff Rhoads.

And finally, Liza. When she started having her Tony Costa nightmares and shared with me the revelation that she had been babysat by a serial killer, my first words were, "There's your book!" Little did I know it would also become mine. After struggling for years with the very tricky (and grueling) task of separating herself from the trauma of her sad and troubled childhood in order to be a dispassionate observer of it, she agreed to let me help. And now, almost three years later and with the book finished, I am in awe—of her bravery, her honesty, her sheer will in forcing herself to "go there," even though it was often painful and always difficult. While many of us have dark chapters in our history, we are grateful they remain buried in our past. Liza's darkest chapters are now published in these pages. That's courage.

Brava, my dear friend, you did it. It's been an honor and a joy to get there with you.

AND FINALLY, A NOTE FROM LIZA RODMAN

So many collaborations had to go well for me to find myself here, in gratitude.

First and foremost, thank you to my family. My husband, Tim, whose sense of humor, code of loyalty, and open heart in this world are the backbone of our family. He makes me believe in every possibility and without him, I would be lost. And to my children, Loren and Sarah and Will, their babies (furry and otherwise), and their partners who have listened to me rattle on about this story for far too many years. I am madly in love with each and every one of you.

A special thank-you to my daughter-in-law, Lindsey, and her friend and photographer John V. Hays for making my first author photo shoot a breeze.

To my family and friends at Waldron Rand. Thank you for enduring the years of my ever-changing schedules and always welcoming me back as if I had never left.

And to my tribe of friends. In my long search for family, each of you is a holy thing. To Emilie Boon and Kim Garcia, thank you for your love and faith; in me, in the power of kindness, and in this thing that binds us called writing. Thank you to Laura Harrington for always cheering me up and cheering me on, Sandy Malone for holding my hand when the nightmares began, and Polly Rutherford and Richard Rutherford for their unyielding belief in me and this book. And to Frank Garcia, for reminding me about the "long view" when I needed it most.

To Gary Whited, who walked alongside me on this journey. Thank you for helping me find my way back home.

And to Jennifer Jordan. Who would have thought the smell of strong coffee brewing across the hall forty-three years ago would eventually bring us here? Every day of our collaboration, both in life and on this book, has felt like destiny. There are so many moments burned into my memory. From our "brave little apartment" on the Oregon coast, to hitchhiking back and forth to Vermont, road trips from Cape Cod to Utah, crying and laughing the whole way. All of it. You have always been my example of what life would be like if I were afraid but did it anyway. I've lived vicariously. And I feel lucky to have had this time together with you. I'm in awe of your tenacity and eye for story. When I was unable, your courage, energy, friendship, and wisdom carried us both over the finish line. Thank you for your strength and perseverance. Together we brought this story out of the darkness and into the light.

And lastly, to my sister, who survived with me, and to our mother, without whom this story could not have been told. Despite it all, I love you both.

September 2020

NOTES

Chapter 1

1 *Vincent Bonaviri, interview conducted by Detective Lieutenant Inspector Richard Cass, March 7, 1969.

2 Frank X. Gaspar, email communication with Liza Rodman, March 27, 2019.

3 Avis L Johnson, Avis and Pete's Illiterate Writers Group, Facebook, September 14, 2009, https://www.facebook.com/groups/59552262922/?post_id=10151258313597923.

4 Frank X. Gaspar, email communication with Liza Rodman, March 29, 2019.

5 *Vincent Bonaviri, interview conducted by Maurice Goldman, March 9, 1969.

6 *Lester Allen Sr., "A Shuddering of Girls," unpublished manuscript, 1970.

7 Avis L Johnson, Avis and Pete's Illiterate Writers Group, Facebook, September 14, 2009, https://www.facebook.com/groups/59552262922/?ref=nf_target&fref=nf.

8 Ibid.

9 Cory Devereaux, email communication with Liza Rodman, September 21, 2019.

10 *Tony Costa, interview conducted by Lieutenant John Powers, November 29, 1961.

11 *Somerville Police report, November 29, 1961.

Chapter 3

1 *Provincetown High School admission record, December 15, 1961.

2 *Lester Allen Sr., "A Shuddering of Girls," unpublished manuscript, 1970.

3 Avis L Johnson, Avis and Pete's Illiterate Writers Group, Facebook, April 23, 2009, https://www.facebook.com/groups/59552262922/?post_id=10151258338477923.

4 Avis L Johnson, Avis and Pete's Illiterate Writers Group, Facebook, May 3, 2009, https://www.facebook.com/groups/59552262922/?ref=nf_target&fref=nf.

5 *Avis Costa, interview conducted by Maurice Goldman, March 9, 1969.

6 *Tony Costa and Avis Costa, interview conducted by Lester Allen Sr., April 24, 1969.

7 *Allen, "A Shuddering of Girls."

8 *Avis Costa, interview conducted by Lester Allen Sr., July 25, 1969.

9 *Allen, "A Shuddering of Girls."

Chapter 5

1 Avis L Johnson, Facebook post, "How to marry a maniac," August 10, 2009.

2 Ibid.

3 *Avis Costa, interview conducted by Lester Allen Sr., July 25, 1969.

4 *Justin Cavanaugh, pretrial notes, memo #1572.

5 *Avis Costa, interview conducted by Lester Allen Sr., July 25, 1969.

6 *Ibid.

7 *Daniel Hiebert, MD, interview conducted by Justin Cavanaugh, March 12, 1969.

8 *Avis Costa, interview conducted by Lester Allen Sr., April 17, 1969.

9 *Daniel Hiebert, MD, interview conducted by Justin Cavanaugh, March 12, 1969.

Chapter 7

1 Bob Anthony, interview conducted by Liza Rodman, April 17, 2019.

2 *Avis Costa, interview with Costa's defense team, March 23, 1969.

3 *Avis Costa, interview with Costa's defense team, March 9, 1969.

4 *Antone C. Costa, "Resurrection," unpublished manuscript, 1970.

5 *Sidney Callis, "A New Drug Available for Treatment of Neurosis: Double Blind Study of Tybamate," *International Journal of Psychiatry*, Volume 2, Issue 6 (November–December 1966): 645–50.

6 *Tony Costa and Avis Costa, interview conducted by Lester Allen Sr., April 24, 1969.

Chapter 9

1 Denise Williams Carson, email communication with Jennifer Jordan, June 8, 2020.

2 John Waters, interview conducted by Gerald Peary, http://www.geraldpeary .com/interviews/wxyz/waters-p-town.html.

3 Denise Williams Carson, interview conducted by Jennifer Jordan, May 19, 2020.

Chapter 11

1   Avis L Johnson, Facebook post, Before the Abandonment, January 16, 2015, https://www.facebook.com/photo?fbid=10152910414213805&set=a .1015108653212380.

2   *Avis Costa, interview conducted by Lester Allen Sr., July 25, 1969.

3   *Avis Costa, interview, conducted by Maurice Goldman, March 9, 1969.

4   *Avis Costa, interview conducted by Lester Allen Sr., July 25, 1969.

Chapter 14

1   Mike Wallace, *CBS Reports*, "The Homosexuals," March 7, 1967.

Chapter 16

1   John Waters, interview conducted by Gerald Peary, http://www.geraldpeary .com/interviews/wxyz/waters-p-town.html.

2   Ibid.

Chapter 18

1   *Vincent Bonaviri, interview (with Cathy Roche) conducted by Maurice Goldman, March 17, 1969.

2   Geoff Becker, interview conducted by Liza Rodman, June 9, 2018.

3   *Tony Costa, psychological examinations conducted by Dr. Jack Ewalt, October–November 1969.

4   Ibid.

5   Cory Devereaux, email communication with Liza Rodman, May 2, 2020.

Chapter 20

1   *Avis Costa, interview conducted by Lester Allen Sr., July 25, 1969.

2   *Avis Costa, interview conducted by Maurice Goldman, March 9, 1969.

3   *Avis Costa, interview conducted by Lester Allen Sr., July 25, 1969.

4   Ibid.

Chapter 21

1   Avis L Johnson, Avis and Pete's Illiterate Writers Group, Facebook, March 12, 2010, https://www.facebook.com/groups/59552262922/?ref=nf_target &fref=nf.

2   *Tony Costa, jailhouse diary, March–April, 1969.

3   *Tony Costa, interview conducted by Lester Allen Sr., March 13, 1969.

Chapter 23

1 Bob Anthony, interview conducted by Liza Rodman, April 17, 2019.
2 *Linda Monzon, interviews conducted by Detective Bernie Flynn and Lieutenant E. Thomas Gunnery, February 14, 1969 and March 17, 1969.
3 *Lester Allen Sr., "A Shuddering of Girls," unpublished manuscript, 1970.
4 *Tony Costa, interview with Justin Cavanaugh and Lester Allen Sr., March 21, 1969.
5 *Antone C. Costa, "Resurrection," unpublished manuscript, 1969.
6 *Tony Costa, jailhouse diary, March–April 1969.

Chapter 25

1 David Raboy, interview conducted by Liza Rodman, February 28, 2019.
2 *Lester Allen Sr., "A Shuddering of Girls," unpublished manuscript, 1970.
3 *Avis Costa, interview conducted by Lester Allen Sr., July 25, 1969.
4 *Town of Wellfleet police report, inventory of stolen items, July 20, 1968.
5 *Antone C. Costa, "Resurrection," unpublished manuscript, 1970.

Chapter 27

1 *Avis Costa, interview conducted by Lester Allen Sr., July 25, 1969.
2 *Lester Allen Sr., "A Shuddering of Girls," unpublished manuscript, 1970.
3 *Antone C. Costa, "Resurrection," unpublished manuscript, 1970.

Chapter 29

1 *Paula Hoernig, interview conducted by Massachusetts State Police, April 6, 1969.
2 E. Thomas Gunnery, interview conducted by Jennifer Jordan and Liza Rodman, September 11, 2018.

Chapter 31

1 *Lester Allen Sr., "A Shuddering of Girls," unpublished manuscript, 1970.
2 Ibid.
3 Ibid.
4 *Vincent Bonaviri, interview with Maurice Goldman and Justin Cavanaugh, March 9, 1969.

Chapter 33

1   *Avis Costa, correspondence with Tony Costa, October 1969.
2   *Paula Hoernig, interview conducted by Detective Bernie Flynn, April 6, 1969.
3   *Lester Allen Sr., "A Shuddering of Girls," unpublished manuscript, 1970.
4   Josephine A. Bunny Rabbitt, Avis and Pete's Illiterate Writers Group, September 14, 2009, https://www.facebook.com/groups/59552262922/?post_id=10151258313597923.
5   *Tony Costa and Avis Costa, interview conducted by Lester Allen Sr., April 24, 1969.
6   Donna Candish, interview conducted by Jennifer Jordan, May 7, 2020.
7   *Edward Kirkland and Donald Singleton, "Christine's Trip to the Morgue," *New York Daily News*, November 26, 1968.
8   Dr. Michael Baden, interview conducted by Liza Rodman, February 28, 2019.
9   *Avis Costa and Tony Costa, interview conducted by Lester Allen Sr., April 24, 1969.
10 *Tony Costa, psychological examinations conducted by Dr. Jack Ewalt, October–November 1969.

Chapter 35

1   Jon Doeringer, Avis and Pete's Illiterate Writers Group, Facebook, September 14, 2009, https://www.facebook.com/groups/59552262922/search/?query=driving%20Tony%20costa.
2   Josephine A Bunny Rabbitt, Avis and Pete's Illiterate Writers Group, September 14, 2009, https://www.facebook.com/search/top/?q=avis%20and%20pete's%20illiterate%20writers%20group&epa.
3   Donna Candish, interview conducted by Jennifer Jordan, May 7, 2020.
4   *Avis Costa, interview conducted by Lester Allen Sr., July 25, 1969.

Chapter 37

1   *Lester Allen Sr., "A Shuddering of Girls," unpublished manuscript, 1970.
2   *Tony Costa, interview conducted by Lester Allen Sr., May 5, 1969.
3   *Antone C. Costa, "Resurrection," unpublished manuscript, 1970.
4   *Lester Allen Sr., "A Shuddering of Girls," unpublished manuscript, 1970.
5   *Tony Costa, interview conducted by Maurice Goldman and Lester Allen Sr., October 14, 1969.
6   James Zacharias, interview conducted by Jennifer Jordan, May 2020.

Chapter 39

1 *Antone C. Costa, "Resurrection," unpublished manuscript, 1970.
2 *Daniel Hiebert, MD, and George Katsas, MD, Autopsy Report—Case A 69–51, March 1969.
3 *Tony Costa, polygraphs conducted by Charles Zimmerman, June–November 1969.
4 *Costa, "Resurrection."
5 Ibid.

Chapter 40

1 Herbie van Dam, interview conducted by Liza Rodman, August 2019.
2 *Tony Costa, polygraphs conducted by Charles Zimmerman, June–November 1969.
3 *Paula Hoernig, interview conducted by Bernie Flynn, April 1969.

Chapter 42

1 Ruth Ann Turbidy, interview conducted by Jennifer Jordan, May 2020.
2 John Wilson, interview conducted by Jennifer Jordan, November 2019.

Chapter 43

1 *Detective William G. Broderick, interview conducted by Leo Damore, 1980.

Chapter 46

1 *Gerald Magnan, interview conducted by Leo Damore, 1980.
2 Ruth Ann Turbidy, interview conducted by Jennifer Jordan, May 2020.

Chapter 48

1 *Detective Bernie J. Flynn, summary of the investigation, March 1969.
2 *Detective George Killen, investigator's notebook, March 1969.

Chapter 49

1 *Detective Bernie J. Flynn, summary of the investigation, March, 1969.
2 *Chief Francis "Cheney" Marshall, interview conducted by Leo Damore, 1979–1980.
3 Ibid.
4 *Detective George Killen, interview conducted by Leo Damore, 1979–1980.

Chapter 51

1 *Detective Bernie J. Flynn, summary of investigation, March, 1969.
2 David Raboy, interview conducted by Liza Rodman, February 2019.
3 *Joanne Watts, interview conducted by Bernie Flynn, March 1969.
4 James Zacharias, interview conducted by Jennifer Jordan, May 7, 2020.
5 Avis L Johnson, Avis and Pete's Illiterate Writers Group, Facebook, September 2009, https://www.facebook.com/groups/59552262922/.
6 *Justin Cavanaugh, case notes, 1969–1970.

Chapter 52

1 *Medical staff, Bridgewater State Hospital admission note, March 6, 1969.

Chapter 54

1 Retired Lieutenant E. Thomas Gunnery, interview conducted by Jennifer Jordan and Liza Rodman, September 11, 2018.
2 *Avis Costa, interview conducted by Lester Allen Sr., July 25, 1969.

Chapter 56

1 *Tony Costa, interview conducted by Maurice Goldman and Lester Allen Sr., April 1969.
2 *Dr. Jack Ewalt, indictment and psychological profile of Antone Costa—#27664—Massachusetts Mental Health Center Evaluation, October–November 1969.
3 *Costa defense team, memorandum prepared for Dr. Jack Ewalt, 1969.
4 *Tony Costa, interview conducted by Maurice Goldman and Justin Cavanaugh, March 25, 1969.
5 *Dr. Harold Williams, psychological examinations, 1969.
6 *Dr. Harold Williams, interview conducted by Leo Damore, 1979–1980.

Chapter 58

1 Stephen Lipman, interview conducted by Jennifer Jordan, August 1, 2019.
2 *Charles Zimmerman, interview conducted by Leo Damore, 1979–1980.
3 *Tony Costa, polygraph conducted by Charles Zimmerman, October 26, 1969.
4 Ibid.
5 *Tony Costa, interview conducted by Maurice Goldman and Lester Allen Sr., August 25, 1969.
6 *Lester Allen Sr., "Shuddering of Girls," unpublished manuscript, 1970.

Chapter 60

1 Stephen Lipman, interview conducted by Jennifer Jordan and Liza Rodman, September 11, 2018.

2 Ibid.

3 *Tony Costa, correspondence with Lester Allen Sr., December 12, 1969.

4 Armand Fernandes, interview conducted by Liza Rodman, August 1, 2018.

Chapter 61

1 *Trial transcript, *Commonwealth vs. Antone C. Costa*, May 14, 1970.

2 *Avis Costa, interview conducted by Lester Allen Sr., July 25, 1969.

3 Ibid.

4 *Trial transcript, May 1970.

5 *Avis Costa, interview conducted by Lester Allen Sr., April 24, 1969.

6 *Maurice Goldman, pretrial notes, April 1970.

7 *Vinnie Bonaviri, interview conducted by Detective Lieutenant Inspector Richard J. Cass, March 7, 1969.

8 *Vincent J. Bonaviri, trial transcript, May 20, 1970.

9 *Leo Damore, author's notes for *In His Garden*, 1980.

10 Evelyn Lawson, Sturgis Library Theater archives, 1908–1984, "Deadly Charm," notes for an unpublished manuscript, 1969.

Chapter 63

1 *Tony Costa, correspondence with Maurice Goldman, December 28, 1970.

2 *Antone C. Costa, "Resurrection," unpublished manuscript, 1970.

3 Leo Damore, interview conducted by Craig Little, "Book Reopens Costa Murder Case," *Provincetown Advocate*, July 1981.

4 Evelyn Lawson, Sturgis Library Theater archives, 1908–1984, "Deadly Charm," notes for an unpublished manuscript, 1969.

5 *Walpole Prison Archives, Antone C. Costa records, 1970–1974.

6 *Tony Costa, jailhouse diary, March 1969.

7 Ibid.

8 Donna Candish, interview conducted by Jennifer Jordan, May 2020.

9 *Dr. A. Nicholas Groth, correspondence with Leo Damore, June 6, 1981.

Epilogue

1 Dr. James Fallon, interviews conducted by and email communication with Jennifer Jordan and Liza Rodman, April–June 2019.

2   Bessel van der Kolk, MD, *The Body Keeps the Score: Brain, Mind, and Body in the Healing of Trauma* (New York: Penguin Books, 2014), page 24.

3   Michele Rosenthal, "The Science Behind PTSD Symptoms: How Trauma Changes the Brain," PsychCentral.com, June 27, 2018.

4   *Tony Costa, interview conducted by Lester Allen Sr., June 2, 1969.

5   *Tony Costa, jailhouse diary, April 1969.

6   Denise Williams Carson and Kris Blaylock, interviews conducted by Jennifer Jordan, May 19 and May 25, 2020.

7   Denise Williams Carson, interview conducted by Jennifer Jordan, May 19, 2020.

8   Celeste Cornwell Dawson and Claudia Federoff Musgrove, interviews conducted by Jennifer Jordan, August 2019 and May 2020.

9   Claudia Federoff Musgrove, interview conducted by Jennifer Jordan, May 2020.

10 Ibid.

11 Grita Perry, email communication with Jennifer Jordan, May 2020.

12 Athena Martinez, interview conducted by Jennifer Jordan, August 2019.

13 Ibid.

14 Grace E. Dickey, interview conducted by Jennifer Jordan, August 2019.

15 Stephen Lipman, interview conducted by Jennifer Jordan and Liza Rodman, September 2018.

16 Denise Williams Carson, email communication with Jennifer Jordan, May 20, 2020.

Authors' Acknowledgments

1   Avis L Johnson, Facebook post, June 4, 2020, https://www.facebook.com/avisljohnson.161/posts/10158345889213805.

---

* Leo Damore papers, Kent State University Libraries. Special Collections and Archives.

BIBLIOGRAPHY
AND ADDITIONAL READING

Alexie, Sherman. *You Don't Have to Say You Love Me: A Memoir*. Boston: Little, Brown, 2017.

Allison, Dorothy. *Bastard Out of Carolina*. New York: Dutton, 1992.

Benson, Michael. *The Devil at Genesee Junction: The Murders of Kathy Bernhard and George-Ann Formicola, 6/66*. New York: Rowman & Littlefield, 2015.

Berne, Suzanne. *A Crime in the Neighborhood*. Chapel Hill, NC: Algonquin Books, 1997.

Brodeur, Adrienne. *Wild Game: My Mother, Her Lover, and Me*. Boston: Houghton Mifflin Harcourt, 2019.

Bugliosi, Vincent. *Helter Skelter: The True Story of the Manson Murders*. New York: W. W. Norton, 1974.

Burroughs, Augusten. *The Wolf at the Table: A Memoir of My Father*. New York: St. Martin's, 2008.

Callahan, Maureen. *American Predator: The Hunt for the Most Meticulous Serial Killer of the Twenty-first Century*. Viking, Penguin Random House, 2019.

Carus, Paul. *The Sayings of the Buddha*. New York: Peter Pauper, 1957.

Colt, George Howe. *The Big House: A Century in the Life of an American Summer Home*. New York: Scribner, 2003.

Conroy, Frank. *Stop Time*, New York: Penguin, 1967.

Coston, John. *To Kill and Kill Again: The Terrifying True Story of Montana's Baby-Faced Serial Sex Murderer*. New York: Open Road, 2016.

Crane, Elaine Forman. *Killed Strangely: The Death of Rebecca Cornell*. Ithaca, NY: Cornell University Press, 2002.

Cunningham, Michael. *Land's End: A Walk in Provincetown*. New York: Picador, 2002

Damore, Leo. *In His Garden: The Anatomy of a Murderer*. New York: Arbor House, 1981.

Doty, Mark. *Heaven's Coast: A Memoir*. New York: HarperCollins, 1996.

Douglas, John. *Mindhunter*. New York: Scribner, 1988.

Fallon, James. *The Psychopath Inside: A Neuroscientist's Personal Journey into the Dark Side of the Brain*. New York: Current, 2013.

Flynn, Nick. *Another Bullshit Night in Suck City: A Memoir*. New York: W. W. Norton, 2004.

Frank, Gerold. *The Boston Strangler*. New York: Signet Books, 1966.

Glück, Louise. *The Wild Iris*. Hopewell, NJ: Ecco Press, 1992.

Groth, A. Nicholas. *Men Who Rape: The Psychology of the Offender*. New York: Perseus Books, 1979.

Hare, Robert D. *Without Conscience: The Disturbing World of the Psychopaths Among Us*. New York: Guilford Press, 1999.

Harrington, William. *Trial: One Murder Case. One Huge Scandal . . .* London: Barrie & Jenkins LTD, 1970.

Hesse, Hermann. *Demian: The Story of Emil Sinclair's Youth*. New York: Penguin Classics, 2013.

Hickey, Eric. *Serial Murderers and Their Victims*. Boston: Cengage Learning, 2013.

Isherwood, Christopher. *The Sixties: Diaries Volume Two: 1960–1969*. London: HarperCollins, 2010.

Janney, Peter. *Mary's Mosaic: The CIA Conspiracy to Murder John F. Kennedy, Mary Pinchot Meyer, and Their Vision for World Peace*. New York: Skyhorse, 2013.

Junger, Sebastian. *A Death in Belmont*. New York: W. W. Norton, 2006.

Kaufman, Bel. *Up the Down Staircase*. New York: Avon Books, 1964.

Kennedy, Kostya, et al., eds. *Inside the Criminal Mind*. New York: Time Inc. Books, 2018.

Krahulik, Karen Christel. *Provincetown: From Pilgrim Landing to Gay Resort*. New York: New York University Press, 2005.

Kunitz, Stanley. *The Wild Braid: A Poet Reflects on a Century in the Garden*. New York: W. W. Norton, 2005.

Larsen, Erik. *The Devil in the White City: Murder, Magic, and Madness at the Fair that Changed America*. New York: Crown, 2003.

Mailer, Norman. *The Short Fiction of Norman Mailer*. New York: Dell, 1967.

———. *The Executioner's Song*. Boston: Little, Brown, 1979.

Manso, Peter. *Ptown: Art, Sex, and Money on the Outer Cape*. New York: Lisa Drew/Scribner, 2002.

McNamara, Michelle. *I'll Be Gone in the Dark: One Woman's Obsessive Search for the Golden State Killer*. New York: Harper, 2018.

Morrison, Helen. *My Life Among the Serial Killers: Inside the Minds of the World's Most Notorious Murderers*. New York: William Morrow, 2004.

Owens, Delia. *Where the Crawdads Sing*. New York: G. P. Putnam's Sons, 2018.

Peck, M. Scott. *People of the Lie: The Hope for Healing Human Evil*. New York: Touchstone, 1983.

Ronson, Jon. *The Psychopath Test: A Journey Through the Madness Industry*. New York: Riverhead Books, 2011.

Rosewood, Jack, and Rebecca Lo. *The Big Book of Serial Killers: An Encyclopedia of Serial Killers*. Dearing, KS: LAK Publishing, 2017.

Rule, Ann. *The Stranger Beside Me: The Shocking Inside Story of the Serial Killer Ted Bundy*. New York: Pocket Books/Simon & Schuster, 1980.

Samenow, Stanton E. *Inside the Criminal Mind*. New York: Crown, 1984.

Sarton, May. *Journal of a Solitude*. New York: W. W. Norton, 1973.

Shapiro, Dani. *Still Writing: The Perils and Pleasures of a Creative Life*. New York: Atlantic Monthly Press, 2013.

Shepard, Sam. *Motel Chronicles*. San Francisco: City Lights Books, 1982.

Shriver, Lionel. *We Need to Talk About Kevin*. New York: Harper Perennial, 2003.

Skloot, Rebecca. *The Immortal Life of Henrietta Lacks*. New York: Crown, 2010.

Steinbeck, John. *East of Eden*. New York: Viking Press, 1952.

Staller, Karen M. *Runaways: How the Sixties Counterculture Shaped Today's Practices and Policies*. New York: Columbia University Press, 2006.

Strayed, Cheryl. *Brave Enough*. New York: Alfred A. Knopf, 2015.

Usdin, Gene L. *Psychoneurosis & Schizophrenia*. Philadelphia: J. B. Lippincott, 1966.

Van der Kolk, Bessel. *The Body Keeps the Score*. New York: Viking, 2014.

Vaknin, Sam. *Malignant Self Love: Narcissism Revisited*. Rhinebeck, NY: Narcissus Publications, 1999.

Vonnegut, Kurt. *There's a Maniac Loose Out There*. July 25, 1969, New York, *Life* magazine.

Vorse, Mary Heaton. *Time and the Town: A Provincetown Chronicle*. Provincetown, MA: Cape Cod Pilgrim Memorial Association, 1942.

Vronsky, Peter. *Serial Killers: The Method and Madness of Monsters*. New York: Berkley, 2004.

Westover, Tara. *Educated: A Memoir*. New York: Random House, 2018.

Wolff, Geoffrey. *The Duke of Deception: Memories of my Father*. New York: Random House, 1979.

INDEX

ABOUT THE AUTHORS

Liza Rodman attended the University of Massachusetts at Amherst and received her bachelor of arts with a concentration in creative writing from Vermont College. She has balanced life as a mother, stepmother, writer, and tax accountant for more than thirty-five years. In 2005, she began researching the story of Tony Costa when she realized her personal connection to the infamous Cape Cod killer. She has gathered thousands of documents, testimonies, and interviews, perhaps more than any other investigator or journalist who's worked on this case. She and her husband live outside Boston and have three children and five grandchildren. *The Babysitter* is her first book.

Jennifer Jordan is an award-winning author, filmmaker, and screenwriter with decades of experience as a news anchor and investigative journalist. She has worked for NPR and PBS, and her work has also appeared in a variety of national and international newspapers and magazines. She has directed and produced several documentaries, including *3000 Cups of Tea*, which revealed the flawed *60 Minutes* report on renowned philanthropist Greg Mortenson. In addition to her own books, *Savage Summit* and *The Last Man on the Mountain*, she has ghostwritten two others. *The Babysitter* is her fifth book.